The *UK Education* Internet Primer

The *UK Education* Internet Primer

Nicholas Mailer and Bruce Dickson

Second edition
Completely revised

The Questions Publishing Company Ltd, Birmingham

Published by The Questions Publishing Company Ltd
27 Frederick Street, Birmingham B1 3HH

Telephone: 0121 212 0919
Email: bookinfo@questpub.co.uk

First edition published 1994 by Koeksuster Publications, reprinted 1995
Second edition, completely revised 1996

Cover illustration by Roger Penwill

Printed in Great Britain by,
Redwood Books, Trowbridge, Wiltshire.

ISBN 0-898149-65-8

Thanks and acknowledgements

Sarah Kaganas, Ma, for – despite her best efforts – holding together the Koeksuster more effectively than we could have imagined possible. And for being right about the publishers and other such issues ;-)

Gillie Dickson for crisps, orange juice and a warm working environment.

David Borchard, our ever busy friend, for putting up with the worst BT could throw at him.

Tim Clark and David Hunt of Research Machines for allowing us to retain at least some faith in British industry.

David Walker of Acorn (or ART) for his inspiring optimism in the face of Golden Delicious reality.

Working friends at Easynet and Mill Hill for interest and encouragement.

Paula Kathuria for the ISP list. Sorry we forgot to mention you in our last edition.

Brad Templeton for Emily Postnews and our nicest piece of Email to date.

Alan Wheatley of University of Wales, Aberystwyth, for his splendid website reviews.

Mark Sealey for constant educational interest (and for encouraging us to do the second edition in the first place).

To the 'Goodwill Recipe Book' for a marvellous Koeksuster Recipe.

About the authors

Both authors live in Mill Hill, North London, at opposite sides of the railway track. Both their childhoods occured, some years apart, in South Africa.

Nicholas Mailer

nickm@koekie.org.uk

Nick has recently graduated from the University of Leeds with a degree in English and philosophy. His highest mark was attained on an essay about Alice in Wonderland. His lowest mark was on a philosophy paper on the Internet's implications for Education. There's higher education for you.

He is currently working in the support department of a large Internet Service Provider. He writes on computing and Internet issues for various publications, including the *Times Educational Supplement*, and has given talks and demonstrations about the Internet in education across the country. As well as the Internet, he is interested in producing a variety of styles of music with computers.

Bruce Dickson

bruced@koekie.org.uk

Bruce currently teaches physics and computing at Mill Hill School, North London. Some years ago, he saw a small piece in a computer journal about the Internet. A friend advised he look into it, he bought a modem and was one of the first teachers to connect his school to the Internet in the UK. He now runs the school's Internet Club.

Bruce has written for various magazines and journals on a variety of topics. His computing interests include getting enabling technology into developing nations, and to this end he is currently researching the possibilities of robust and solar-powered palm-top computers whose satellite connections to the Internet will, in the not too distant future, offer disadvantaged children all over the world the opportunity to learn from and contribute to the world's culture.

Preface

The Internet has an historical significance similar to carving, writing and printing. The skills required to get the best from it are leading to a radical reappraisal of everything schools have been teaching with and about computers. As with all revolutions, there is less than a decade before patterns ossify and habits set it in steel. The first years of that precious period are behind us, and the reactionaries are beginning to wonder how to gate off whole fields of learning to prevent access or, at best, replant them to their own advantage.

We have written the second edition of this book in the hope that a critical mass of learners and educators will seize the potential of the Internet before it can be turned into yet another corporate entity, yet another sanitised, sanctioned medium of tedium. It is more than a shopping network. It is more, even, than a vast virtual library. It represents, perhaps, a turning point in the evolution of humankind from solo creator to that Hegelian state of profound synergy in which every learner is a teacher, every writer a publisher, every consumer a producer and every creator an artist. It represents a new realm where individual minds are shared resources. This is not just a Brave New World, but a unique opportunity for all of today's cultures to mingle with and build on the peaks of all previous recorded societies.

Already, all on-line academics can be aware of research being conducted by other groups across the world. Soon, no sincere human intellectual venture will wither for want of wide and appreciative acknowledgement and criticism. We have met previously lonely academics whose personalities have flowered after making the first Net contacts. Far from trapping anoraks in bedsits, it seems the Internet could give a vital reality to the paper freedoms of inclusive democracy.

No man is an island. Let us rejoice that technology might now unite the archipelago.

Contents

Invitation

If you have any suggestions or comments, we would like to hear from you.

Please send Email to

`koekie@koekie.org.uk`

Or, if we have failed to convert you from snailmail, write to

Koeksuster Publications
St Augustine's
High Street
Mill Hill
London NW7 1QY

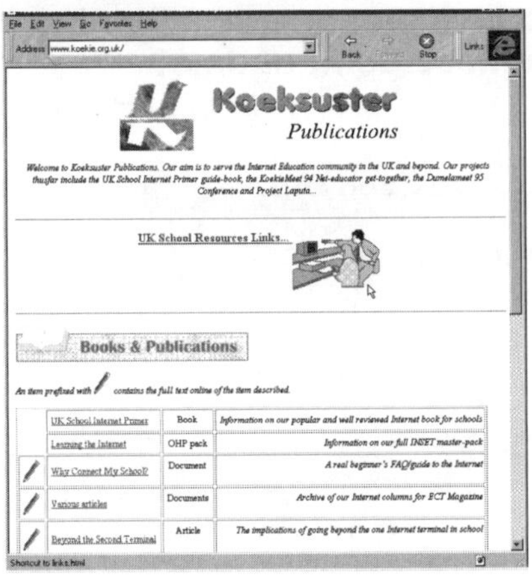

Visit us online

Why not pop in to our web pages at

`http://www.koekie.org.uk/`

We'll try and keep updated education links, copies of our educational scribblings as well as some classroom competitions. Also, our "Ask Any Question" service, *Project Laputa.* Hope to see you there!

'Tis education forms the common mind,
Just as the twig is bent the tree's inclined.

Alexander Pope

`http://www.wam.umd.edu/~wendyjc/pope/popehp.html`

Too much rigidity on the part of teachers should be followed by a brisk spirit of insubordination on the part of the taught.

Agnes Repplier

`http://www.library.upenn.edu./special/mss/repplier.html`

Is it a fact - or have I dreamt it - that by means of electricity, the world of matter has become a great nerve, vibrating thousands of miles in a breathless point of time?

Nathaniel Hawthorne

`http://www.tiac.net./users/eldred/nh/hawthorne.html`

Authors' introduction

This book is not a manual for a particular piece of software or an instruction pack for any proprietary service. When we like what we see, we say so, and conversely. We make no bones about being Internet enthusiasts, but we believe its success and potential lie not in technical wonder at the system itself, but in the creative sparks it strikes in the mind of the learner. With this book, we seek a path between the crags of hype and the quagmires of pessimistic technophobia.

We were delighted with the thoughtful response of the educators who enjoyed the first edition, which appeared sometime in the late Jurassic age (1994). As the first UK Internet guide for educators, it broke some new ground in widening education beyond the school gate and national border. Nevertheless, at that time, few companies we contacted in the course of our research had plans for Internet development. It was something for the distant future. CB radio for the nineties. A scurry amongst technicians. A token of possibility. A blip.

Since then, the Internet has become common currency for business people, politicians and many of the non-university academics we hoped to attract with the first edition. In 1994, we wrote about the peak of the wave approaching. How wrong we were. The impending tsunami still cannot be forecast. The "blip" is already beginning to change society.

The choice for the UK is clear. We can, if we wish, be at the heart of the Internet revolution. We have the language and the tradition of the yeoman inventor. We have a viable national curriculum and relative political stability. We must not throw all this positive potential away by continuing to ride in our deepening rut of cultural parsimony. The metered phone line, even with the compromise solution of ISDN, is not conducive to broad and effective communication. The underfunded higher education network infrastructure is a disgrace. No cohesive network policy exists for school education. Our pupils, then, instead of learning from the give and get of online experience, acquire little from our metered meanness beyond the diminution of communicative spirit, the quick fix mentality and a fearful reluctance to explore alternatives beyond the daily snatched glimpses of a world in evolution. The politician who backs her or his rhetoric with genuine substance in this area will walk tall in the cultural fruition that ensues.

A note on terminology

Computers generally, and the Internet in particular, have produced an explosion of new terminology, acronyms and expressions. Beginners have been known to go mad trying to follow manuals which expect them to know their URL from their http.

We have tried to minimise the inevitable confusion in the following ways: new terms are italicised when first introduced; they are either explained immediately in the text, or in a glossary entry at the back of the book. We hope the index will prove comprehensively helpful also. Internet jargon is in a state of flux – some has become sufficiently common to merit a loss of capitalisation, others not. Still more terms oscillate between the two – so if you see World Wide Web in some places and world wide web in others, fear not.

What is the Internet?

Introduction to the Internet: its structure, history, users and services, including Email, Usenet newsgroups, FTP and the World Wide Web.

Chapter 1

Several years ago, it was virtually unknown outside the echelons of academe. Suddenly, the Internet (or "The Net") has become a media buzz-word. It seems that no Sunday supplement is now complete without an article either eulogising the virtues of the Net or deploring a supposed tide of electronic anarchy. Sometimes both. But what is behind this latest darling of the chattering classes? What is this thing called the Internet? Where did it come from, where is it going, and what is its educational value?

The answer to these questions can be quite elusive because of the very nature of the Internet. Computers have been talking to one another for decades, with the information trundling down telephone lines, zooming across data cables and bouncing off satellites. Electronic communications became commonplace with fax machines, television's teletext and specialised commercial computer service-providers, like Prestel. The commercial services offered facilities like real-time share updates, and limited access to electronic mail and discussion forums. Perhaps more significant in the pre-Internet world of communication were the electronic bulletin boards (*BBS*), many still going strong. These were usually amateur operations – a computer in a bedroom, serving information down the telephone lines.

The Internet is a network of networks without a defined centre.

It is a lingua franca.

The Internet paradigm is similar, but in several significant respects, it is radically different. It is characterised by:

- No absolute centre from which services radiate
- No over-arching controller or ombudsman
- A truly global interconnecting network

Unlike most other media, the barrier between user and operator, provider and consumer, is virtually non-existent. There is no editor-in-chief on the Internet, only the millions of users around the world who contribute to it. The Internet is a criss-cross of hundreds of sub-networks, thousands of information server machines and millions of individual users. The thousands of independently owned but commonly connected machines on the Internet all communicate with one another via an agreed communications protocol. By doing so, they have access to the same backbone of services. When one computer communicates with another, the data bounces across the network like a pin-ball, finding the most efficient route for connection. Finding analogies to the Internet can be a tortuous process, but the closest example seems to be the English language – a global system of communication originating in one country, but owned by none. An evolutionary system whose users shape it far more radically than any hierarchical academy. An agreed set of basic communication standards, through and above which an infinite variety of transformative dialogues can be engaged. The Internet can be thought of as an electronic *lingua franca*, the story of the Tower of Babel in reverse.

That the network has evolved this way is no coincidence: it was initiated as such by the American military (it is one of the few positive leftovers of the Cold War). The *Advanced Research Projects Administration* (ARPA) were concerned that a computer network with a well delineated centre of operation would be highly vulnerable to attack – just eradicating that centre would annihilate the whole network at a stroke. They went about designing a more pragmatic, less centrist networking philosophy, with a multitude of possible connections through a number of independently connected server machines: a network that could not simply be "turned off" without destroying physically every single one of those hundreds of thousands of information servers and the infrastructure that supported them. That is why the term "information superhighway" is not merely irritating, but is a completely inappropriate metaphor in describing the *modus operandi* of the Internet. The one thing the Internet is not is a well-defined trunk route between A and B.

Metaphors

Infobahn, Cyberspace, Information Superhighway: no doubt you've heard them all bandied about by the press when discussing the Internet. These are twee, inaccurate and cloying, and probably should be avoided

The Internet's greatest strength can also be interpreted as its most telling weakness. It is this freedom from overall central control that has allowed its rapid growth and its diverse user-base. But because there has been little large-scale central planning of its information sources, it is sometimes quite a daunting task to find someone or something on the network. Fortunately, in the teleological way in which the Net tends to operate, there are now appearing high quality online catalogues and search utilities to much of what is available and what is valuable.

Another problem which is more difficult to solve is the suitability of some of the data for some of the users. What is important to realise is that whether this is considered a problem, and how it is dealt with, is an issue of philosophy as old as communication itself. The press-exaggerated areas of pornography and subversive undercurrents, ranging from Anarchism to right-wing Revisionism muddy the fact that, although pockets of these activities do exist, it is important not to become hysterical about them: they are no more or less prevalent than in any other form of communication, from printed magazines to chats in pubs. The benefits of an overwhelmingly co-operative community to complement an enormous base of genuinely interesting information constructed by and for that community far outweighs any of these unfortunate by-products of free speech.

Although the Internet has no controller, it has a sense of history - the men and women who pioneered the protocols and philosophies that make up the Internet gain a respect that sometimes verges on the hagiographic, like the Internet site illustrated right. Vint Cerf is often dubbed the father of the Internet, because he was one of the main designers of its "language", TCP/IP.

A summarised history

1965 The US Defence Department begins ARPANET project
1968 First generation of networking hardware
1969 ARPANET connects four US universities
1971 23 hosts on ARPANET
1973 First computers outside US connect to ARPANET
1974 First commercial division of ARPANET, Telenet, is opened
1976 Queen of England sends Email over ARPANET
1977 Theorynet - the first Emailing list
1978 TCP/IP protocol in development
1979 Usenet Newsgroups established
1981 New host added to ARPANET every 20 days
1982 Term "Internet" used for the first time
1983 TCP/IP becomes the universal language of the Internet
1984 There are 1000 hosts on the Internet
1986 First Freenet established, to give free access to the Net to all
1987 Over 10,000 hosts on the Internet
1988 IRC (real-time chat system) created
1990 ARPANET is retired
1991 World Wide Web created in CERN, Geneva
1992 Over one million hosts on the Internet
1993 Mosaic, the first popular Web browser, is released
1995 Java, an Internet programming language, is released by Sun
1996 Ten million hosts on the global Internet

How Many Users?

Because of the nature of the Internet, quantifying its users is a difficult task. Different figures - from 40 to 100 million users - are offered, but its exponential expansion ensures that any figure will be innacurate soon after its ennunciation.

Internet addressing

Every house on every street has an address - otherwise getting from A to B would become rather complicated. Every computer on the Internet has an address too. The Internet is based on the client-server model. That is, there are machines and programs which serve out information, termed *servers*, and other machines and programs, perhaps at the other end of the world, called *clients*, which receive them. In order that the right client speaks to the right server and vice versa, there needs to be some clear and unambiguous way of identifying each one.

There are, in fact, usually two synonymous addresses - one clear and unambiguous to humans, the other to computers. As with postal addresses, where there is the full street address as well as the postcode, the Internet has a textual address termed a *domain name* as well as a numerical address, termed an *IP address* (or IP number).

The router and gateway machines, whose jobs are to ensure that information moves from A to B as efficiently as possible, need to use the IP number form of address, but humans prefer the more prolix domain name - so another machine, called a *Domain Name Server* (DNS), consults a database automatically and converts from one to the other - without the end-user even knowing.

Here's an example of a full domain name:

`www.acorn.co.uk`

Fairly intelligible - **www** stands for world wide web, so this machine serves world wide web pages. At **Acorn** Computers. Which is a **co**mmercial service. In the **U**nited **K**ingdom. More on domain names and what they signify in the Email chapter.

When the user refers to `www.acorn.co.uk`, the local DNS machine converts the address to the IP number, which in this case happens to be:

`136.170.131.2`

An IP number will always consist of four numbers (separated by full stops) between 0 and 254. Because certain combinations signify special cases, not every combination can be used for addresses (similar to telephone numbers - for example, no general UK telephone number can begin with 999 or 100 for obvious reasons).

TCP/IP

To connect to the Internet, your machine must speak its "language", (or, in Net-speak, use its *protocol*), TCP/IP.

IP stands for Internet Protocol. Your data is packaged with the destination address. The protocol drives it along the most efficient route.

TCP stands for Transmission Control Protocol. It makes sure your data arrives correctly and all in one piece.

These protocols were built to connect across many different physical networks. A TCP/IP suite is available for most computers.

Little technical knowledge is required these days to use the Internet successfully.

Services on the Internet

The Internet offers a vast and constantly changing range of different services. Some are a product of the Internet's infrastructure; others are offered by various information providers and academic institutions. Many are offered by the Internet's users. The main focus here, though, is a summary not of any particular content-providers, but of the services and systems used to access that content over the Internet. Each is dealt with fully in later chapters.

Email

Electronic mail is the most basic and, perhaps, most essential service of all. It allows communications between any two users of the Internet. After subscribing to an Internet service provider, or obtaining your Internet access from another source (through an academic institution, perhaps), you are given an Email address. You use a program on your computer to compose and deliver mail to other users as well as to read the mail in your electronic postbox. The great majority of providers do not place an additional charge on this service, allowing you to post or receive as many messages as you want from anywhere in the world.

In addition to simple text Email, you can send programs and data. You can subscribe to Email mailing lists and interest groups where users can post to everyone else subscribed to that group. There are also many official bulletins or "zines" available, which are posted at regular intervals and cost nothing.

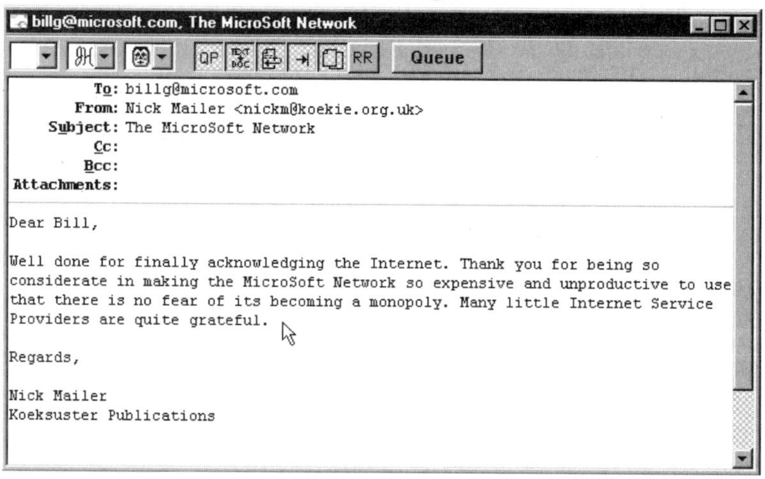

billg@microsoft.com, The MicroSoft Network

QP RR Queue

To: billg@microsoft.com
From: Nick Mailer <nickm@koekie.org.uk>
Subject: The MicroSoft Network
Cc:
Bcc:
Attachments:

Dear Bill,

Well done for finally acknowledging the Internet. Thank you for being so considerate in making the MicroSoft Network so expensive and unproductive to use that there is no fear of its becoming a monopoly. Many little Internet Service Providers are quite grateful.

Regards,

Nick Mailer
Koeksuster Publications

Sending Email is quick and simple. Unlike a fax, one does not pay more if one is sending a message abroad. In the illustration (right) a new message is being typed. Clicking on "Queue" will send the message next time a connection is made to the Internet.

Usenet news

This is the Internet's answer to the electronic bulletin board. It is not a news service in the traditional sense: as usual with the Internet, there is no central news provider. Instead there are literally thousands of different newsgroups, ranging in content and tone from particle physics to music fan clubs. Using a special newsreader program, every Internet user can post to newsgroups, and their contributions can be read by others who have subscribed to that newsgroup.

These forums are at the heart of the Internet community, and although some of the newsgroups or postings within are of dubious value, it is unlikely that you'll find absolutely nothing of interest. Some groups have an official moderator, others are a free-for-all. Many groups are frequented by experts in their field, and several celebrities are known to contribute.

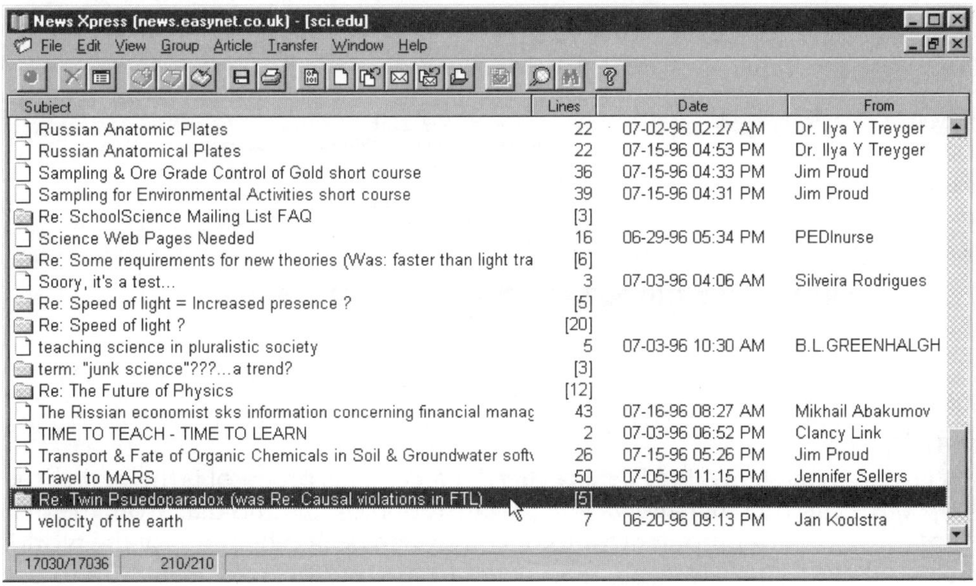

News Xpress (news.easynet.co.uk) - [sci.edu]

File Edit View Group Article Transfer Window Help

Subject	Lines	Date	From
Russian Anatomic Plates	22	07-02-96 02:27 AM	Dr. Ilya Y Treyger
Russian Anatomical Plates	22	07-15-96 04:53 PM	Dr. Ilya Y Treyger
Sampling & Ore Grade Control of Gold short course	36	07-15-96 04:33 PM	Jim Proud
Sampling for Environmental Activities short course	39	07-15-96 04:31 PM	Jim Proud
Re: SchoolScience Mailing List FAQ	[3]		
Science Web Pages Needed	16	06-29-96 05:34 PM	PEDInurse
Re: Some requirements for new theories (Was: faster than light tra	[6]		
Soory, it's a test...	3	07-03-96 04:06 AM	Silveira Rodrigues
Re: Speed of light = Increased presence ?	[5]		
Re: Speed of light ?	[20]		
teaching science in pluralistic society	5	07-03-96 10:30 AM	B.L.GREENHALGH
term: "junk science"???...a trend?	[3]		
Re: The Future of Physics	[12]		
The Rissian economist sks information concerning financial manag	43	07-16-96 08:27 AM	Mikhail Abakumov
TIME TO TEACH - TIME TO LEARN	2	07-03-96 06:52 PM	Clancy Link
Transport & Fate of Organic Chemicals in Soil & Groundwater soft\	26	07-15-96 05:26 PM	Jim Proud
Travel to MARS	50	07-05-96 11:15 PM	Jennifer Sellers
Re: Twin Psuedoparadox (was Re: Causal violations in FTL)	[5]		
velocity of the earth	7	06-20-96 09:13 PM	Jan Koolstra

17030/17036 210/210

The illustration (above) is an extract from the titles of some current "postings" in a scientific education Usenet Newsgroup discussion-forum. Topics include faster than light travel paradoxes, the philosphy of learning and organic chemicals in the environment.

Telnet

This is one of the oldest ways to access other machines on the Internet. It is the trans-Internet *terminal emulator.* Telnet can be used to log into these machines via the *command line* (if you've used MS-DOS, you've used a command line), where you can type commands and control the machine, usually through the *Unix* operating system, which is popular in academic circles. Sometimes, Telnet can be used to access specific services, like remote access to library catalogues. Although quite an esoteric tool these days for the general user, it remains vital for administering and monitoring via remote control the machines which serve and transmit data on the Internet.

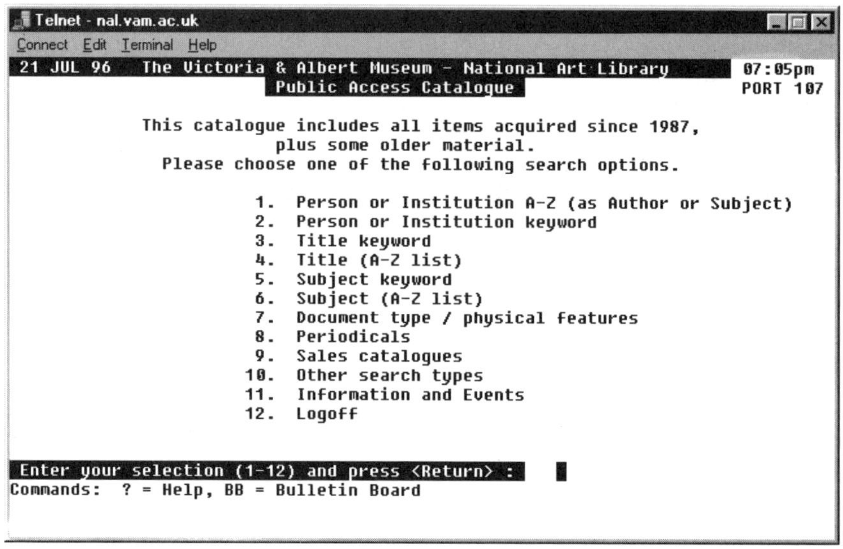

Telnet - nal.vam.ac.uk

Connect Edit Terminal Help

```
21 JUL 96   The Victoria & Albert Museum - National Art Library      07:05pm
                           Public Access Catalogue                    PORT 107

            This catalogue includes all items acquired since 1987,
                        plus some older material.
              Please choose one of the following search options.

                     1.  Person or Institution A-Z (as Author or Subject)
                     2.  Person or Institution keyword
                     3.  Title keyword
                     4.  Title (A-Z list)
                     5.  Subject keyword
                     6.  Subject (A-Z list)
                     7.  Document type / physical features
                     8.  Periodicals
                     9.  Sales catalogues
                    10.  Other search types
                    11.  Information and Events
                    12.  Logoff

 Enter your selection (1-12) and press <Return> :
Commands:  ? = Help, BB = Bulletin Board
```

A very worthy public use of Telnet is for accessing online library catalogues all over the world. The illustration (right) demonstrates a Telnet connection to the Victoria and Albert Museum's library - you can search for a title and detect whether it is on loan from any Internet connection in the world.

FTP

This stands for *File Transfer Protocol.* This protocol is the part of the Internet that allows you to transfer programs and data from the disc of one computer to another. They can be at other ends of the world, as long as they are connected to the Internet and are set up to use the File Transfer Protocol.

There are thousands of publicly accessible FTP sites - machines which companies and individuals have placed on the Internet from which anyone may download programs or *utilities.* To access these machines, you use a program to connect to the host computer, and then you can browse the files and directories via remote control as though the machine were right next to you. You can download any files that are publicly accessible, usually by logging on to the host machine as "anonymous" (the process is therefore known as "*anonymous FTP*"). Often these files are in a compressed state to save space and the time it takes to download them. The decompressor program will also be available online.

These FTP sites contain a wide range of data, including literary works, song lyrics, MIDI music files, public domain programs, utilities and graphical images. Because there are so many FTP sites, there are various search services like *Archie* which direct you to all the FTP sites containing data related to a keyword you provide.

It is from FTP sites that most users obtain the majority of the software they use to access other Internet services. Many users are initially surprised at the amount of free or inexpensive shareware available.

IRC and MUDs

These are two contentious areas of the Internet. IRC stands for *Inter Relay Chat.* It is a protocol which allows users to communicate with many others simultaneously and in real time (with no delay between exchanges, in other words). If Email is Internet's answer to the postal system, IRC is its answer to CB radio. You log on to IRC via an IRC client program. This attaches to an IRC server, a machine which distributes the various "channels" of immediate discussion to others around the world. Some educational organisations use the IRC structure, but ensure that unhelpful disruptions are avoided through password access and close supervision.

MUD stands for *Multi User Dimension* (or 'Dungeon', as these systems are often used for online textual Dungeons and Dragons games). The idea of the MUD is similar to IRC, except that a MUD does not span the whole of the Internet, unlike IRC, but is a specific service run on a specific machine. There may be "gateways" to other MUDs, but the idea is that the server contains a self-contained "virtual" world.

MUDs are accessed via Telnet (see above) or special client programs, which cater to the structure of MUDs more successfully. You give yourself a nickname on a MUD and can chat with people in virtual rooms, which are "built" by the users.

Some MUDs have game content, where riddles and puzzles are solved collaboratively. Because our society frowns upon such apparently time-wasting activities as chatting and game-playing, especially when there is a phone bill to pay, some institutions actively discourage these services and ban them. It is easy to understand the strong counter-reaction to MUDs and so on, mainly through their adverse effect on able people; but glowing reports have been received from virtual MUD classrooms and other novel experiments. Also, IRC has proved itself a very useful and immediate forum of information from people in areas of conflict, where traditional methods of communication are restricted, and for rapid access to those with specialised knowledge.

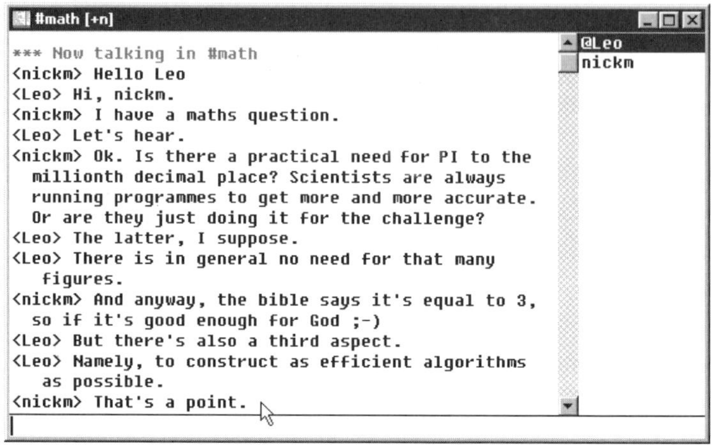

An impromptu (but genuine) discussion between two people - one in England, the other in Sweden - on an IRC mathematics "channel".

World Wide Web

The web, for some people, is almost synonymous with the Internet. In a sense, this is true: one aspect of the world wide web is that you use one computer program to access many of the services outlined above through a unified address. Those documents constructed especially for the world wide web are what excite most people, though. Web server machines all over the world furnish the user with bright, colourful pages of text, graphics, animation and even sound.

You browse web pages by selecting hypertext links. In practice, this means clicking upon a word, phrase or picture, which will transport you to a page related to that word or phrase. Whether the page is on the same server machine or on another thousands of miles away makes no difference to the user - it looks like just another link in this infinitely inter-connected mesh: hence the term world wide web.

A popular program for browsing the world wide web is *Netscape Navigator*, which allows one to "plug-in" extended multimedia features, and includes access to *Java*, a programming language not unlike C++ (an extremely popular language used for all manner of programming tasks). Java runs small (at the moment) programs across the Internet, these often being incorporated in a wider set of web pages.

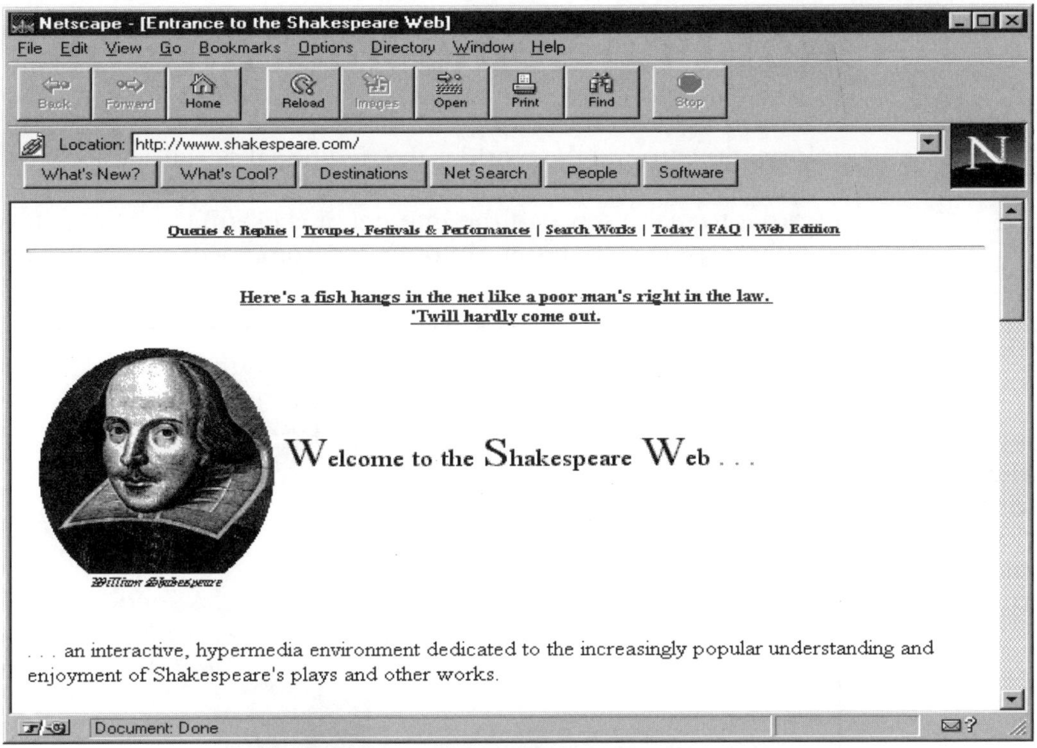

The Web turns the Internet into a playground of intuitive exploration. While good for classifying and cataloging textual material (as illustrated above) its real power comes in the synthesis of text and image (see left), where the techniques of traditional publishing combine with interactive, networked presentation.

Routing some information

A surprisingly useful analogy of the way the Internet routes its information around the world is the traditional postal service.

In order to make sense of the Internet, it is useful to examine the parallel steps in getting some information from, for example, Britain to Japan.

The Post - information is routed around the world in a matter of days (if you're lucky).

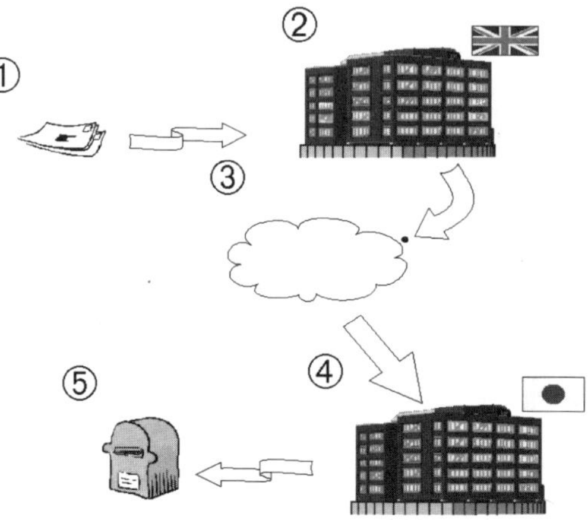

The postal service

1) Information is packaged in an envelope, which displays an address and makes sure the package arrives in one piece.

2) It arrives at the local sorting office. If no postcode is on the envelope's address, the post office converts the street address to the postcode using their database.

3) The enveloped information can go through any number of processes before arriving in Japan. It may be routed through several countries, may go through the air or over the sea. If an intermediate stop is unavailable, the postal service will make sure it takes another route.

4) It arrives in Japan, filtering through various local sorting offices

5) It arrives at its final destination. If the destination is a block of flats, it is up to the flat's caretaker to determine how the deliveries will reach the right doors.

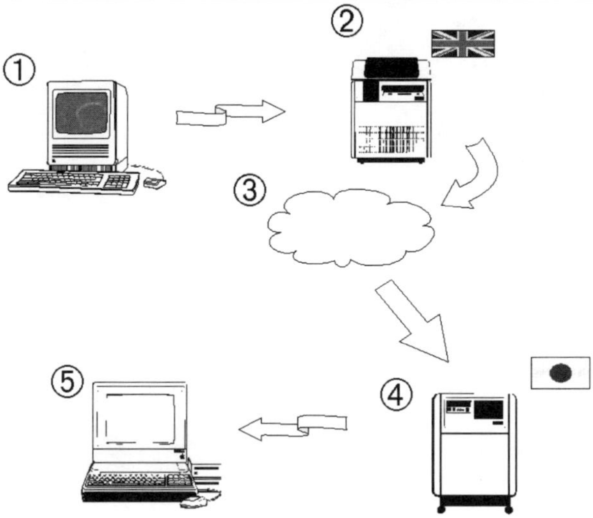

The Internet

1) Information is sent as a TCP/IP "packet", encapsulating the address and information to validate the package once it has arrived at the other end.

2) It arrives at a local "router" machine. The Domain Name Server (DNS) converts the address into its corresponding IP number.

3) It will be routed through any number of networks on its way to Japan, over many different kinds of physical links. If a usual link isn't available, it will try to be routed via an alternative.

4) It arrives in Japan, eventually reaching the router which can deliver it to its final destination.

5) If there is a local area network (LAN) at the destination (for example, an office or campus-wide network), it is up to the local network administrator to ensure the information arrives at the appropriate machine.

The Internet - information is routed around the world in a matter of milliseconds (if you're lucky).

What does the Internet offer for Education?

The exciting possibilities opened up to any learner by the Internet.

In particular, a look at the possible learning strategies one might undertake, and an overview of online resources in the humanities and sciences.

Chapter 2

> **The URL**
>
> Throughout this book, you will be presented with Internet addresses called URLs (Uniform Resource Locators). They are usually preceded by *http://* For example, *http://www.bbc.co.uk/* will, through a web browser, take you to the BBC's pages.
>
> Once online with your world wide web browser software, type the full address into the location box at the top of its window, or select "Open Location" (or a synonymous option) from the browser's File menu.
>
> After typing in the location and pressing the return key (or clicking on OK or whatever option your browser offers), the web site mentioned in the book should be displayed on your screen.

The Internet is an education in itself. Learning about the community and how it works, communicating with fellow pupils across the globe and discovering niches of experimentation; even if it had no specific educational resources, getting to grips with the Internet would be an heuristic exercise in itself. But, of course, it offers a very wide range of specifically educational resources. Academic establishments still play a very important part on the Internet, so there is a vast pool of talent represented by the people and data available.

In the United Kingdom, universities and other educational establishments connect up to the Internet though the *Joint Academic Network* (Janet) and its more powerful successor, Super Janet. There are equivalent networks connecting to the Internet all over the world. This means that there is much communication between students and staff of universities. More and more schools, too, are now launching into the Internet, so their presence is beginning to be felt.

Internet users

Until the 1990s, there were only a few kinds of Internet users – mainly higher academic and military researchers. At the beginning of the 90s, with the development of new and friendlier services, and with the establishment of commercial and domestic Internet service providers, a wider range of people began to realise that the Internet offered a greater potential than the hodge-podge of limited communications services on offer thus far. With more powerful software, it became easier to connect a microcomputer to the Internet with a modem, so the number of hobbyists and home users online increased rapidly. Commercial interest grew exponentially such that by the mid-nineties, those businesses with no interest in providing some kind of Internet presence were in the minority.

With the development of cyber cafes, and initiatives to connect developing nations, the user-base is becoming more diverse all the time. While there is still a predominance of white, educated males, this sector does not represent the hegemony it does in other technological areas, and the influence of multi-cultural interaction on a level playing field suggests that the Eurocentric information elite might not remain the problem some commentators suggest. English is the most popular language on the Internet, but this does not preclude the many resources available in and for other languages.

The Internet is entering a new phase of development, in which those who have little technical knowledge are beginning to be enticed by its promises. Several multinational companies wish to exploit and expand this new wave of interest by creating inexpensive "information appliances", which attach to the television and allow for relatively easy access to the Internet. It remains to be seen how the hyperbole will be translated into practical reality.

Why connect our schools?

There are several ways of answering this question. One can be practical and utilitarian, and argue that the future employability of any pupil will be determined to a large degree by his or her ability to communicate, and that the range of communicative possibilities these days includes online literacy. We deplore the fact that some children leave school unable to read or write. Literacy with the medium through which much of their future reading and writing will take place is just as important, and that includes the Internet.

Of course, such utilitarian justifications soon lead to more inspiring ones – the very notion of education and learning itself can be enhanced by a sensitive and imaginative use of the Internet's power to connect, in a sense beyond the technical. This is, perhaps, an apposite place to introduce a word which, beyond all others, encompasses the Internet: eclectic.

For some, the eclectic is something to be feared. Moreover, that free-ranging and intuitive learning experience we enjoy before our schooling is often seen at odds with a formal education. Yet few may doubt the effectiveness of such pre-linear discovery. It is this exploratory form of knowledge that the Internet is best at supplementing. This does not necessarily mean the result of Internet research will be qualitatively different to other forms of learning – whether it is or isn't depends on the disposition of the researcher – but it does mean an education through the Internet is likely to encompass a wider assemblage of related information, topics and skills.

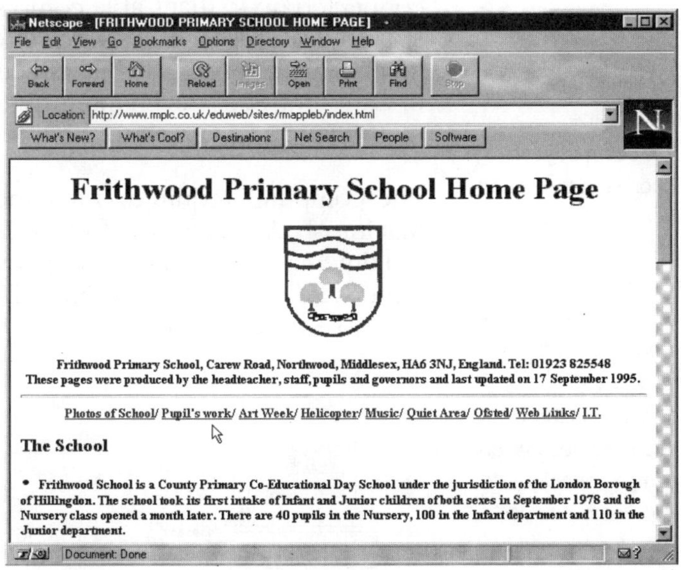

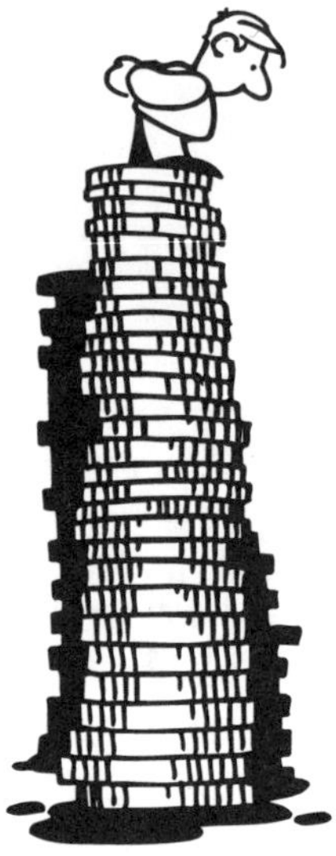

Is it expensive?

Often, teachers hesitate in giving the go-ahead to an Internet connection because of the apparent expense involved. Later chapters deal with costs in detail, but it should be stated immediately that the bottomless pecuniary pit is a misconception: an Internet connection can be very economical if managed prudently.

You get a subscription to an Internet Service Provider (ISP) and connect (usually) over the normal telephone line with a modem – a device which converts the squawks and sounds which like travelling down phone-lines into digital data, which is what computers prefer, and vice versa. Modems cost from about £75 for a slower model to about £150 for a well priced fast model (which transmits at 28.8 thousand bits per second – twice as fast). Modems even faster than this are now becoming available, and are compatible with some ISP's systems.

As mentioned above, you get your connection (which includes at least one Email address) from an Internet Service Provider (ISP). These are now very competitive, so you can stay online for as long as you want for around £10 a month, all inclusive. Unlike any other media, there is no additional charge, no matter which sites in the world you are browsing – all you pay is your fixed subscription fee and a standard local telephone call. If you are in a Cable TV area, and an ISP is also connected up to that Cable company, you may get free local calls or special deals for schools, which effectively means you can stay online for absolutely no cost – whether you're chatting to someone in Camden or Canberra. See later chapters for further details on ISPs and different methods of connecting to the Internet.

The computer required is a standard system – PC, Acorn, Apple Macintosh, Amiga and so forth (all of which can connect). The usual multimedia attachments are required if you want fancy web browsing. Otherwise, your ISP will supply all the necessary software, with more available for downloading.

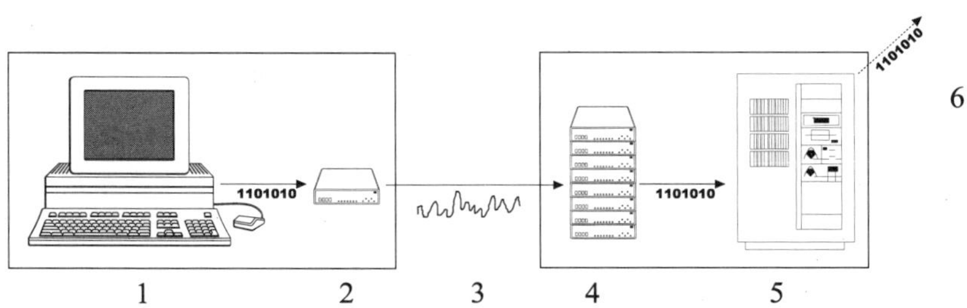

Below right: Connecting to your ISP.

1) The computer sends digital data to the modem.

2) The modem converts the data into fluctuating electrical representations of sound-waves.

3) The sound is transmitted down the telephone line.

4) A modem at your ISP converts the sound back to digital data.

5) The ISP's server machine decides the best route around the Internet that data should take.

6) The data is then routed to its destination over high capacity leased lines. You do not pay for this part of the connection – your ISP pays a fixed rate.

Learning strategies

Because the Internet and its information is so diverse, there is no single simple model of integrating the system into a learning environment. Most schools and other academic institutions will integrate the Internet into a pre-existing scheme. This is all very well, but being overly rigid rather strait-jackets the Internet's possibilities. For a truly successful synthesis of the Internet into a programme of learning, one needs a little flexibility of approach.

The traditional curriculum

Internet can complement the traditional curriculum quite happily, supplementing the drier and more abstract Key Stages with some real-world, interactive examples. However, you are doomed to disappointment if you believe that the Net can deliver simple, pre-packaged "Curriculum Quanta", nicely digested for your particular exam board's chunks of the National Curriculum.

If this is your approach to the Internet, you will become discontented. The information on the Internet comes from a wide variety of academic and commercial sources. Some will be more suited to American curricula. Some will be suited to no current curriculum at all. For productive online experiences, it is up to the imaginative teacher and the receptive pupil to extract the relevant information, perhaps even learning more from the extraction than if the information is spoon-fed. The curriculum becomes a focus and a framework, rather than a fetish.

Schools which believe that education signifies more than just ticks on a National Curriculum checklist will gain much from the Internet. Those whose red pens are only poised to delineate and proscribe will not.

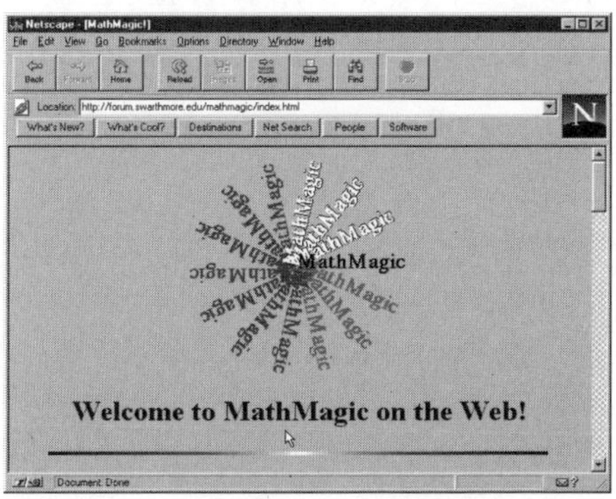

Below left: An educator who turns his or her nose up at a site merely because it uses the word "math" rather than "maths" will be missing many learning opportunities.

The MathMagic site is an example of a superb international resource which can, with imagination, be used well in any flexible curriculum.

`http://forum.swarthmore.edu/mathmagic/`

Making an example of it

Some areas of the curriculum are, obviously, more difficult to teach than others. This is not always simply a product of the topic's inherent complexity or obscurity, but because the pupil finds it difficult to plug the idea into his or her world-view. Or, indeed, to any world-view. The plea "but how does what I'm learning fit into real life" is familiar to all but the most enthusiastic learner. The question reflects not simply a yearning for some guarantee of financial utility, but is a request for some example of how and where that academic postulate fits into human society beyond the closed circuit of abstract academe.

The Internet provides such exemplar material. Because of its wide-ranging scope, the forums and web sites are rich with diversity of experience, with the combined academic and commercial user-base ensuring that even obscure topics will receive extensive attention in a lively, discursive context.

Interactive exploration

A really successful Internet scholar will allow the interactive nature of the system to shed light on his or her very notions of what it is to learn. On the Internet, every teacher is, to an extent, a learner. Every learner has something to teach. In the classroom, such sentiments have a specious quality. On the Internet's level playing-field, they represent a contingent reality. The blithe Net learner will begin with fewer preconceptions, where learning becomes an investigation into a wide variety of connecting areas.

The strategy involves less unquestioning consumption of approved "Facts", be they textbooks or class-notes, and more context-analysis. With a kaleidoscopic, truly interactive media like the Internet, the question which one learns to ask is not only, "what is being said?" but, "in what context is it being said? Who is saying it, and why are they saying it?" Those who believe that children and pupils are unable to cope with such discrimination have their fears diminished after observing them online for just a short time: they often appear to be more media-savvy than their elders!

Humanities

At first the major users of the networks that make up the Internet were those in the scientific community. For example, the world wide web's protocols were developed by CERN (the particle accelerators in Geneva) as a way of distributing complicated and linked on-line documents. One of Usenet's first major users was *Bionet*, a large sub-network of biologists who use the forums to discuss virtually every aspect of their science. Nevertheless, the scientific hegemony has loosened its grip, with more and more humanities-related departments and organisations coming online. Of course, amongst the trivia and jargon, there are Usenet newsgroups dealing with subjects including philosophy, sociology and music. There are feminist discussion groups, areas discussing the ideas of Jaques Derrida, history newsgroups and so on. The variety is endless, with new groups being formed every day. Because of the high academic concentration within the official Usenet groups, it is likely that a question asked in a newsgroup will be discussed by those currently at the pinnacle of academic investigation in that area.

There are also many discursive electronic mailing lists and online magazines dealing with aspects of popular culture, available by Email. Because these are written by users for the tens, hundreds or thousands of other "subscribers", the creative 'zines are an ideal opportunity of airing pupils' work to a greater audience.

The world wide web, because of its user-friendly interface and powerful multimedia and hypertext links is a very fruitful area for humanities sites. The Vatican Library is available as a web site, with diverse displays, including the Dead Sea Scrolls. An electronic version of *Le Louvre* includes special exhibitions, textual information and so forth. The former Soviet Archives are available for the open perusal of history students all over the world. There are more and more specialised electronic exhibitions coming online. The Holocaust Museum in Washington, for example, gives full access to various exhibits and access to a database of text, images, audio sound-samples and even full-motion video clips from newsreels and archive footage. These can be played back via an MPEG player (a Full Motion Video player that makes use of the special compression routines).

Below: Le Webmusuem remains an extremely popular online art gallery, with magnificently researched and presented exhibitions and beautifully scanned pictures.

`http://sunsite.unc.edu/wm/`

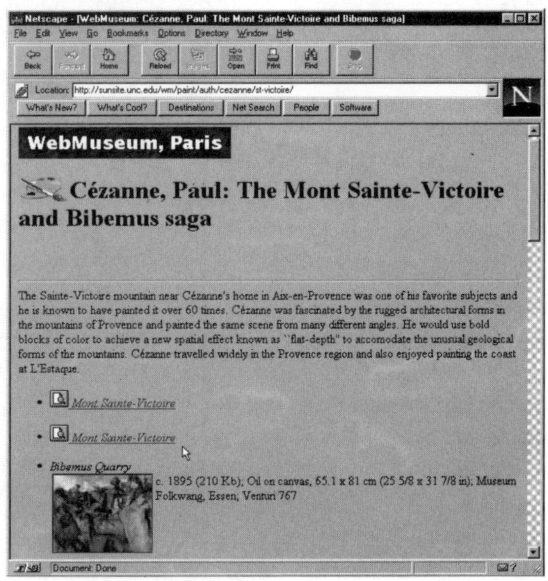

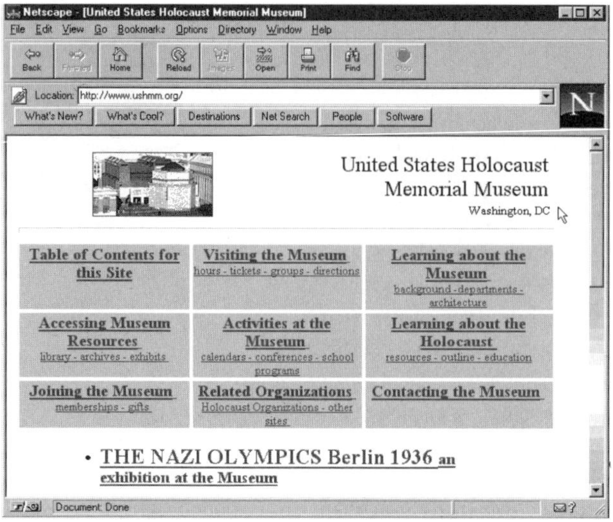

There are large libraries of humanities resources – catalogued and archived for easy access. The Bible, dictionaries and Roget's Thesaurus are online and can be keyword-searched. A significant development is *Project Gutenberg* and related schemes. These societies' aims are to provide as much out-of-copyright material on the Internet as possible. They already have many works of literature, including the Complete Works of Shakespeare, Frankenstein and the American Constitution. Such repositories are supplemented by many others, including huge archives of classical music MIDI files, interactive creative-writing courses and so on. Again, eclectic in the most popular of senses, ensuring every interest is represented.

Above: one of several Holocaust memorial sites online, this one affiliated to the Washington museum.

`http://www.ushmm.org/`

Very innovative are the organisations which use the MUD multi-user chat environment to run virtual-classes. *LinguaMOO* is an example, on which cultural events, poetry "readings" and even dissertations take place between pupils and students all over the world. This global dimension

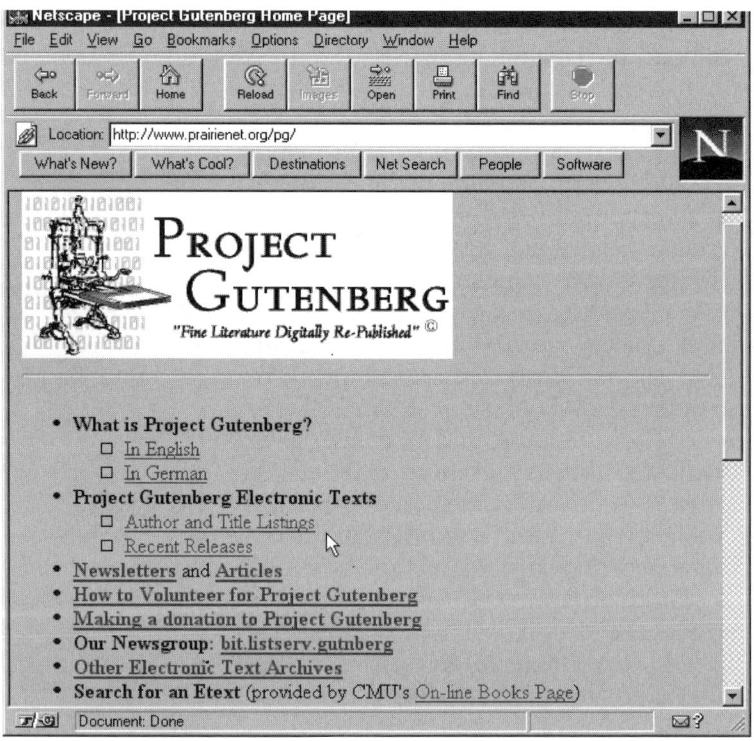

Right: Project Gutenberg remains exemplary in its commitment to getting literary texts online and freely available for all.

`http://www.prairienet.org/`

is very important. Through the Internet, politics and language students can gain immediate first-hand experience of other cultures throughout the world. For the latter, online language laboratories have been running successfully for some time, with the virtual cultural exchange leading to some strong international friendships.

Collaborative efforts extend to artistic spheres – musical composition between pupils around the world (swapping MIDI files and adding their own cultural variations) have produced some very interesting results. Again, it must be stressed, this is something any school can become involved in. As with all other Internet projects, interactivity is the key to success. Learning becomes, once again, not some troublesome annoyance tacked on to general experience but the experience itself. With every pupil in every school now able, through the web, to become a world-publisher, those involved with humanities can return to the ideal of active involvement in a shared culture rather than passive consumption of an imposed one.

Below: Because MIDI files do not take up much memory, you can download, say, a beautifully transcribed Fugue from one of the many music repositories and play it back through your MIDI keyboard or sound-card.

`http://www.prs.net/midi`

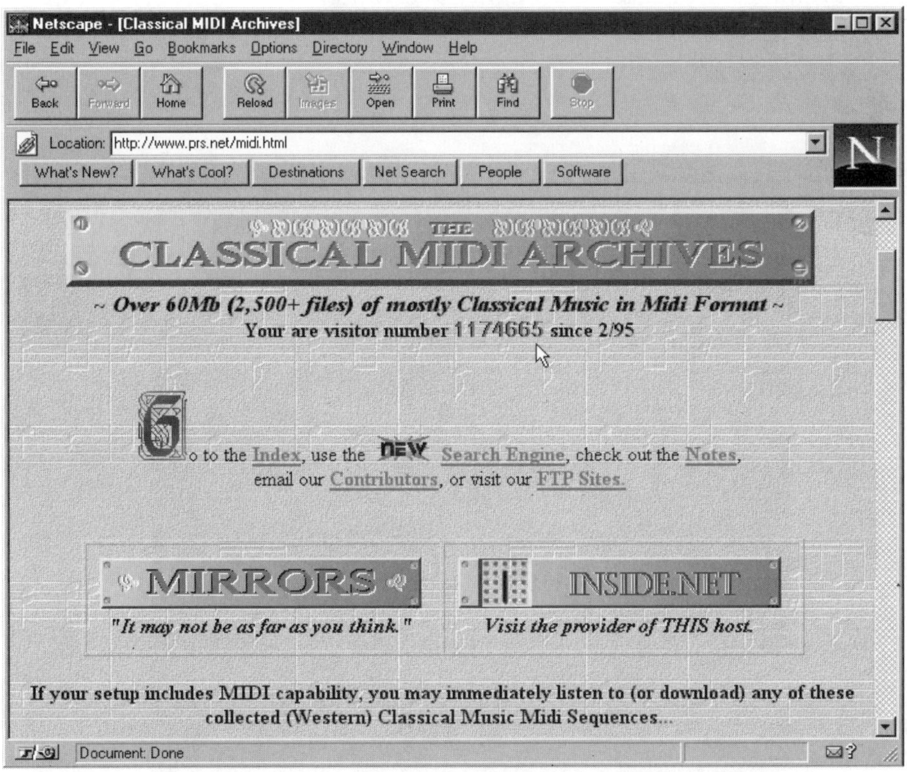

Sciences

The Internet is rich in scientific sources and ongoing scientific discussion. In fact, it has been said more than once that if you want to find the cutting edge of scientific thought, it will be discovered, rough and ready, within the Usenet newsgroups long before it enters any journal.

It should be remembered that the newsgroups are used as a means of communication between scientists, and so the school user will have the privilege of spying on real scientists as they do real work. If their language becomes too technical, a polite request to clarify what is meant will, nine times out of ten, meet with a comprehensible response. There are newsgroups concerning virtually every area of scientific study, at every level of sobriety. New and controversial theories can receive a critical airing on the Internet, even when spurned by the notoriously close-minded traditional journals. This does not mean that the Internet is only good for arguing about faster-than-light travel or Zero Point energy – common or garden scientific issues are discussed every day in the context of practical situations.

Below: NASA is one of the most active web sites of all. As well as a huge range of educational resources, there are many special projects, including live Internet coverage of current space missions and the like.

`http://www.nasa.gov/`

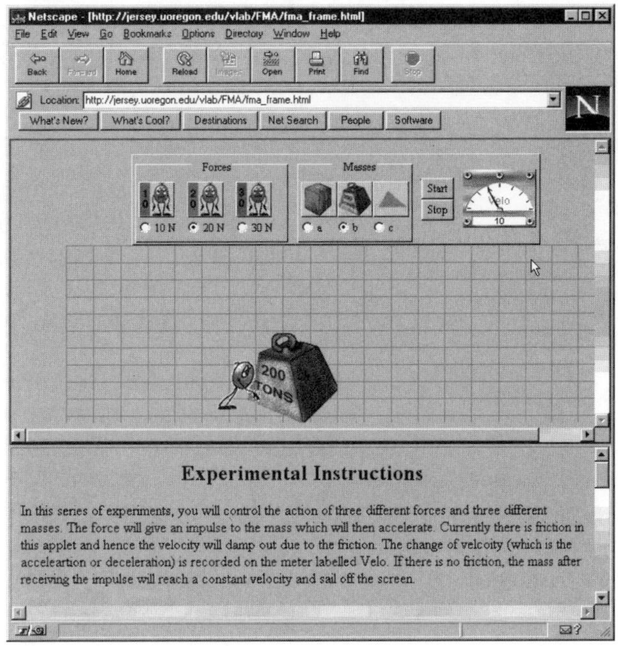

Above: As Java, a programming language which can run programs across the Internet, is beginning to be built into world wide web browsers, sites are becoming even more interactive. The website illustrated above is a part of a full virtual laboratory. This interactive experiment illustrates Newton's Laws.

`http://jersey.uoregon.edu/vlab/FMA/fma_frame.html`

In the current commercial dazzle, it is useful to remember that the world wide web was initiated as a tool of scientific communication. There is an enormous amount of scientific educational material online. Much of it is highly pictorial. Of course, one of the primary contributors is CERN itself. At a less heady, but just as interesting level, sites have been set up specifically for school children. Java, an interactive programming language which integrates into the world wide web, allows small programs to run in a web browser's window over the Internet. This has facilitated virtual laboratories, with usable measuring equipment, automatic graphs and any number of other exciting innovations.

Mathematics, that make-or-break subject, is one of the Internet's most valuable areas. There are lesson plans, enjoyable mathematical puzzles, and volunteer groups set up specifically to help children all over the world who are struggling with particular mathematical areas. Both pupils whose work is suffering due to feelings of intimidation in a classroom environment, as well as those who have progressed beyond the curriculum, will find a happy niche through the Internet.

Of course, there is a large amount of computing and computer science material online. There are many Usenet newsgroups concerning every aspect of every popular system. These range from technical discussion areas to the infamous "advocacy" newsgroups, where owners of different machines argue the benefits of their system over others. There are groups for individual software packages, for researchers in Artificial Intelligence, and a newsgroup for every popular programming language – which is very useful if you have a problem implementing a program. As usual, there are many knowledgeable souls who are more than willing to help. Perhaps the Internet's most impressive achievement to date is the creation of a popular operating system through it. A Norwegian student decided he'd like to write a version of the powerful Unix operating-system for normal PCs. He decided it should be free (unlike "official" versions, which can cost thousands). Through discussion and collaborative programming via the newsgroups and other Internet channels, *Linux* was born. It proved faster than most other operating systems on the PC, and better than most of the expensive versions of Unix it was designed to replace. What's more, because of the newsgroups, it is better supported as well! Now, any school computing department can set up a very cheap, very powerful Unix workstation, even network, safe in the knowledge they will not be alone in the deep-end.

In the area of general computing, every computer company now offers support and updates to programs through FTP sites. The world wide web is an exciting computing environment in itself, and watching it develop is the best computing education one can hope for – it encapsulates virtually every aspect of computer science.

Shareware and free computer programs abound on the Net. You can search for what you want with one of the web's powerful and freely-available *search engines*. With access to the world's computer libraries, it is possible to keep the school's computer system up to date. If you suddenly need to view a particular kind of computer graphic, for example, you can simply download an appropriate viewer. You'd like a new Email-reader? Download it, and consult its web page for documentation.

The computer resources on the Internet show conclusively how inaccurate is the usual picture of the computing enthusiast as an antisocial, isolated nerd. Instead, one finds a vibrant, helpful community excited by this supreme human invention and happy to share in its achievements.

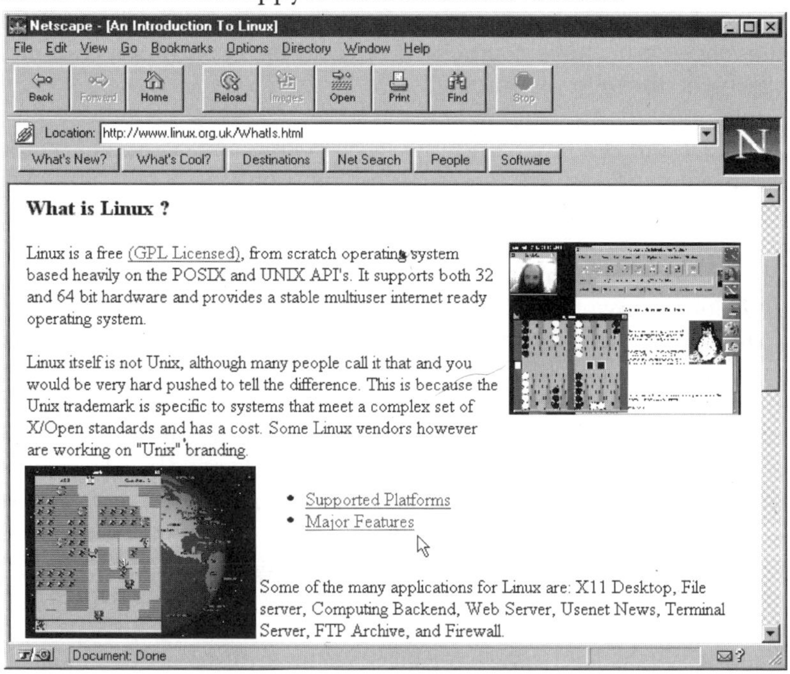

Right: A good-quality, free version of Unix which turns any PC into a work-station was constructed through Internet co-operation. Linux is very well supported, and allows any pupil to delve into advanced computer science with little expense.

http://www.linux.org.uk/

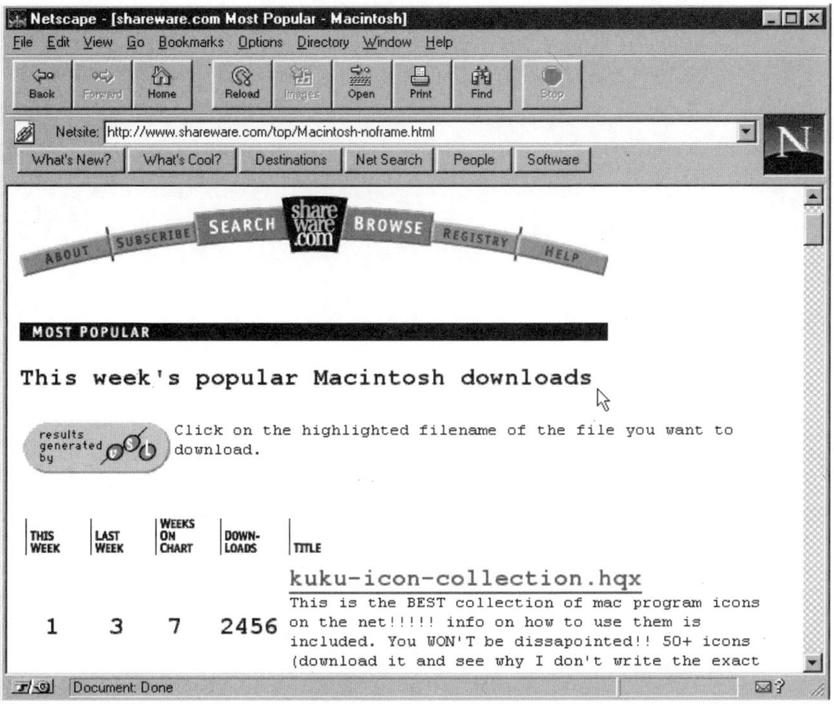

Left: Good quality public domain and shareware programs can be downloaded, free of charge, for every computer system. An easy way to start a software library, and essential for getting the programs that make use of the Internet's services.

`http://www.shareware.com/`

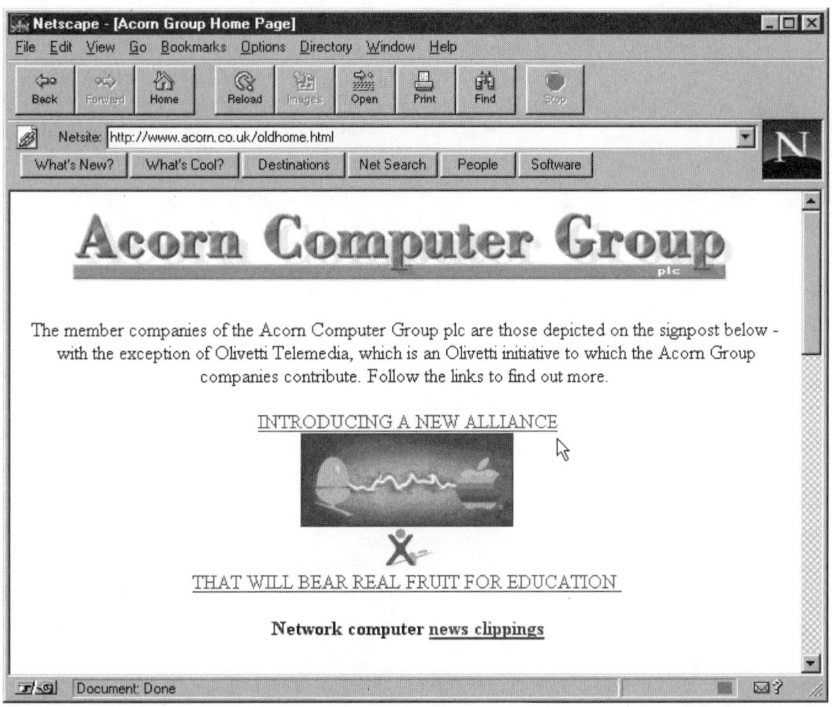

Right: Be it ever so humble, every computer company has a presence on the Internet, with support, updates and information available at the press of a button.

`http://www.acorn.co.uk/`

Dealing with Problems

The Internet has been demonised in some circles.

It is important to keep things in perspective.

In this chapter, you can find successful strategies for dealing with contentious issues.

Chapter 3

Mad cow disease is one of the few modern bogeymen the media have not blamed on the Internet – this may be because journalists are now more accepting of the Net as eyes, ears and memory tool and less as punchbag. Rarely at first was there discrimination between the Internet, commercial services and single Bulletin Boards – the whole world of computer communications was painted as a sin-filled Bohemia: children downloaded pornography by the bucketful, terrorists communicated freely in Usenet Newsgroups, anarchists' websites broadcast their plans to engulf the planet in a tide of nihilism.

As more articles and television programs were produced, the more overblown were the claims. Sadly, some educators were influenced for quite some time, and even today irrational fears about the perils of the Net influence decisions. There is a slight danger that we will swing the other way and become too enthusiastic about its potential, but the judicious governor, head and teacher triad has for a long time been making sensible decisions about allocating resources.

Those who have spent any time on the Internet will be well aware that the subversive and negative elements are only a small part of it, and do not contaminate the whole beast. The problem is, these hyperbolic claims have tainted the Internet in public perception as well. The public includes parents and parents complain about things to head teachers. Therefore, besides there being a genuine need to protect children from some things with the power to deprave and corrupt, it is also essential that the governing body of the school and the parents can be confident and secure in the knowledge that, in general, their children are receiving far more good than harm from the Net.

Fortunately, it is now possible to demonstrate the positive aspects of the Internet sufficiently to convince most sceptics that, even taking into account the inevitable tricky considerations, a blanket ban on the Internet in a caring school environment will be a grave disservice to the children, who will be experiencing the online world without the benefit of any helpful academic context at all.

Minor irritants

What on the Internet deserves censorship depends very much on the age group of the pupils and the general level of tolerance amongst staff and parents. Because the Net is such a free and wide-ranging forum, there are some sections which would be deemed undesirable at some times. These include various Usenet newsgroups, some Email magazines ('zines), and a few areas on the world wide web. The nature of the material within all of these is quite different. For example, Usenet contains in its alternative hierarchy several "oddball" groups popping up and disappearing all the time. One such example is **alt.nuke.the.usa**, which seems to consist of Americans and British people throwing rather colourful ASCII invective at one another.

Then there are the *flame* newsgroups, intended for people who wish to vent their spleen. Search engines, the quick-acting programs that researchers use to find study material, can very easily be set up to seek out any of these by name, class, or content. It is unlikely that protection programs will do more than delay access. As pupil publishing power increases, whether done from school or home, some unseemly comment, a sort of electronic graffiti, is likely to be circulated more widely than it does on the playground. It is not enough to invoke the laws of libel here – parents and schools will be expected to take responsibility for the output of their charges. Nevertheless, these sorts of areas are unlikely to deprave and corrupt school pupils – it's all very much at the level of the playground.

However, it can be argued that this sort of thing should remain on the playground – at least pupils will be getting some fresh air and not running up large phone bills. These network activities might be considered as being in the "third division" set of items which need to be controlled or censored – they are not in themselves likely to create any permanent problem but must be controlled by subtle diversion to those areas which are, ultimately, more fulfilling. If this is not done, school governors will, rightly, become anxious at the proportion of puerile material emanating from this powerful medium of communication. Within this category, too, will be the MUDs and IRC. They are notoriously addictive and their control is probably needed in a school.

More contentious areas

In the second division are the Usenet groups which contain visual and verbal erotica, and various socio-political pressure groups who have sites on Usenet and the world wide web, ranging from homosexual lobbyists to animal rights activists. Groups like these usually contain material no more extreme or insidious than that readily available in the traditional media, but almost all schools will, understandably, desire their access to be regulated. It will be at the discretion of the head empowered by the governing body whether any regulated access, as a part of a social or personal educational programme, should be given to the more responsible groups with educational content as opposed to those that are simply there to titillate or horrify.

Some of the *moderated* areas provide a sensible and objective introduction to various contentious subjects, including child abuse and drug rehabilitation, and may be a more effective medium than salacious playground gossip or tabloid agony aunts. Every night national television services carry post-watershed if not post-videorecorder material that explores these areas to the full in documentary, drama and jest. Responsible schools who are used to dealing with and extracting from such contentious areas will have little problem adapting their strategies to the online paradigm.

Nasties

The "first division" is, thankfully, a small one. The pockets of violent racism, pornography and anarchist and drugs "cookbooks" represent a smaller proportion of the Internet than some press reporting would have you believe. Nevertheless, the novelty of the Internet as a communications medium has meant that these areas have been given an unworthy amount of attention by that same press. Fortunately, this means that sites are now increasingly vigilant in their monitoring of such activities. Often it will take no more than an Emailed note to a site manager, informing him of some of his users' activities, for those activities to be stopped.

Because the people attracted to such activities seem, in general, to have little imagination, their rantings become tedious and the initial frisson of discovering forbidden fruit will soon dissipate from the majority of pupils' minds. One of the great benefits of a medium whose primary means of communication is uniform ASCII text is that it deprives extremists of their most powerful weapons: oral showmanship, the cult of personality, and rousing invective. As for online pornography, the time, tedium and effort of downloading and decompressing such material can be hindrance enough in itself; the main problem here is currently home-accessed material that is passed around at school as school-acquired. Because of the large file sizes and the relative paucity of hardware at present, erratic downloads can be detected in a vigilant school environment, and experience shows that it is often straightforward to track back to its roots in a community where the children know the parents would join the school in being against such things.

Although, in general, it is quite difficult to censor the Internet, the school environment actually makes this easier. There rarely will be more than a couple of machines with modems. This will enable a fairly regular monitoring of activities. It is useful if the modem is internal or, if it is an external model, is never allowed out with the possibility of connection to an active phone-line when there is no-one available to supervise. This will ensure that the modem is used only on the machines designated for it.

Prevention

For even more effective protection, password locks can be set up immediately if your programs are loaded off a school *local area network*. If they are loaded off the hard disc, there are several password protection programs available in the public domain which can be downloaded which prevent the machine from booting until the password is entered. Of course, you will have a password given by your Internet service provider which gives access to the actual services, which you must keep safe too.

The best password protection programs are those which include logging facilities, where each pupil has a separate username and password. This allows a DoT style "driving test". In practice, this means only allowing pupils to use Internet facilities on their own after they show themselves to be proficient and responsible users, after a trial period and, perhaps, a small formal test. Then the pupil is awarded her or his Internet Driving License. Psychologically, the licence is an achievement to be defended, not a right to be taken for granted. In a similar manner to the DoT, some rights granted by licence are lost when a misdemeanour or careless behaviour occurs. If all are removed, the user is banned from the system for a set period of time and must needs prove him or herself suitable again via re-test.

Instilling this self-discipline should ensure little overt censorship is required. Nevertheless, limited forms of control can be achieved. Some service providers ensure that their Usenet news feeds do not update several groups which may contain dubious material. In other ways, de facto censorship can be achieved. The downloading of pornographic images, for example, requires large amounts of disc space – often several megabytes per full colour animation. They can also take a longish time to download, so that bloated phone-bills and over-attractive hard-discs would soon reveal the culprits. Of course, various software disc-locks and hard-disc partitioning programs can help too, although you will be penalising the pupil who has genuine uses for large permanent store.

An unsatisfactory method from where we sit is the so-called "walled garden" or "Net Nanny" approach: the Provider claims to give the teacher control over every access and every message. Not only is this stultifying to the individual, but it limits the interaction with other people on the Net, and finally it hands back to the teacher the problem of censorship of every passing message and package, and guarantees pupil frustration as every hiccup in the system will be blamed squarely if unjustly on the luckless censor. One Provider tried thought police, reading every message, and swiftly went bankrupt. Their intellectual descendant, a large American concern currently offering apparently-free access to every school in the UK, uses the sort of filtering program that blocks any word containing unsuitable combinations of letters, in combination with online "cyber police". Again, there is some criticism stateside of other similarly draconian tactics. It will be interesting to see what kind of freedom our children in schools benefit most from handling.

Practical measures

Nothing will make an online site more attractive than an edict forbidding its access. It might be wise, then, to demythologise some of these contentious areas. A history teacher might, for example, explicitly introduce his or her class to an historical revisionist section of the Usenet. The teacher will encourage the class to give any postings, which usually attempt to deny the Holocaust, the close scrutiny with which they would treat any historical source. With careful guidance and an availability of reliable historical counter-sources, even GCSE students will soon begin to realise that this brand of revisionism is peppered with fallacies, distortions and lies. By allowing pupils to explore the meticulously constructed online world wide web Holocaust Museum exhibition as well as the moderated information sources on Usenet, they will, with guidance, be able to work out for themselves the true motivations behind this brand of Revisionism. The lesson will be far better learned than if it was given in a shower of threat-filled invective, warning pupils to stay away from revisionist areas of the network. Or else.

In a similar way, it is unreasonable to expect that a complete ban on MUDs and IRC is practicable, especially when they are both undeniably fascinating forms of communication and entertainment. Much more effective will be the reasoned regulation of their use. Perhaps allocating a strict quota and restricting MUD usage to after-hours may be a solution. Maybe only allowing MUDs to be used in classroom situations (using foreign language MUDs in Modern Language classes) is an idea. Several institutions have self-funding MUD clubs, where each member of the club contributes a small sum of money to pay for the time they spend on-line. They then take turns to log in at specific times. It is surely better to instil in the pupils a sense of self-discipline than to ban MUDs outright, especially when more and more of them will be purchasing modems of their own.

A supportive ISP (Internet Service Provider) is always useful too. Try and go for one that has some sympathy for schools. The *Internet for Learning* service provider tailors its service for schools, monitoring the newsgroups and so forth. There are also many other providers who, although not necessarily specifically aimed at the education community, will be more than happy to help a school, adapting a package to suit its particular needs.

With an information source and communications medium as vast in size and possibility as the Internet, it is only human to feel an exaggerated threat – to allow a sort of cyber-agoraphobia to erect a restrictive “Great Wall of China” around a small group of officially sanctioned activities. That has great disadvantages, though. It could place the Internet in a boring equilibrium in the minds of the pupils, with the staid, carefully selected range of preplanned activities soon losing their appeal, putting the pupil off the Net and the communications revolution it represents. More worryingly, the condemnation and banning of even slightly subversive or unusual elements of the Internet will, as usual, send these activities further underground and shroud them with a mystique, ensuring a logarithmic increase in their popularity. Instead of a frank and communal exploration of the Net, what will remain is little more than a clandestine scavenging for its own sake. Open-minded experimentation is desirable; but appraisal and responsibility must be encouraged to complement and temper it.

Protection software

A number of software packages are now available which give a helping hand in guiding children to more productive Internet resources. These are often based upon frequently updated "blacklisted" sites. These will be barred from the school's computer. With the installation of this software, one should not become complacent, though. It will never replace the vigilant guide and the sensitively motivated pupil.

Cyber Patrol

The software will download updated lists every seven days automatically. It places the restricted sites in categories, so teachers can decide which resources should be banned.
`http://www.cyberpatrol.com/`

Surf Watch

Written as an alternative to Internet-wide censorship, this popular software package now includes a comprehensive list of prevented sites, and also allows regular updates.
`http://www.surfwatch.com/`

Net Nanny

Perhaps the most comprehensive of all tools – this monitors all Net transactions – Email, FTP, news and more. It includes editable "banned word" lists, as well as the usual prevented-sites database.
`http://www.netnanny.com/`

PICS

Not protective software, but an industry-wide scheme for classifying web content. Like the age restriction on films, this is seen as an alternative to draconian system-wide censorship. Web pages will be given these ratings, and PICS compatible web browsers (the latest are) will allow teachers and parents to set the age level of various groups. An example in the consortium's literature is a pupil studying John F Kennedy. Pupils could go to the Playboy website and read the interview, but be prevented from accessing the other predictable areas of the site. Sites that aren't rated are "locked" from view, unless a supervisor's password is entered.

Further information is available at **`http://www.classify.org/`**

Towards adequate INSET

The powerhouse of any school's ability to inspire its pupils is, of course, a correspondingly inspired faculty. In normal classrooms we have all met the kind of pupils who interpret Shostakovitch and Shakespeare while the curriculum delivers rhythm and rhyme. Ever so polite they are too, usually. Today, a home Internet terminal can give each competent pupil who feels restricted by an overly-narrow curriculum a modicum of personal access to every Nobel prize-winning laboratory, thinktank, and university. The UK's enquiry, research, and experiment based technical education system will encourage all our young high fliers to make good use of the high ground. We teachers will now have to begin to learn from their contacts and their insights. This must be one reason why we are having to negotiate more with an increasingly alert pupil population, needing to lay out the syllabus and to justify our demands to ourselves and to our *protégées*. No team, no teaching. Learning becomes a lifelong process. Platitudes, yes, but only solid Internet experience in initial teacher training and in INSET, with firm confidence in using the Net for self-teaching and for directing the studies of other learners, can replace steam power with intellectual internal-combustion. And eventually, perhaps, cold fusion.

INSET

This stands for In service Education Training. It means, in a basic sense, teachers teaching themselves – keeping up to date with the latest in educational philosophy and technology.

As education spreads from the classroom, parents and even pupils are playing a greater role in these training sessions.

Fortunately, Internet INSET can be very cheap: at some schools, pairs of pupils might give lunchtime lecture demonstrations. The lecturer works from a pack of prepared overhead transparencies, so needs little preparation. The demonstrator shows off as much as possible of what is being discussed from a rickety old telephone connection. The technical *pièce de résistance* is the display TV screen, hooked up to a PC. Audience enquiries usually drive the show. The lecturer jumps through his or her acetate pack to whatever part of the Net is asked for. Teachers are totally irrelevant to the performance, although they are welcome to come and learn. Challenged by youth, we learn too slowly to keep up with the pupils in fair competition. Nor is the playing field level: teachers can usually get away with one year's rehearsal before next year's command performance in class; this time it will all be different again next year as the Internet will have developed, and new young pupils will be faster at learning about it again.

INSET, then, becomes something not simply for teachers and by teachers, but for the school community as a whole. As the distinction between the learner and the teacher is blurred in succesful Internet interaction, so it is between trainer and trainee.

A quick list of topics for a longer INSET briefing might be:

- What the Net is.
- What services the Net offers.
- How to use these services.
- How they can be adapted for education.
- How to deal with attitudes towards the Internet.
- How to get on-line at home.
- How to make the Internet available to teachers.

Separate sessions might be run for managers, governors, parents and the IT staff who will be in the firing line.

Training the trainers

All areas of the school community should be given the opportunity to feel comfortable with and about the Internet. The technological aspects need to be demythologised, and the interactive nature needs to be explained and internalised. As such, it is not enough simply to hold a teachers' INSET day – there needs to be management commitment. Also important are introductory sessions for parents, governors and auxiliaries. Not just because this will help them catch up with the pupils, but also so they can feel they have a stake in the school's experiments, and so that when the odd things go wrong, they are a part of the supportive community, and not finger-waggers castigating an inner elite.

We have run Internet learning sessions with a diverse range of groups, from a few colleagues around a terminal to a plenary demonstration in an auditorium of one hundred. In our experience, groups of twenty to thirty are most effective: this allows adequate interaction between speaker and listener, with the number sufficient to allow mutual interaction. With too large a number, though, demonstrators lose the Socratic connection with the audience.

Training or introduction sessions can be held either as a part of a greater school event (an open day, cultural evening, AGM or ordinary PTA meeting) or as a stand-alone occasion. Public interest in the Internet and its educational application almost guarantees that a series of events may be necessary, with, perhaps, each evening tailored subtly to suit a particular audience. It is advisable, though, not to limit an event to too narrow or exclusive an audience. The Internet is eclectic and fully cross-curricular, and scientists will have to learn to live with linguists, not to mention historians and artists. Ageism is out too: a range of pupils in any evening not only allows for some valuable contributions, but also ensures that they know they are included in the school's plans. The more they know at this stage, the more they will direct their research and energy towards aiding and fulfilling the school's evolving plans.

The demonstration team, which may well include pupils, can also have a range of knowledge to complement the audience's. In the ideal world, the team contains the experienced Net user, who is able to guide online demonstrations and answer technical queries, an IT co-ordinator, who may have less online experience, but is familiar with school policy, facilities and opportunities, and an enthusiast, perhaps from outside the school caucus, who is able to inspire and encourage with examples of positive social interaction through the technology. A lucky school will have all three characteristics in one individual. A luckier school will have three such individuals able to complement one another in their tasks. Having more than one demonstrator will also help to head off problems such as technical failure, or heckling doom-sayers in the audience. Our two-man teacher and student team has used this effectively in all manner of configurations: partly to engender old-hand vs young-upstart banter and partly to cover the educator-learner generation gap, to cover issues from both behind and in front of the chalkface.

Good team preparation can include visits to cyber-cafés, and mock sessions and trial runs. Even more useful is online browsing – bookmark useful sites, download jargon lists, audit newsgroups and so on. If you intend taking your audience on a pre-planned online tour, ensure you have alternatives ready in case a particular server is down or running slowly. If there is time to plan, start a Usenet thread a week before the demonstration, perhaps concerning a subject or issue surrounding the current school's experience. Reveal the answers and contributions to the thread on the day of the demonstration. For example, if a field-trip is being planned in another country, try posting a question and making contacts in that country's "soc.culture" newsgroup – as well as being a good example of the ease of global communication beyond the hype, the school's visiting party may find some real live friends waiting to meet them as a bonus!

The demonstrator needs to appeal to a wide range of competencies – there will be some in the audience who are technophobic, who need a gentle and non jargon-filled introduction to the Internet, with particular emphasis placed on continuation and integration rather than revolution and differentiation. There are others whose technical background requires acknowledgement without allowing its domination of the evening,

Communications Decency Act

The CDA is an example of what can go wrong when a government reacts with badly formed legislation to problems about which it understands little. The recently passed act was slipped into an American Telecommunications Reform package. It is ambiguously worded, claiming, to paraphrase, that a service provider will be criminally liable for anything deemed inappropriate by the American government found on the Internet through its services. This is like threatening to throw the manager of British Telecom into prison because of dirty phone-calls made by his customers.

What is more, it is technically un-enforceable – no provider can monitor the millions of transactions passing through its machines every day: only the complete destruction of the Internet would allow such an Act to be practical.

It is ironic that in the month the CDA was passed, the Chinese regime had a crackdown on its Internet-using citizens, imprisoning several ISP employees.

More information on this and other free speech issues is available at `http://www.eff.org/blueribbon.html`

alienating the rest. The audience majority is likely to consist of caring parents and teachers, often silent, but always receptive. Many will also be business people and professionals, partly motivated by the need or desire to adopt Internet practices in their employment. Warning – don't let a strong individual hijack the meeting – invite them to stay afterwards if they want their particular key word search to be satisfied.

Where the meeting takes place and what apparatus is required depends upon the size of the audience and what the school has available. A classroom with an overhead projector and coffee-machine is perfectly adequate. Of course, online facilities add a whole other dimension to the proceedings, with the Usenet-gosh effects followed on very quickly by the web-wow: there is no doubt that the apposite keyword search can illuminate the Internet and its mechanisms more effectively than an hour's exposition. Nevertheless, it is important to ensure that discussion time is freely available, and is not squeezed away by continuing "surfing" – there will be plenty of time for people to follow their interests at a later stage. In this meeting, people with axes need space to grind them, or they will be wielded at a less opportune occasion.

Of course, with more than a handful of people, a single computer screen is ineffective. There are several ways around this. Firstly, out of room demonstrations to small clusters, say, in coffee breaks. Secondly, computers can be adapted to use television screens as their monitors. Several of these around the hall or classroom may be the preferred solution. Thirdly, an electronic tablet, lying over an overhead projector, can be used to display your computer's output. Experience shows that the output is often lower quality than might be hoped for. A loan projection device needs early delivery and trial, partly to ensure it has the right leads. For a larger audience, a powerful overhead projector is needed. With the normal classroom OHP, larger audiences will strain to see the display. Fourthly, there are specialised and powerful integrated projectors which display a large and bright image. These, though, are very expensive, so it's beg, borrow or review time. Whatever the projection technology, technical failures are very likely, so there needs to be an effective backup plan with conventional overhead projector acetates. It is surprising how effective an evening with no more than coffee and discussion can be. A flip chart can be useful to list issues for discussion, both before the meeting, and those arising during it.

While the event is running, it is important to keep an eye on and react to the audience. Once again, more than one presenter is useful. A responsive team will avoid rambling ever onward while the audience is still coping with the mental jumps. It is important to instil in beginner speakers the discipline of self-interruption driven by eye contact and body language. There are many times when something the demonstrator rushes over because it seems trivial or obvious can contain in its proper explanation a solution to current misconceptions and future problems. Although a specific question-and-answer session is always useful, it is vital that the timetable of an event be sufficiently flexible to be driven by audience questions throughout.

For a first introduction of what the Internet offers, a general example-driven overview is useful. This can consist of an outline of Email, newsgroup and web usage, with a little time given to interactive real-time services such as online chat and virtual classrooms. The overview should be illustrated with examples of typical inter-classroom projects, from the simplest Email exchanges between pupils and experts, through interactive language learning and cultural sharing, to collaborative, concurrent science experiments. Video conferencing, for example, through CU-See Me, can be mentioned, and instant audio via the web can be demonstrated. Technical issues, like building web pages and installing *firewalls*, should, at most, have cursory attention: again, head off trouble from hobby-horses by guaranteeing time in a terminal or future q&a session. Directing the rider to a minuting secretary in the room can guarantee that the points are not forgotten. If hard questions arise, do an online keyword search or Email a friend during the demonstration. If all else fails, Email us at **koekie@koekie.org.uk.** The response will probably arrive after the demonstration, but both action and followup will be illustrative.

If the meeting is for more advanced users, the questions will be more demanding of academic detail and penetrating in technical analysis. The number one question will very likely be associated with web page creation: "How DO we get our prospectus online?" A thoughtful reply will not simply refer to HTML and its various editors, but to the need to give more to the community than just an advertisement, perhaps taking a look at the examples of some of the schools already online, and asking what pupil strengths the school wishes to display. More advanced users will also expect to see more of the cutting edge: familiarity with the issues of the day (currently the Java language being integrated into the Netscape and Microsoft Internet Explorer browsers) need to be researched so that effective discussion can be two-way, including taking into account the implications of one particular standard taking off while another, perhaps more inclusive, standard is left behind.

Communicating with Email

Email is a quick and easy way to send messages across the block or around the world.

Unlike most other forms of communication, there is no cost proportional to distance travelled by the message.

Chapter 4

Quick Introduction

Any individual can have his or her own Email address.

Email sent to one individual can only be read by that individual, unless explicitly copied to another, or sent to an electronic mailing list.

Sending international Email does not require an international phone-call.

Email takes a few seconds to send to a server, which then takes over. If Email cannot reach its host, you will usually be notified.

Programs and other attachments can be sent via Email.

Electronic mail is the most widely used facet of the Internet. Some people are happy to subscribe to ISPs which offer nothing but Email facilities. It is probably one of the fastest growing forms of communication ever, and it is easy to see why. Electronic messages can be sent around the world at the press of a key or click of the mouse. You do not need to worry about the geographical location of the recipient or the local time. The costs are minimal when compared with traditional communication media, including *snailmail* (the colloquial Internet term for the traditional paper post service) and international telephone calls. Also, nine times out of ten, the message arrives at its destination after, at most, a few minutes.

Not having to worry about geographical location is quite significant, and is probably one of the system's greatest strengths. It means that communication with a person five thousand miles away can be as quick and spontaneous as with a person only fifty miles away. For years, academics have communicated across the Atlantic and Pacific via Email, with research, questions, answers, abuse, gossip and salutations helping more than anything else to create something close to that elusive global village.

It is not only universities and other higher education institutions which have come online. Recently, more and more schools, not only in the United States, have begun to realise the value of Email as an educational concept and practical tool. Not only does it allow quick and effective communication with other schools and academic institutions, but also it allows pupils to communicate directly with the world about which they are learning. It is quite possible that the author of a pupil's physics or history textbook has an Email address. If the pupil has any comments or questions about the book or sections of it, Email offers an informal and semi-anonymous way of doing so. Because of the still-prevalent symbiotic relationships on the Internet, it may be refreshing to find the extent to which owners of addresses are willing to help.

Because ASCII text is a great equaliser, the implicit hierarchies which are usually so detrimental to effective communications are lessened. The recipient of the note cannot make initial judgements based on appearance, handwriting style, accent, disability or gender. Indeed, many hard-of-hearing and deaf people have commented that Email is one of the few forms of spontaneous communication where the first response is not an embarrassed condescension.

Using Email: an example

An ordinary teacher in an ordinary computer room – let's call her Jane:

1) Jane loads her Email package.
2) She gets her computer to dial up her ISP.
3) It connects.
4) She instructs her Email package to check for new mail.
5) It transfers mail from her ISP, saving it on her local hard disc.
6) She gets her computer to hang up the phone.
7) She reads her Email.
8) She types a reply to some Email, which is queued on her hard disc.
9) She dials up her ISP again.
10) She instructs her Email package to send all the queued messages.
11) They transfer to the ISP's machine, from which they will be routed.
12) She gets the computer to hang up the phone once the messages have finished transferring to her ISP's mail-server.

Data via Email

As well as mailing lists, you can send and receive computer programs and data via Email. It is even possible to read and contribute to Usenet newsgroups over Email, and download software from FTP sites (see later chapters). In order to achieve this, you post a specific request for a specific program to a server machine, using a command given in the service's documentation. It then posts back the requested program or data.

In order to send or receive programs and binary data via Email, it needs to be encoded first, because Email can only transport alphabetic characters. The encoding process converts binary data into thousands of alphanumeric characters, sent via Email and reconverted at the other end. There are several ways of achieving this. A popular way is through an encoding system called *MIME* (Multimedia Internet Mail Extensions). It is now built into most popular Email software, so that the process of attaching a file to your Email and converting it back again is automatic and happens behind the scenes.

Another popular method is called *UUENCODE* (and, conversely, *UUDECODE*). This is especially useful if you are sending pictures or data to a machine running the Unix operating system, as this is built in. Many mail readers on other systems now offer this facility too.

ASCII

The Internet's great success has been achieved largely through agreeing to certain technical rules, and applying them universally. This "open standards" approach did not only occur with the Internet – one of the most useful agreed standards includes dealing with text across different computer systems.

Computers encode everything in numbers – text, pictures and sounds. Each letter of the alphabet is allocated a number internally. ASCII (American Standard Code for Information Interchange) standardises which number equals which letter, no matter what computer or program you're using, rather like Morse Code standardises which dot-dash combination specifies which letter.

Email, Usenet newsgroups and (to an extent) the world wide web make use of standard ASCII text, so that text can be sent between different systems. Unlike a word-processed document, which contains much more internal formatting information, ASCII is simply the plain text – nothing else. That's why, when you send attachments via Email, it converts the file into a stream of text characters, which are decoded at the other end.

ASCII is not the only text-coding standard used on the internet. In some ways, it is limited, particularly in representing non-Latin alphabets and special characters. Nevertheless, you can be pretty sure that ASCII text will be read and written throughout the world.

Mailing lists

Even if Email is the only service to which your school has access, you are not limited to simple one-to-one communications. Electronic mailing lists have sprung up over the years, and there are now thousands of them, spanning every conceivable educational and non-education topic and interest. Subscribing to a list is a simple matter of sending a request. It costs nothing, and once you have subscribed to a non-moderated list, every time you post to that list, your posting will be received by everyone else subscribed to it. On moderated lists, a volunteer screens each posting to the list, perhaps providing a digest of the previous day's postings each morning. Some mailing lists allow you to receive periodical newsletters and online magazines. All of them are invaluable ways of meeting many people who share your interests, and provide good starting points to collect useful addresses.

Protocols

In computing, a protocol defines an agreed set of technical standards, such that some compatibility can be guaranteed between systems using them.

Under this definition, the evolving rules of English grammar and spelling might be termed an emergence of the "English Syntax Protocol"!

On the Internet, the most significant protocol is TCP/IP, which ensures that communication can take place. Additional protocols ensure an open-standards approach is taken when constructing specific features and services.

On the Internet, open-standards are the norm. Few successful protocols have been proprietorial, in the gift of one organisation.

Finding mailing lists

With so many mailing lists and focus groups all over the world, there is likely to be a group of people concentrating on the area that you want to discuss. The problem is in finding them. Initially, you will probably ask like-minded friends and colleagues who are already on the Internet. They may well be able to recommend a mailing list or two.

After exposure to the Internet, the newsgroups and the web, it becomes easier to find mailing lists. The many catalogues of resources on the web include information on mailing lists. Those on the relevant Usenet newsgroups will recommend particular lists too. Finally, the many Internet magazines contain printed catalogues of resources. These often include reviews of selected mailing lists.

Mailing List Software

You will sometimes hear of mailing lists referred to as *listservs*. This is because listserv is the name of some software used to administer electronic mailing lists.

It is not the only software that does that – other names you'll hear might include *majordomo* and *mailbase*. All have their own features and commands, some of which can be accessed by the mailing list subscriber. Email the list maintainer for further information about what's available.

Subscribing to a mailing list

How you actually access a mailing list depends on the system which is being used by the list's maintainer. In general, though, it is simply a matter of sending a small line of text to a central Email address.

For example, say you wanted to subscribe to the **`UK-Schools`** mailing list, which is for teachers and others interested in the use of the Internet in British schools. If your name was Jane Smith, you'd send an Email to **`mailbase@mailbase.ac.uk`** with **`join uk-schools Jane Smith`** as the sole text of your message. You'd then start receiving the group's mail. To post a contribution to the whole list, you'd Email it to **`uk-schools@mailbase.ac.uk`**, and everyone else will be able to read your comments. So, one Email address is for administration, the other is for posting to the list. This is usually how it works.

If you wanted to leave the mailing list, you'd send the message **`leave uk-schools`** to **`mailbase@mailbase.ac.uk`**.

Addresses

Email addresses can seem rather daunting at first, with strings of baffling letters, numbers and punctuation marks. Nevertheless, as standardisation progresses, it is becoming easier to classify them. Here's a typical address:

jbloggs@comlab.ox.ac.uk

To the left of the **@** symbol is always the individual user's Email account – in this case, "**jbloggs**". To the right is the Internet domain of the machine or system upon which that Email account lives. The address tells us where in the world the Email account resides – just as a normal postal address. Instead of the different parts being separated with the commas and spaces like street addresses, Email uses full stops. As with normal postal addresses, the first part of the Internet domain is usually the most specific. In this case, it is "**comlab**", which we may assume is some sort of computing laboratory within an institution. This is not a standard domain name or identifier – we're just using common sense! "**ox**" shows us that the institution in question is Oxford University. "**ac**" stands for academic, and confirms that this address belongs to an academic institution. "**uk**", of course, indicates that the institution is in the United Kingdom. A final two-character indicator is common in most addresses, revealing the country or domain of origin. The table shows some of the more common ones.

Common Country Domains

Country	Domain
Australia	au
Austria	at
Canada	ca
Finland	fi
France	fr
Germany	de
Iceland	is
Ireland	ie
Israel	il
Italy	it
Japan	jp
Korea	kr
Netherlands	nl
New Zealand	nz
South Africa	za
Spain	es
Sweden	se
Switzerland	ch
Taiwan	tw
United Kingdom	uk

For the United States, "**us**" is sometimes used, but American addresses usually have no country domain. Like the UK not having "UK" on its stamps, this is a privilege for starting the whole thing up in the first place.

There are other domain indicators to look out for in an address which indicate the nature of the institution from which it has emerged:

domain	indicated area	examples
ac	academic	bristol.ac.uk
co	commercial	channel4.co.uk
com	commercial	microsoft.com
edu	educational (usually US)	harvard.edu
gov	governmental	nasa.gov open.gov.uk
mil	military (usually US)	navy.mil
net	network organisation	demon.net
org	non-profit organisation	greenpeace.org mensa.org.uk

There are some newer domains that are specific to the United Kingdom. Some of these are quite recent, and so you might not come across them in a while:

`ltd.uk`	Limited Liability company address
`mod.uk`	Ministry of Defence address
`nhs.uk`	National Health Service address
`plc.uk`	Public Limited Company address
`sch.uk`	School address

Here's another address – this time one that genuinely exists, and you should have no trouble understanding:

`president@whitehouse.gov`

There are other weird and wonderful naming conventions on the Internet, especially when communicating between sub-networks. It is not necessary to worry about such things, though, because of the continual standardisation which is occurring.

POP-3

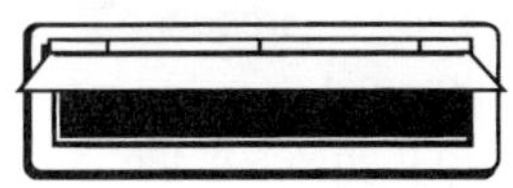

As with everything else on the Internet, there are agreed technical standards concerning the delivery and transmission of Email. The most popular protocol, which is adopted by most ISPs, is called *POP-3*. This stands for *Post Office Protocol* (version 3). Why Post Office? Because your ISP's mail-server machine acts like the PO-boxes at your post office. For each Email address, there is a separate POP-3 account – basically a chunk of your ISP's hard-disc space on a machine connected to the Internet.

When you dial up, your mail software looks for this mail server machine on the Internet. You then type in the password for your POP-3 account (for security, so other people can't read your mail), at which point the mail is transferred to your machine and saved on your hard-disc.

For example, consider the Email address **`jane@rmplc.co.uk`**: the **`jane`** mailbox lives at her ISP (**`rmplc.co.uk`**) on a machine called **`mail`**. So, the machine's full name would be **`mail.rmplc.co.uk`**. The full POP-3 address would, in turn, be **`jane@mail.rmplc.co.uk.`** So, when people send mail to **`jane@rmplc.co.uk`**, the mail will actually be routed to the **`jane`** mailbox on the **`mail.rmplc.co.uk`** machine.

When Jane connects to the Internet, her Email package transfers the mail from the **mail.rmplc.co.uk** machine to her own, saving it on her hard disc for perusal at leisure.

A major benefit of POP-3 is the fact that your Email account lives on a machine at your ISP which is connected to the Internet, so your mail can be accessed from anywhere on the Internet – you don't need to dial up your specific ISP. So you could be in a cyber-cafe across the world – all you'd need to do was input your POP-3 account's address in the preferences of the local software.

The only disadvantage with POP-3 is that each individual's Email address has to have its own account on your ISP's mail-server machine. For each user who wishes to receive Email, you need another POP-3 account set up. Some ISPs will give you a certain number of POP-3 mailboxes with your account, but it would be uneconomical to purchase one for, say, every pupil in the school. For that, you need an SMTP mail account, where you receive an Internet domain, and any mail for your domain (regardless of which particular name happens to appear to the left of the @ sign) is delivered to an Email server at your site, at which point it is up to you to distribute the Email (see SMTP below).

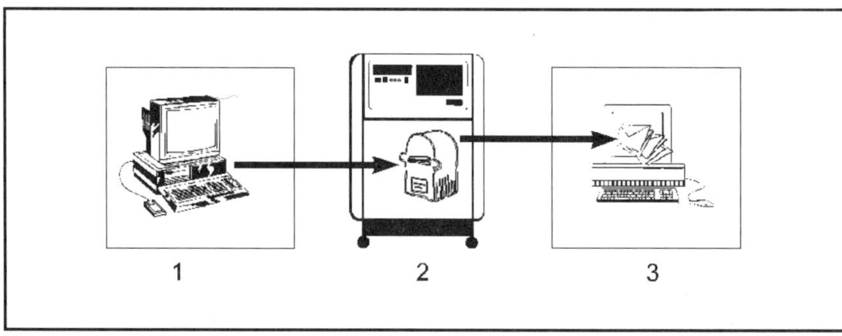

Right: POP-3 mail delivery.

1) The Email is posted across the Internet.
2) It arrives at the destination ISP's mail server and is placed in the POP-3 account.
3) When Fred logs in, the mail is transferred onto his hard disc and deleted off his ISP's server.

SMTP

If you have an *SMTP* account, you will probably receive your own Internet domain. For example, if your Internet Service Provider happened to be *Demon Internet*, and your school was, say, the *Hollyhead Primary School*, your domain might be **hollyhead.demon.co.uk**. You would set up a computer that was identified as **hollyhead.demon.co.uk** on the Internet (with its corresponding IP number address), and run a program on that computer called an *SMTP server*.

When you dial up to your ISP, all the mail for your domain is forwarded to the machine running your SMTP server. SMTP stands for *Simple Mail Transfer Protocol.* Its simplicity lies in the fact that the ISP's server machine doesn't really care (and doesn't attempt to determine) if the Email has been sent to **`jane, postmaster, year 5`** or anyone else at the **`hollyhead.demon.co.uk`** domain. The ISP simply routes all the mail along to Hollyhead Primary's server (which lives somewhere in a cupboard). Jane's colleagues and pupils then accesses this SMTP server from other machines connected to their local school network (as long as they use TCP/IP – and most these days can) and check for mail for any individual user, be that user **`year 5`**, **`dinnerlady`** or whatever – it's up to Jane to have set up the various users on her SMTP server, each with its own password. The server would then bounce back any mail addressed to a user Jane had not set up.

The significance of this way of doing things is that you can, effectively, have as many Email addresses as you want. What you do with what comes before the **`@`** is up to you, not your Internet Service Provider.

An SMTP mail account can be thought of as being analogous to traditional post being delivered to a site office in a block of flats. The post office, when determining a delivery, simply examines the building's street address (the domain) and delivers all the post to the block's site office (SMTP server) where it is sorted. The post office doesn't care to whom the piece of post is addressed it is up to the site agent (SMTP server as set up by your network administrator) to put the relevant envelopes through the relevant doors.

Users are able to check their Email locally because the machine running the SMTP server software is also running a POP-3 server (often from the same program), which sets up locally accessible mailboxes for each user.

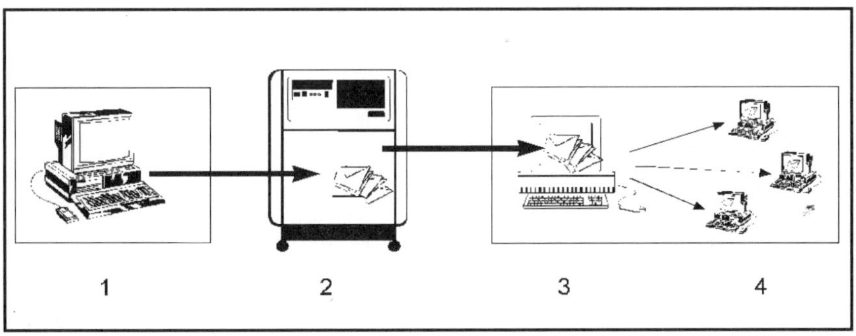

Below Left: SMTP mail delivery.

1) The Email is posted across the Internet.

2) It arrives at the destination ISP's mail server – a stepping stone in the system – which attempts to forward it to a subscriber's own local server when it has dialled up.

3) When that server logs in, it collects all the mail for the domain and sorts it to individual usernames.

4) Individuals collect their mail over the school's local network – the local server has set up a POP-3 account for each of them.

Sending Email

Although there are hundreds of different software packages which can be used to receive, reply to and send new Email, there are several basic similarities shared by most. Generally, each message is preceded by several lines of text, including a **TO** line, a **FROM** line (which is, of course, already given), a **SUBJECT** line, a **CC** line and perhaps a **BCC** line. Some packages have an **ATTACHMENTS** line, which will specify any binary files you are sending with your Email note.

The **TO** line is simple enough – it is where you must type the address to which you wish your letter to be sent.

The **SUBJECT** line allows a one-line summary of the content of the letter, so the recipient can easily find it again.

The **CC** (carbon copy) line allows you to input an additional recipient for your letter.

The **BCC** (blind carbon copy) line has the same function as the CC line, except the first recipient will not see that the message was carbon copied.

All packages will also allow you to reply to existing mail, optionally including the text of the letter to which you are replying indented or bracketed. This allows your own annotations to be added to the original.

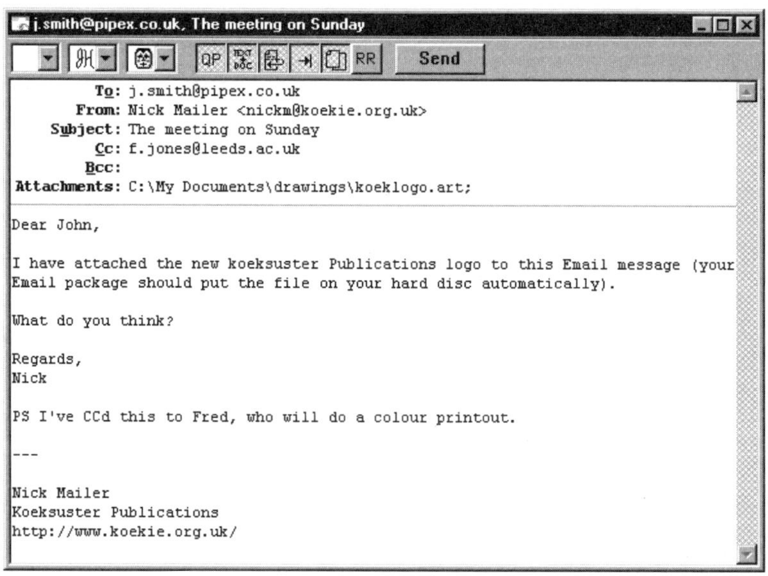

Right: Here, all you have to do is fill in the header, type your message and click on Send.

The text at the foot of the note is known as the signature. You can set up your mail package to "stamp" your signature at the bottom of every message you send. It usually contains your name, address and so forth – some people put witty aphorisms, disclaimers or even pictures made out of text.

As a rule, try and keep your signature to no more than four lines.

Some sending problems

If the mail does not arrive at its destination, it is said to 'bounce', because it returns to your mail box with automatically generated comments about where it's been and why it could not arrive at its final destination. Often, the cause of bounced mail is an incorrectly typed or discontinued address.

Because of their length and complexity, it is all too easy to mistype Email addresses. This can be particularly tedious if you correspond regularly with one person. Fortunately, most Email packages let you set up address books, nicknames and aliases, so that you only need to input the full-winded Email address once.

Below: An Email message has bounced. The mail-server sends a lot of technical details, but the gist of it is that the address we typed didn't exist.

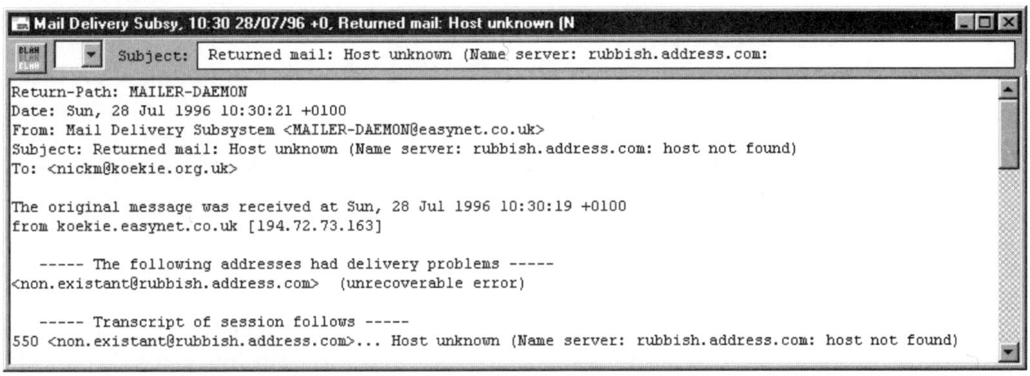

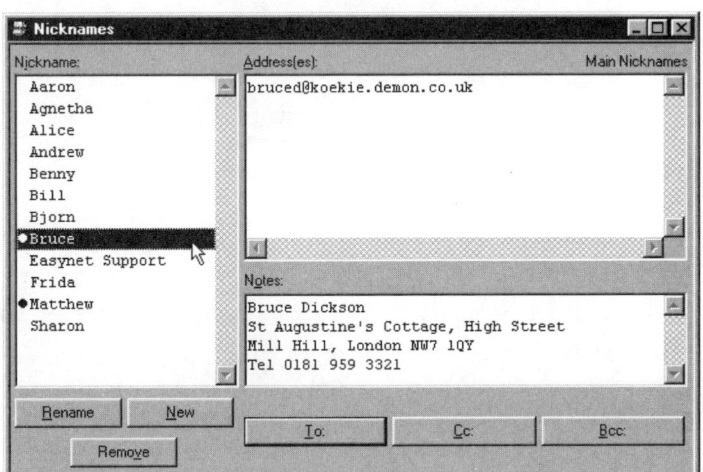

Left: Typing long Email addresses can be tedious, so most mail packages allow you to set up nicknames, which can be used instead, as an alias for the full address.

Email uses

One-to-one

Pupils and staff communicate with "keypals" across the world in their own time. There are organisations who will introduce potential keypals from around the world. Such a scheme can be used for cross-cultural and even inter-lingual communication. The ease and inexpense allows for some never-before possible collaborations.

Class-to-class

Each member of a class corresponds with a keypal in another school as part of a co-ordinated project. The class then comes together and produces a digest of their weekly activities, perhaps.

Many-to-one

Some organisations run projects where "experts" come online and can be questioned by pupils – "Robin Hood", "Henry VIII" and a now-adult WWII evacuee, for example, are contributors to a recent scheme. Sensitive answers lead to further investigation by pupils, freshly inspired to discover more about a subject that might have previously seemed detached.

Mailing lists

There are many online Email discussion groups, where one member's mailing is distributed to all other members. The group is controlled by a moderator who kicks off discussions and administrates. A pupil-administrator could print out interesting digests for others in the class to read – a real-word comprehension exercise.

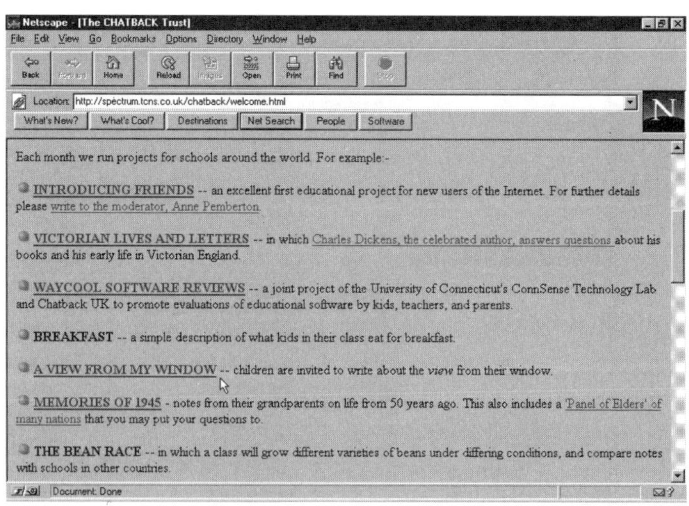

Right: The homepage of the Chatback Trust, an organisation dedicated to making the most of trans-national Email connections. The projects are genuinely inspiring.

http://spectrum.tcns.co.uk/chatback/welcome.html

Email in schools

Email can be used in many ways in the school environment. Communicating with academics is a boon. Responses to mailing lists can be useful in classroom situations, with careful online questioning to nudge the discussion to topics you are currently teaching. You can then integrate into your teaching examples of the way real-life people are dealing with problems as you speak. You can encourage your class to formulate a response to a particular query or discussion arising from the list and post it. This, in turn, will be replied to. This ongoing and wide ranging continual assessment of ideas should help inject a living reality into the subjects learned in the classroom.

Some schools will be able to set up a separate username with a private disc area for each pupil – these days, this is economically viable, especially if the school has an SMTP-based Email setup (see above). Even if not every pupil has a personal address, it is vital that as many pupils as possible are given the opportunity to send, receive and manage the mail stream. Familiarity with Email will be vital for those progressing to higher education, where it is used regularly as a means of communication between tutors in the same university as well as friends and colleagues at other institutions.

Appointing a pupil-manager to distribute and organise school Email is useful. Having such a go-between means that those pupils, and more probably, members of staff, who are technophobes, will still be able to send and receive messages via Email. That way, they can be introduced to the technology without having to press a key – the school message service can print out Emails, put them in pigeon holes and fulfil requests.

Also, even if every pupil doesn't have an Email address, it is useful to have a separate account for the member of the teaching staff who is to be the system manager. It will be required to allow for confidential correspondence between colleagues, as apart from the more public flux of information in and out the school.

An Account of an Account

You may have noticed the word "account" used quite a bit already – an Internet account, an Email account and so forth. This does not indicate any financial matter, but rather, denotes a space on a machine at your ISP, protected with a password and with sufficient electronic infrastructure to make use of a particular service.

For example, if you have an Email account, it simply means that there is some space on a hard disc for your mailbox, with routing information such that all messages directed to you are stored there. Again, it does not signify any financial transaction – many people can and do have free Internet accounts, at Universities for example, but they are still termed accounts.

Etiquette

As with all suggestions concerning etiquette, these are not hard and fast rules, but simply suggestions based on practical considerations. It is important in a school environment for the staff to have sufficient confidence in the pupils to uphold certain standards online. As heads are wont to say in assemblies, "when pupils are out in public wearing school uniforms, they tacitly represent the school". This is also the case when logging in through the school's account. Messages should be kept short, polite and succinct. Succinct because no one enjoys staring at text on a screen when 90% of the content is redundant. Also, though generally not the case, some people pay for all the Email they receive, literally by the word, so they do not wish to pay for some ten line witticism in a signature. Formality seems stilted in the context of Email, but shoddy spelling and grammar still reflect badly.

When responding further to specific points in a received Email message, it is useful to include parts of the original letter, indented, with replies underneath. This is helpful, because simply launching into a reply with no reference to the question may confuse the original sender, especially if he or she reads and writes a large amount of Email every day. All too often, though, people simply indent the whole original letter and tap a few new lines underneath. This makes the reply far more difficult to read. It is best to get into the habit, and to teach pupils to get into the habit, of quoting only those specific areas relevant to the response, with, perhaps, three full-stops or a conventional "[stuff deleted]" message.

If your pupils are abusive or offensive to people through Email, the aggrieved parties will soon be inundating your network manager's mailbox with complaints. Where contentious issues are discussed, it is regrettably easy to bash out a hasty response, click on "send" and regret it immediately. *Flame wars*, as these battles of purple prose are dubbed, begin like uncontrolled nuclear reactions – no one thinks of putting in the moderators until it is too late. Often a reasoned, calm and polite response to some ranting can knock some sense of shame into the ranter, and return some sense to the discussion.

If you receive junk Email, advertisements and so forth, reply to the service provider from which the message emerges. For example, if you receive a message encouraging you to join a pyramid scheme or some such unfortunate enterprise from, say, **makemoney@aol.com**, send the complaint to **postmaster@aol.com**. The great majority of ISPs set up the postmaster mailbox to receive complaints about Email, and will be quick to respond and rectify the matter.

Email software

Email software can be downloaded from FTP sites and Web pages. There are also commercial versions, which usually offer features like mail filtering and spelling checkers. This is a selection of some of the better offerings.

Pegasus Mail (free)

Very comprehensive and easy to use
Win3.1 Win95 Mac
`http://www.pegasus.usa.com/`

Eudora Light (free)

Almost industry-standard on the Mac and PC. Also available in commercial version, Eudora Pro
Win3.1 Win95 Mac
`http://www.qualcomm.com/`

ANT Marcel Mail/News (commercial)

Part of the ANT Internet Suite
Acorn
`http://www.ant.com/`

Voodoo (shareware, free demo available)

High quality – does more than many PC packages.
Amiga
`http://www.hut.fi/~oahvenla/Voodoo/`

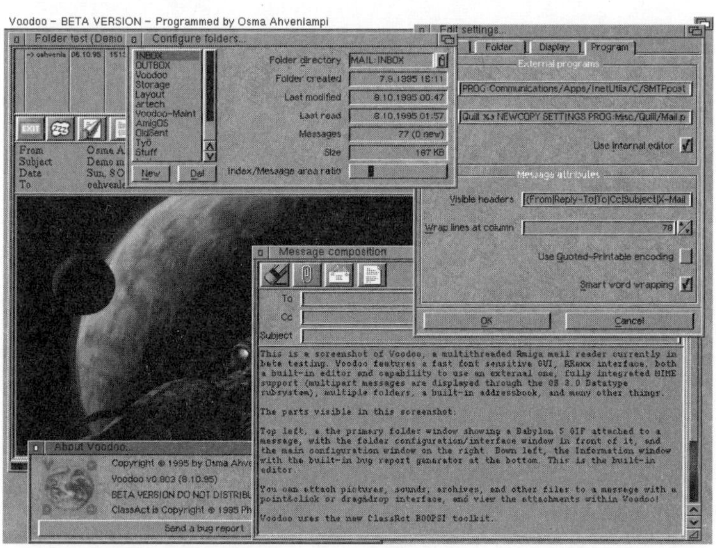

Left: Voodoo on the Amiga is an example of how minority machines still have much good-quality Internet software produced for them.

This is a particularly important point in the United Kingdom, where Acorn machines have long been used in schools, and for which Internet software is now available.

The News on Usenet

Usenet Newsgroups are the Internet's discussion forums.

From research to trivia, inquisitive schools will gain a huge amount with sensitive and selective use of this often overlooked Internet resource.

Chapter 5

> **Why News?**
>
> The news-based terminology ('articles', 'subscriptions' and so forth) for what is, in the main, a collection of forums, seems strange. The jargon is due to the system's history: it was initiated in 1979 by students who wanted to share news about Unix.
>
> The "news" metaphor became strained, as discussion began to surplant the "official" news postings. Nevertheless, the terminology stuck. The news network was, initially, distributed rather crudely.
>
> In 1986, the *Network News Transfer Protocol* (NNTP) came along, which effectively integrated Usenet into the greater Internet. You may hear of an "NNTP server" – which, you will now realise, is synonymous with an Internet usenet news-server machine.

Usenet News is at the heart of the discursive Internet. It is the public forum where issues are mooted and arguments flare, where shallow trivia flows amongst deep insight. It is the closest emulation we will ever have of that town square in Athens millennia ago. This electronic town square is frequented by millions of individuals from around the globe. No one controls it and nothing can prepare you for the vast amount of freely flowing information you will encounter.There is no question too profound or ephemeral for detailed discussion on Usenet. From "The Goons" to organometallic physics, all life is here.

The nature of Usenet

To call Usenet a "news service" is perhaps misleading. There is no general news distributor, no professional journalist, no centre: all the "news" is posted by the users of many networks, these days mostly a part of the "Greater Internet". It is more helpful, therefore, to conceive of the service as a mixture of online conferences and public noticeboards. The postings are distributed throughout the world via a spreading chain of news server machines. Each server receives the latest updates and routes it along to another "news peer". This allows the postings to flow all over the world in quite an efficient, if unpredictable, manner.

To access Usenet, you require a program called a newsreader. This package should allow you to read articles from your local news server, as well as posting your own contributions and comments. The server will hold many thousands of newsgroups, each dealing with a different topic. You subscribe to groups of interest and can read the postings from others, reply to them, or post something completely novel. Subscription does not denote anything financial – it merely means selecting a group from a list and instructing your news program to keep up to date with your reading habits on that group. There are now tens of thousands of groups distributed over the world, so it makes

sense to work in a system of voluntary selection.
A collection, over time, of replies and counter-replies concerning a particular topic is termed a "thread". The nature of human discourse ensures that threads move very quickly away from the initial topic and that discussions evolve rapidly. Because people are constantly posting to Usenet, old postings cannot be kept indefinitely. The older items are dropped to accommodate the new.

Newsgroups

Because there are so many groups, their identifying titles are classified in order to make it easier for computer and human to deal with.

Firstly, there are the moderated and the unmoderated groups. Moderated groups cannot simply be posted to by all and sundry: an official moderator who presides over the group decides what gets on and what doesn't. The moderated group is usually a well-ordered information area, often intended for the dissemination of official information or digests from other groups. Unmoderated groups are a "free for all", where no-one controls or censors what appears.

Secondly, there are two major types of newsgroups – universal (or "world") and alternative or local. The universal groups are available from news servers all around the world. The selective alternative groups, on the other hand, are a pick-and-mix bag, where the specific news server passes on only what it wishes. Although many are very popular, others appear on only a few servers around the world.

Each ISP runs its own news server, and it pays to ask what sort of news service you can expect – how many groups are available, how diverse are the number of sources that "feed" the server and, importantly for schools, does the ISP reject newsgroups whose sole and unsubtle aim is to propagate pornography?

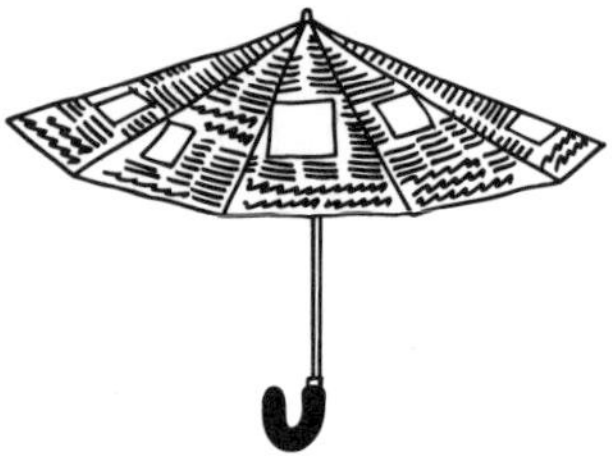

Newsgroup titles

Like an Email address, all group titles consist of significant words and abbreviations linked together with full stops. Unlike Email addresses, though, the separate parts of the group name become more specific as you move from left to right. The first part of the newsgroup's name hierarchy, therefore, indicates the very general area of discussion. These are the main major world newsgroup categories, which you should find on all news servers, and an example of a group under each category:

comp	Wide range of computing topics

comp.simulation covers all areas of modelling.

misc	Eclectic mix of miscellaneous topics

misc.kids shares parental ideas.

news	Deals with newsgroup issues

news.newusers.answers helps newbies to learn about Usenet.

rec	Discussions of recreational, artistic and hobby areas

rec.arts.books reviews and airs all things literary.

sci	Scientific topics and research

sci.physics.fusion is for researchers of nuclear fusion.

soc	Social and sociological subjects

soc.history discusses a range of historical topics.

talk	Debating issues

talk.philosophy.humanism debates this philosophy.

Alternative hierarchies

These are a few broad categories of some newsgroups you may or may not find from your service provider. Even if these categories are present, there is no guarantee that every newsgroup under the broad heading will be available:

```
alt
```

Alternative newsgroups. From the fascinating to the puerile – although there are some very useful newsgroups in this category, many of them as widely distributed as the major hierarchies, there are also pornographic areas, which should be avoided – specifically educational ISPs do.

```
bit
```

These redistribute the postings of some electronic mailing lists.

```
biz
```

Commercial and business concerns are dealt with under this heading.

```
clari
```

ClariNet is a commercial service providing professional actual news and information over Usenet. Access to these groups will cost your service provider a fee, which it may feel unnecessary when taking into account the number of free news resources available over the world wide web.

```
k12
```

A selection of newsgroups for k12 (kindergarten to year 12) educational projects. Some are for specific class-to-class projects.

```
school
```

The school newsgroups deal with a range of school-related issues.

Understanding titles

Understanding a newsgroup's title is largely a matter of common-sense and intuition. Because of the free nature of Usenet, there are quite a few different customs and ideas on how to create a descriptive name of a group. If you're unsure, you can always read a few postings from the group, which should clarify things. The more you use and explore Usenet, the more familiar you become with its naming customs. Here is a group name:

`comp.sys.amiga.advocacy`

This is how each section, successively, narrows down the area of discussion in the group.

`comp`
This is a group devoted to discussing aspects of computing.

`sys`
The topic surrounds a particular computer system.

`amiga`
That system is the Amiga Computer.

`advocacy`
This group's *raison d'être*: advocating the benefits of the Amiga.

Here's another, similar title:

`comp.sys.mac.marketplace`

This group is a forum for the buying and selling of Apple Macs. There are a number of such newsgroups, and it is important to restrict such commercial activities to them.

Here is a final illustration of the nomenclature, this time in a non-computing environment:

`soc.culture.indian.telugu`

This newsgroup, as you may have guessed, deals with the culture of the Telugu people of India.

The newsreader

It is important that the program you use to access the Usenet news-stream is well written and makes good use of your computer's features. Most computers now support graphical interfaces that use the mouse, windows, menus and so on. For quick editing and selection of groups, it is unlikely you will need or want to encounter the Unix newsreaders with their monstrously unfriendly line-editors.

Since most newsreaders are in the public domain and are readily available for downloading from the Internet, it makes sense to experiment with as many as are available for your machine. It might make sense to use simpler, more user-friendly programs for beginners or younger pupils and progress to packages with a greater number of features afterwards.

A newsreader should provide, in a window, a list of all the thousands of groups available. Subscription should be no more than a click of the mouse. To help you navigate through the enormous list, most new packages allow a keyword search facility.

A newsreader allows you to save any news article onto your own disc, where it can be treated just like any other ASCII file.

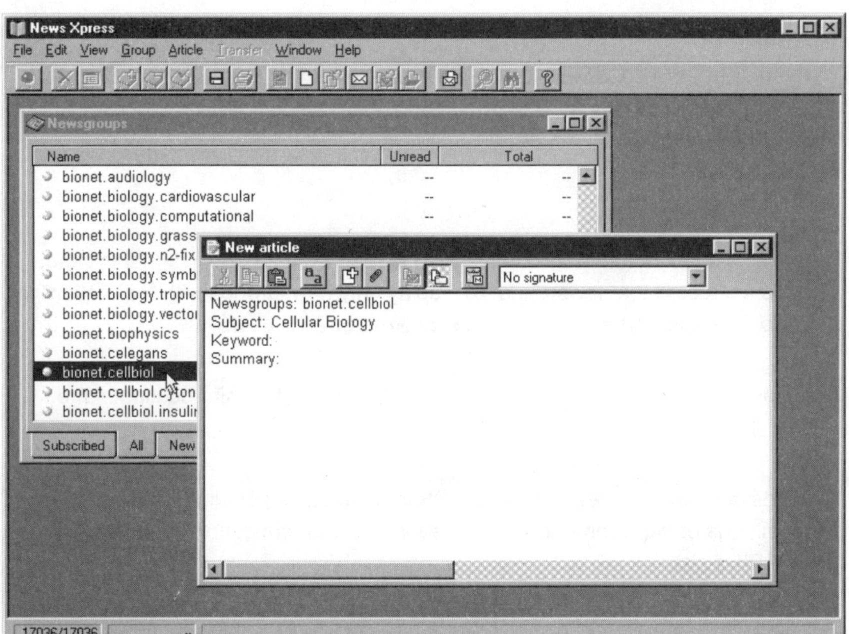

Left: Modern newsreader packages make full use of the windowing environment – you can have several groups open at once, keep your group-list up while you type a new message and so forth – a far cry from, the first Unix command-driven news-reader.

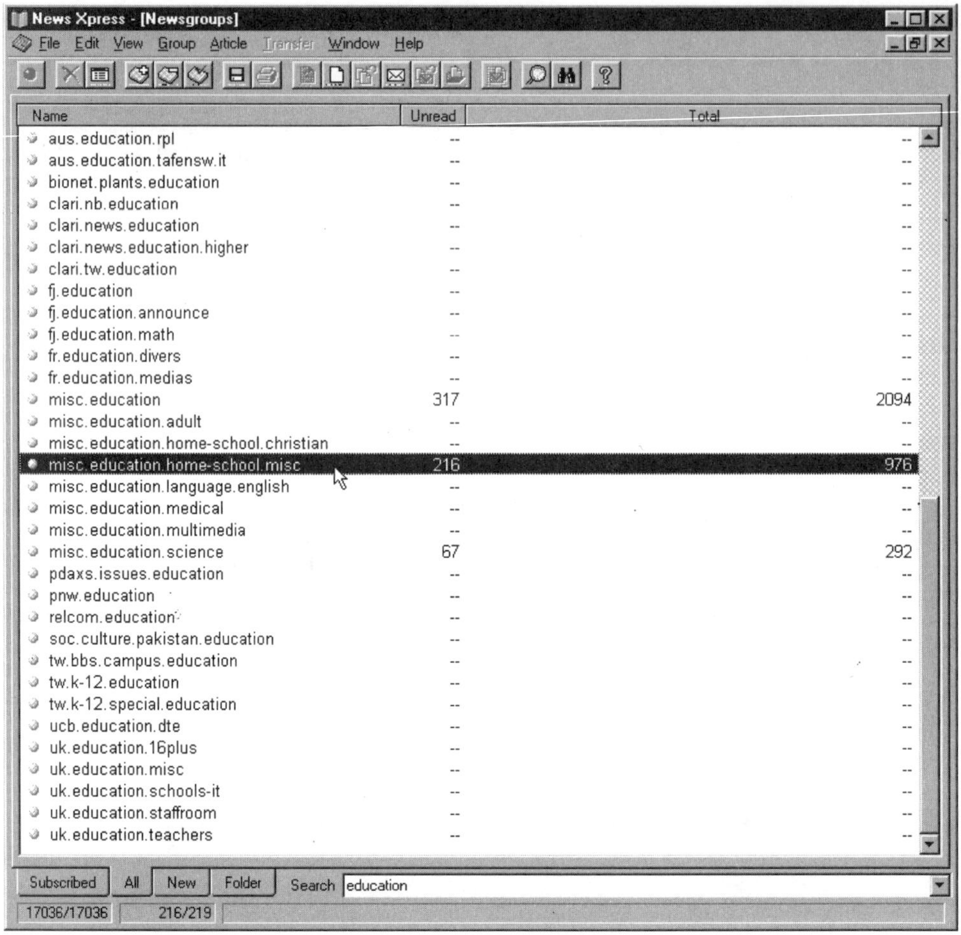

1) Above: We select a newsgroup we wish to read from a large list. In this case, we have instructed the newsreader to display only newsgroups with "education" in their title. We select `misc.education.home-school.misc`

2) Opposite top: The current articles appear. We select the third posting in the "Latin?" thread.

3) Opposite below: We read the article. Note the original posting is indented with: symbols. This being Usenet, the response to the Latin education query is by an Isotope Physicist!

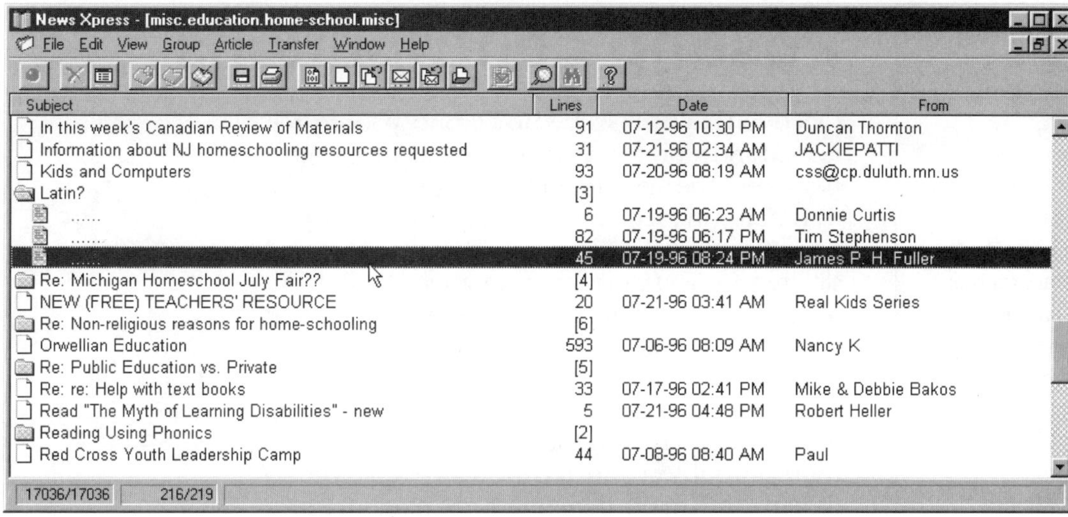
News Xpress - [misc.education.home-school.misc]
File Edit View Group Article Transfer Window Help
Subject Lines Date From
In this week's Canadian Review of Materials 91 07-12-96 10:30 PM Duncan Thornton
Information about NJ homeschooling resources requested 31 07-21-96 02:34 AM JACKIEPATTI
Kids and Computers 93 07-20-96 08:19 AM css@cp.duluth.mn.us
Latin? [3]
...... 6 07-19-96 06:23 AM Donnie Curtis
...... 82 07-19-96 06:17 PM Tim Stephenson
...... 45 07-19-96 08:24 PM James P. H. Fuller
Re: Michigan Homeschool July Fair?? [4]
NEW (FREE) TEACHERS' RESOURCE 20 07-21-96 03:41 AM Real Kids Series
Re: Non-religious reasons for home-schooling [6]
Orwellian Education 593 07-06-96 08:09 AM Nancy K
Re: Public Education vs. Private [5]
Re: re: Help with text books 33 07-17-96 02:41 PM Mike & Debbie Bakos
Read "The Myth of Learning Disabilities" - new 5 07-21-96 04:48 PM Robert Heller
Reading Using Phonics [2]
Red Cross Youth Leadership Camp 44 07-08-96 08:40 AM Paul
17036/17036 216/219

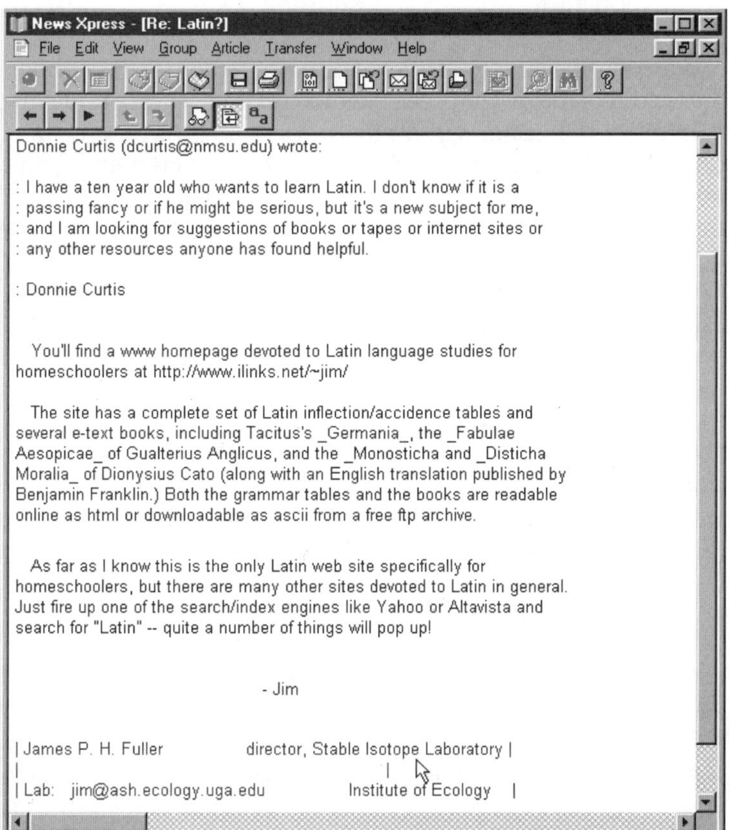
News Xpress - [Re: Latin?]
File Edit View Group Article Transfer Window Help
Donnie Curtis (dcurtis@nmsu.edu) wrote:
: I have a ten year old who wants to learn Latin. I don't know if it is a
: passing fancy or if he might be serious, but it's a new subject for me,
: and I am looking for suggestions of books or tapes or internet sites or
: any other resources anyone has found helpful.
: Donnie Curtis
You'll find a www homepage devoted to Latin language studies for
homeschoolers at http://www.ilinks.net/~jim/
The site has a complete set of Latin inflection/accidence tables and
several e-text books, including Tacitus's _Germania_, the _Fabulae
Aesopicae_ of Gualterius Anglicus, and the _Monosticha and _Disticha
Moralia_ of Dionysius Cato (along with an English translation published by
Benjamin Franklin.) Both the grammar tables and the books are readable
online as html or downloadable as ascii from a free ftp archive.
As far as I know this is the only Latin web site specifically for
homeschoolers, but there are many other sites devoted to Latin in general.
Just fire up one of the search/index engines like Yahoo or Altavista and
search for "Latin" -- quite a number of things will pop up!
- Jim
| James P. H. Fuller director, Stable Isotope Laboratory |
| Lab: jim@ash.ecology.uga.edu Institute of Ecology |

Creating a Newsgroup

Believe it or not, anyone on the Internet can create a newsgroup. The democratic tradition which has grown involves taking an online vote. If it is in your proposal's favour, the group will be created. Otherwise, the "create newsgroup" message will be ignored by most news servers.

The process is more rigorous for the world newsgroups than for the alternative groups, explaining why there are more "odd-ball" groups in the alt hierarchy.

Further information on the tortuous road to creating a new newsgroup is regularly posted to the news.announce.newusers newsgroup.

There are nearly 20,000 newsgroups at the moment, so think very hard before embarking on the creation of a new one!

Posting contributions

Once you have subscribed to a group, you are free to read and reply to previous contributions, or post new ones. The mechanics of posting are very similar to Email – in fact, some packages make use of an integrated Email editor. There are several differences. You can reply to another contribution, including parts of the original posting indented, or post a new contribution. Obviously, there is no need to type out an Email address to which you wish to send your contribution – you are posting directly to the Usenet Newsgroup. Like Email, though, there is a subject line. It is crucial, even more so than with Email, that this is as succinct and unambiguous as possible.

When replying to an existing posting, the software can be set up to indent the reply with a > symbol prefixing each line. This allows you to comment in between the indented lines. Some packages are clever enough to change the colour of the indented text, which makes it even simpler to recognise. Whatever the case, it remains important not to produce reams of unnecessarily quoted text when you are just commenting on one or two relevant lines. All packages will allow you to delete as necessary, using the mouse to cut, copy and paste just as you would in a word processor.

There is, unlike Email, a "distribution to" line or something similar. This is asking you how far and wide the contribution should travel. You type in a proscriptive area (ie: local, uk or world) indicating the intended breadth of distribution.

"Local" will go no further than your local news server – perhaps the posting only needs to be seen by subscribers to your ISP, or only on your campus. At the other end is "world", which will ensure your posting is distributed across the globe. In between, there are countries and domains, which should be used when your posting concerns only a specific locality.

As with Email, most people have an automatic signature. The signature is your opportunity to display some of your personality to the public, and will be taken as such, so be careful with what you produce. Although most contributors display their Email addresses in their signatures, the Email address appears automatically next to the subject title in the group's titles window.

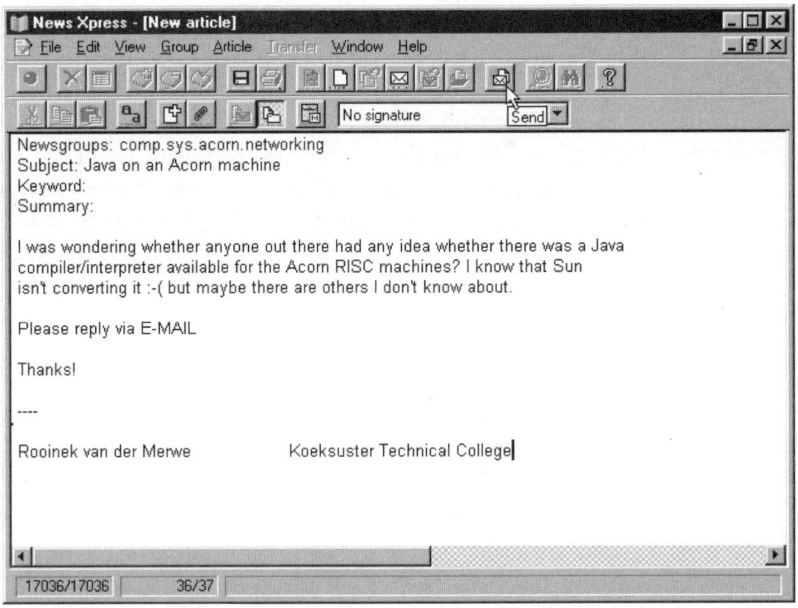

Left: Posting to a newsgroup is a simple matter of filling in the header, typing your message and clicking on send. It is just as easy as Email.

Usenet information

There are many varieties of information that can be found within Usenet groups. Different groups have different traditions and styles. Unmoderated groups are usually mixtures of informal discussions and "official" information postings. A moderated group is more likely to contain "official" information or newsletters. There are several flavours of moderation, though – sometimes organisations like NASA will post space-shuttle schedules into read-only groups. Other moderated groups will consist of selections of the "best of Usenet" collections and the like. It's all rather varied, as usual, and can only be appreciated by sampling the different kinds of newsgroups and comparing the approaches in each.

Here are some of the postings you will encounter:

FAQs (Frequently Asked Questions)

Most major groups set up a FAQ file: a list of Frequently Asked Questions and their answers. These are useful sources of information, and are often genuine compilations of, as the name of the resource suggests, questions which have often been posted to that newsgroup.

FAQ files can be found in several locations: first and foremost, in their related Usenet newsgroups. They are updated periodically (usually about once a month). They can be identified by the word FAQ in the subject line. Secondly, there are several independent groups set up specifically as receptacles for FAQs from all over Usenet. Because there are so many different FAQs, it helps if your newsreader has a search facility. These groups often have the word "answers" as the final part of the title. Each general newsgroup title has an "answers" area:

Maintaining the FAQ?

An individual, or group of individuals, will decide to maintain a particular Frequently Asked Questions file. If someone in the group is too busy, it usually gets passed on.

The volunteer maintainer's duties include posting the file to appropriate newsgroups every month, keeping it updated and sending copies to appropriate FAQ archives.

It comes as a surprise to those who have not experienced this communal information gathering process as to how professional and richly detailed the average FAQ file is.

```
comp.answers
misc.answers
news.answers
rec.answers
sci.answers
soc.answers
talk.answers
```

It is very likely that alternative newsgroups also have their "answer" area. For example, **`alt.answers`**. All these groups are moderated, so they provide for a very well-ordered information resource.

Finally, there are FTP and web archive sites where collections of FAQs are kept available for downloading. There are very many sites which are expanding and changing at all times. Therefore, the best way of tracing down a particular archived FAQ file is by the the various FTP and web searching services.

Once you have found a useful FAQ, it makes sense to download it and keep a copy on your local hard disc or network and make a hard copy. Not only will this provide a useful introduction to the particular newsgroup, but it will answer specific factual questions. Often, each answer is attributed to a different person, with his or her Email address printed below the answer. This provides an invaluable facility for pupils, for follow-on questions not dealt with in sufficient detail by the FAQ. Nevertheless, common courtesy should prevail – even well balanced FAQ contributors could become unhinged if they are greeted with a mailbox full of vague, rambling Email questions from forty pupils!

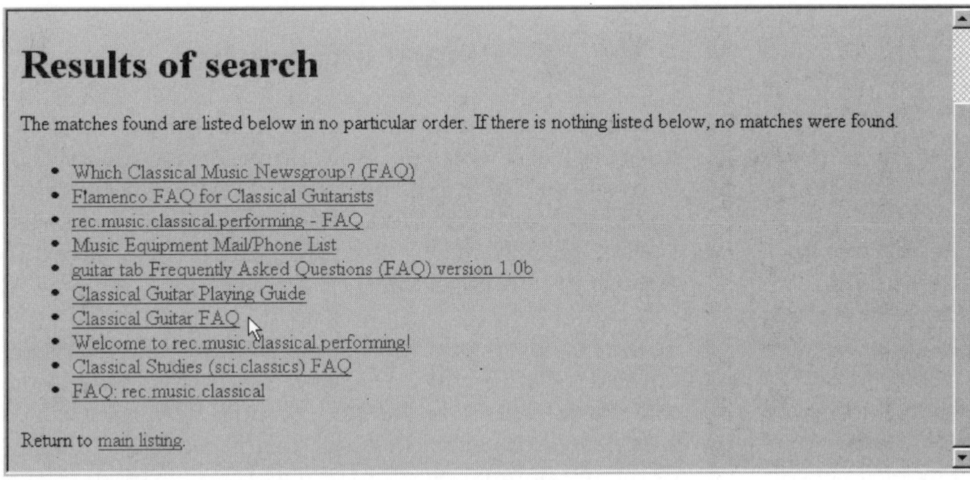

Results of search

The matches found are listed below in no particular order. If there is nothing listed below, no matches were found.

- Which Classical Music Newsgroup? (FAQ)
- Flamenco FAQ for Classical Guitarists
- rec.music.classical.performing - FAQ
- Music Equipment Mail/Phone List
- guitar tab Frequently Asked Questions (FAQ) version 1.0b
- Classical Guitar Playing Guide
- Classical Guitar FAQ
- Welcome to rec.music.classical.performing!
- Classical Studies (sci.classics) FAQ
- FAQ: rec.music.classical

Return to main listing.

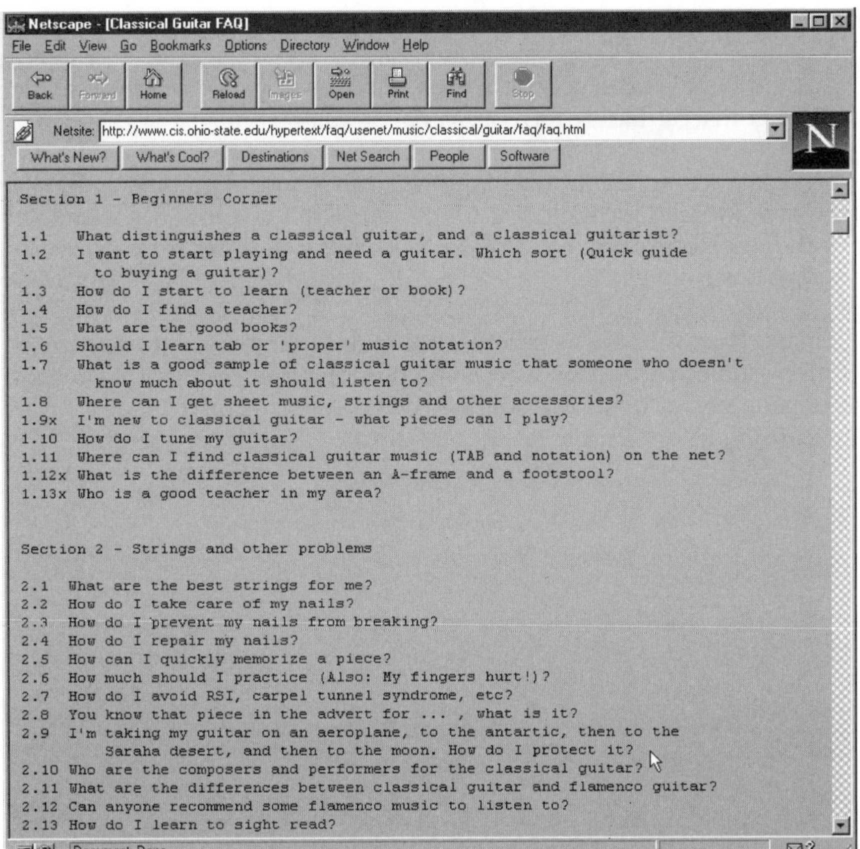


```
Section 1 - Beginners Corner

1.1   What distinguishes a classical guitar, and a classical guitarist?
1.2   I want to start playing and need a guitar. Which sort (Quick guide
        to buying a guitar)?
1.3   How do I start to learn (teacher or book)?
1.4   How do I find a teacher?
1.5   What are the good books?
1.6   Should I learn tab or 'proper' music notation?
1.7   What is a good sample of classical guitar music that someone who doesn't
        know much about it should listen to?
1.8   Where can I get sheet music, strings and other accessories?
1.9x  I'm new to classical guitar - what pieces can I play?
1.10  How do I tune my guitar?
1.11  Where can I find classical guitar music (TAB and notation) on the net?
1.12x What is the difference between an A-frame and a footstool?
1.13x Who is a good teacher in my area?


Section 2 - Strings and other problems

2.1  What are the best strings for me?
2.2  How do I take care of my nails?
2.3  How do I prevent my nails from breaking?
2.4  How do I repair my nails?
2.5  How can I quickly memorize a piece?
2.6  How much should I practice (Also: My fingers hurt!)?
2.7  How do I avoid RSI, carpel tunnel syndrome, etc?
2.8  You know that piece in the advert for ... , what is it?
2.9  I'm taking my guitar on an aeroplane, to the antartic, then to the
       Saraha desert, and then to the moon. How do I protect it?
2.10 Who are the composers and performers for the classical guitar?
2.11 What are the differences between classical guitar and flamenco guitar?
2.12 Can anyone recommend some flamenco music to listen to?
2.13 How do I learn to sight read?
```


There are now quite a few searchable FAQ repositories on the world wide web. This one is from `http://www.search.com/`

Above: We typed in “Classical Guitar” as keywords for a search. A few seconds later, we were presented with the list of titles, inviting us to select any one of them to read the FAQ.

Left: We select the Classical Guitar FAQ. Listed here is a small excerpt from its table of contents, let alone the contents itself!

Binary information

Some groups are intended for the distribution of encoded binary information. Effectively, this allows contributors to use the Usenet newsgroups to distribute programs, data and graphics files. As with Email, the files are first encoded. The most popular method of encoding on Usenet is UUENCODE. Most newsreaders today have this encoding and decoding method built in.

To the eye, an encoded posting appears as a long list of seemingly random characters, with only an explanatory header remaining legible. If the newsreader doesn't decode these postings automatically, these can be saved as text files onto a local disc and run through a decoding program. At this point, the original program or data is reconstructed. Sometimes, if the data to be distributed constitutes an especially large file, its encoded text-file is so large that it is necessary to split it up, because some service providers limit the amount of information that can be distributed at one time. Big binary files are, therefore, sent to the newsgroup in sections. These then have to be put back together again before they can be decoded. Doing this manually is extremely tedious, so it makes sense to use a newsreader package that can handle this concatenation automatically.

Some particularly fancy packages will preview your graphic within the newsreader as it downloads. Of course, if it is a sound, a program or some other form of binary data, you will have to view it or run it externally, just as normal.

Ensure that your ISP is careful in which binary newsgroups are on offer – some are used for distributing pornographic or copyright images. Fortunately, educational service providers scrutinise the news flow carefully, and will remove access to these kinds of groups.

Why do we need to Encode?

As with Email, the Usenet news distribution mechanism can only cope with alphanumeric informationt – plain ASCII text. Programs, graphics and other files contain more than plain ASCII text in their contents – if you listed the "guts" of the file, you'd find quite a few strange nonstandard characters.

To transmit the file over Usenet or Email, therefore, the additional weird characters need to be converted to common-or-garden ASCII where, for example, two normal ASCII characters together will be an encoded representation of one of the strange, untransmittable characters.

```
Lines: 316
Message-ID: <31fd3c55.22069872@news.clinton.net>
References: <4t0bre$oid@news.onramp.net>
NNTP-Posting-Host: opus-117.clinton.net
X-Newsreader: Forte Agent .99e/32.227
Status: N

begin 644 gopher1.gif
M1TE&.#EA@'+@';,"""/\"'#_'/__""__\'_P#_______P"""""
M"""""""""""""'"P"""'@'+@'4,$^_#(2:N]..O-N_]@*(YD:9YH
MJJYLZ[YP+,]T;=]XG@%Z[__'H'!(+!J/2!&'IV$FG]"H=$JM6J^QI?.RQ'J_
MX+!X3'9JS^BT>LUNN]GEN'Q.K]M1Z'!'S]_[^X!_@H%]2P,!'P"'B8N*B(Z,
MCV>$@Y64=YB9FIN<,FZ-:XV'E'JBCZ:1B6A<DZF0EK"DL%N=M;:WN&)Y:*AI
MIX^!;X:_KJ!LQ<2*RGO(D;+/6KG2T]35-EJR9Z[,K[V%PFV]XI+@V'O)XXQ^
M:=;M[N_P&VK0:>G*P>7Y^FZEW>C*IOK$&TBP8+5=V<SU:;9,X3YS^[Y-JF1J
M&$-\!C-JW%AG^R(]A(.2<?NH!QR^)?@HH9PEZ'W'ES!C6IG'\HU*<Z*TV#N9
M[%N@1"5C58(CLZC1HTA\#7WHT:%$I_Z'"H465.*!+DBS:MU:I&E0IDRIK@-K
M,AK7LVC37E/:E"Q9L6(G[E-+MZ[=#S3ATG3+E]_4I<+N"AZ\E8W>FT_[*H9Z
M&#'[PI'COVO3.&[?KRW]*JW\%_,9R:!#=Z+<N31FS^5\+DUI^IQ4/L#^JA%-
MN_:<B*TY/^7L]>\HUU%?):1GN[AQ*6''KM2=N_0:63D9B@/8_"2MX]BSKU5\
M6C9(YB1AV1L?&SQ+[>C3JUALF+'R]N:M0P]._C74Y=57J=_/^Y]#V>0?E14?
M2PNA8Z'KUCWGGF7]-<A?:N\)^%V$P@P87BD'T@=8!:0U]IF#(-:63V+O=:>:
M7O\YA!]S$]7GR$UFL=);@"'6&-F(F:W4EF,H^I5@7OFIYJ)]J&$PHW<V)BE8
MA3EFMIN3S7%'X8JMU?,/@S(&*8B27!9F4WY45@4EC.RI.*&'K0A74XP<'MEC
MEW#*]*6%8YE7)DAA1HG3+PE%0\MU9K+V59R$:L0DG8A.J<^%[N&G8"].?9A
M$PON,FFAZ05P@*:<;NIIIYKV]>FHJ(5%ZJF@7G5GHN;]QJIW5/:V&4"GK+DH
```

The UUENCODED gobbledegook (extract above) decodes into a piece of clipart (left).

Usenet in education

With imagination and planning, Usenet can be a valuable educational tool. For this to be the case, it is vital that it is not allowed to become a secret known only to a small computer-science clique. Whoever sets up Usenet in the school has the responsibility of introducing pupils, heads of departments and teachers to the service in public and private demonstrations. Separate sets of newsgroups should be subscribed to for every department. Relevant FAQ files and interesting postings from the subscribed groups might be given to the department as a starter kit, along with instructions on how to use the school's newsreader package.

A pupil or member of staff should be appointed school newsmaster, whose responsibilities will include investigating new newsgroups, saving valuable FAQ files and other useful postings in a local archive (either on a local area network or on an accessible hard disc), distributing any relevant printed material from or about Usenet and setting up a time-share schedule as more departments begin to use the service. If your school has a local area network, there are immeasurable benefits in setting up local newsgroups, run from and accessible only by computers on your school's network. Each school department could have message boards, chatting areas and selections from external Usenet groups. The ability to log in to a local news service provides all these practical benefits as well as giving pupils the experience of the workings of the news network in a secure local environment. Having local newsgroups on a local area network allows whole classes to experiment with news facilities instead of just the lucky few individuals who happen to have access to the school modem at any particular time.

Because they are forums of information and discussion, some Usenet groups can be used as natural extensions to the classroom. It is advisable that pupils become proficient in using Usenet-type conferencing (and the Internet as a whole) for research – they may well be expected to use the service when they progress to higher education establishments. University departments are using locally created newsgroups to communicate with their ever-increasing number of students. These are also used as forums for questioning other students and lecturers as well as making comments on the course. In a small school environment, this might seem artificial, but on a vast campus with many thousands of students, it is essential.

Today, accessing a Usenet feed is not difficult – every dialup ISP will give you access, and if you do not feel like downloading and setting up a newsreader package for each computer on your local network, you may well find that your world wide web browser has one built in. Setting up a local mail, news and web server will allow you to experiment with a full "intranet", using the facilities of the Internet in a local context. With the added Internet connection, your Intranet will not become stagnant or insular – a fresh stream of ideas is important, even if some of them seem trivial at first. This is a point some business managers, ever keen to create little "off-shore", non-connected Intranets fail to notice.

Usenet projects

Integrating the worldwide Usenet into classes can be achieved in many ways. At one end, pupils can be encouraged to use the news network as a kind of living encyclopaedia. Pupils, or groups of pupils, could ask pertinent questions on relevant newsgroups as part of their research into a project. Additional credit could be given by the teacher for evidence that Usenet has been utilised in a novel and efficient manner. At the other end, the service can be used by whole classes. Teachers can dip into Usenet discussions on topics about which the class is currently being taught. That real people in the real world are discussing such topics will, no doubt, be a welcome revelation to some pupils. The class could be encouraged to formulate a response to a particular point that has come up in the discussion, or to ask something new.

For lively discussion, particularly useful when preparing for formal debates, the "talk" newsgroups are useful (and sometimes heated) areas for collecting varied opinions.

Again, it must be emphasised that for such a system to be fair and productive, there needs to be some form of universal access policy, even if it is to just a selected and monitored subsection of the full Usenet newsfeed. Fortunately, because Usenet is all ASCII, you do not need a fancy computer or particularly fast connections to allow pupils on your computer network to post responses to Usenet threads. Provision for such a service may seem risky – a rogue posting could reflect badly on the school, and there is the highly remote possibility that children might learn Anglo Saxon phrases not already common playground currency. On the other hand, if one has such little confidence in one's pupils, one shouldn't really have any kind of Internet connection at all.

Searching Newsgroups

Several free archive services have now been set up which allow you to search the contents of thousands of newsgroups going back months. The search completes in a few seconds. This turns the newsgroups into a very useful research tool.

Most of these archive services are accessible from the world wide web. You type in some words, selecting other parameters, like dates, relevance criteria and so forth. It then returns relevant recent articles.

An example of such a service is DejaNews at `http://www.dejanews.com/`

Useful newsgroups

It would be nearly impossible to provide a list of newsgroups worthy of subscription. Your news service provider may not distribute the particular listed newsgroups. It may be that a listed newsgroup is restricted to a particular region. Also, new groups are popping up every day, so the only effective way of finding useful groups is by investigation and word of mouth. It is simple to "sample" newsgroups, so it should soon become clear which newsgroups to keep an eye on and which to steer clear of.

Nevertheless, there are several which you might want to subscribe to when you achieve your connection:

`news.announce.newusers`

This is a moderated trove of information for the user new to Usenet. It contains FAQs, lists, advice and useful contact addresses. This should be your first Usenet port of call. Indeed, you may well not even need to subscribe to it, as most packages do so by default.

Save information found here on your local disc and make printouts. There are articles on every aspect of the Usenet, from technical issues to conventions, from the deadly serious to the uproariously humorous.

`news.newusers.questions`

Here you can ask any questions not adequately dealt with in the FAQs from the above group. There are many people who are willing to help. Perhaps to repay the communal favour, you could answer some questions on this group when you become more knowledgeable.

`uk.education.teachers`

This newsgroup, as its title suggests, is especially for teachers in the UK. There is a regular stream of contributors, so it is a superb place to make initial contacts – you'll soon realise you're not alone. There are other **`uk.education`** groups as well, whose perusal will yield much apposite information.

Useful hierarchies

There are general newsgroup hierarchies with a standard or specialised purpose throughout the Usenet system.

`.advocacy`

Advocacy groups are, in theory, there to advocate the benefits or unique features of something under discussion (usually a computer system). In truth, the discussions waver from highly dry and technical point scoring to catty name-calling. An example is **`comp.os.ms-windows.advocacy.`**

`.answers`

As has been mentioned, newsgroups with this suffix are repositories for all FAQ files on Usenet. For example, **`comp.os.answers`** would be good place to look for FAQs delaing with computer issues. A useful place for finding Usenet-specific FAQs is **`news.answers`**.

`.binaries`

These newsgroups are for the transportation of programs and data over the Usenet. They are encoded in a form suitable for transmission as text, often via UUENCODE (see above). The postings are saved on to a local disc and decoded into their original program or file. Often small public domain programs and utilities as well as graphical files find their way into binary groups. An example is **`comp.binaries.atari.st`**, which contains binary postings for that machine. Educational ISPs will ensure that newsgroups used to distribute pornographic images are unavailable.

`.d`

Groups with the **`.d`** suffix are areas where other groups can be discussed. These extra discussion areas are necessary where the mother group is moderated, or is intended as an archive of particular information only, where discussions would be unwelcome clutter. Examples are **`rec.humour`** and **`rec.humour.d.`** The former is a receptacle of jokes and humorous articles. The latter contains comments and diatribes on the humour content (or lack of it) of the former.

.test

It is only natural to want to send a test-post to Usenet, an electronic equivalent of the "testing 1..2..3.." microphone mantra. Nevertheless, it is not done to post an "Ignore: this is just a test!" message to a group dealing with astrophysics. The proper areas for such messages are the **`.test`** groups – for example, **`misc.test`**.

Alternative newsgroups

There are actually several forms of alternative newsgroups. Some are regional, others are specialised and others deal with material and issues considered unsuitable in world newsgroups. Some alternative newsgroups are commercial – for example, the clari groups which are feeds from professional news gathering sources like United Press – and require that the service provider pays for access to them.

The most common form of alternative newsgroup is, of course, the **`alt`** hierarchy. This is a complete free-for-all. There are newsgroups created because their name sounds funny, newsgroups created out of frustration, newsgroups whose postings are so surreal they might be considered Dadaist "happenings". Nevertheless, there are diamonds amongst the dross. Finding these areas is a matter of investigation and luck. If a school is to undertake an exploration of the **`alt`** groups, an official school "newsmaster" (either a teacher or trusted senior pupil) is vital, and not just a luxury.

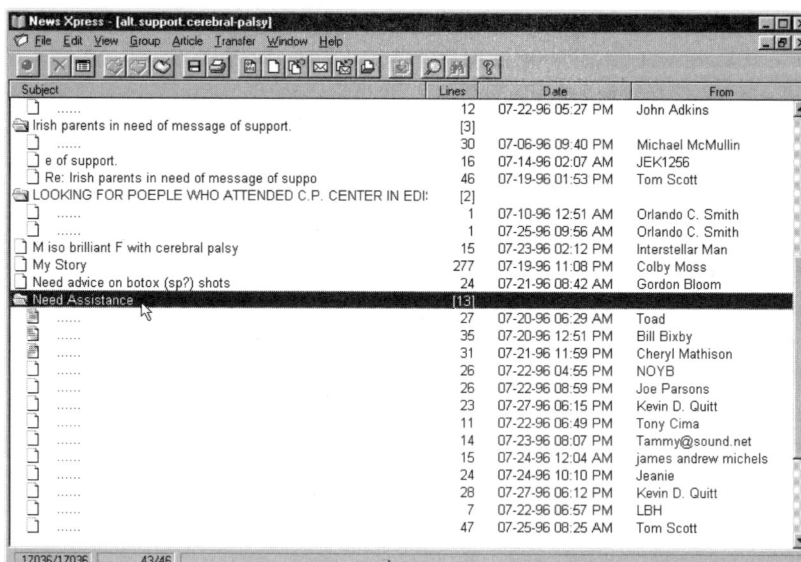

Right: Although alternative groups are sometimes pilloried as odd-ball, this cerebral palsy support group was described by one subscriber as a "life-saver". Notice the number of responses to the plea for help.

Flame wars and kill files

Groups dealing with contentious issues are more likely to contain heated arguments. When the argument overheats, it becomes known as a flame war. Flame wars can begin in any group, but are more prevalent in groups frequented by activists. Computing advocacy groups are notorious for their flame wars, which usually boil down to little more than "my computer's better than yours" slanging matches. In fact, some groups are there specifically to attract diatribes (**`alt.flame`** seems an obvious example!)

Nevertheless, the selective nature of Usenet means that you need not pay any attention to such trivia: you can use your newsreader to eliminate threads and even particularly unpleasant authors from appearing on your screen. Once an author is placed in this personal blacklist database, known as a "kill file", you will not be troubled by his or her postings again. It is best not to become embroiled in flame wars. They rarely conclude with any productive solution, and although they can be fun, there is so much of genuine interest on Usenet that spending too much time on flame wars is a waste, particularly in a school environment.

The worst result of a flame-war is mail-bombing. This is where an annoyed opponent will post a very large message to you via Email, so it takes a long time to download, or clogs up your system completely. You ISP will be able to remove the message from the mail-queue quite easily, but such antisocial behaviour should be reported to the offender's postmaster.

You should remember that your whole personality is being expressed through the medium of plain "vanilla" text. As such, it is astonishingly easy to misconceive innocent statements for something nastier. Conversely, you should take account of all possible meanings of a particular statement you have made – are ambiguous interpretations going to cause unnecessary friction? If in doubt, clear it up before posting. If you or your pupils post something which has been taken the wrong way, send an apology through the newsgroup and via Email, explaining the true intentions.

You must be careful not to start up any unwanted flame wars. It is considered especially bad form to criticise a contributor's English – it may not be his or her first language.

Newbies

The Internet has minted a certain number of new words. One of them is "newbie". This refers to someone who is new or inexperienced, usually with a particular aspect of the Internet, or as a whole. It is not a term of abuse, but usually appears in statements like "I'm a newbie, so I don't know how to ..."

> **Conclusion to a Recently Posted FAQ on Usenet**
>
> IF YOU'RE UNHAPPY
>
> If you are unhappy, what are you doing reading netnews? Take a break. Stretch. Walk outside in the sunshine or the snow. Relax your brain, watch some TV for a while, listen to the radio. If you need to communicate with someone else, give them a phone call, or see them in person.
>
> It's good not to spend too much time all in the same place with a fixed focus – rest your eyes once in a while by looking around at something else.
>
> Don't worry about missing anything, it'll all get re-posted if it's any good.

There are other strange conventional abbreviations and punctuation combinations you will notice, but IMHO you should RTFM, if you wish to learn more.<g> BTW, Email me with further examples. TIA.

In English, that reads "In my humble opinion, you should read the 'flipping' manual if you wish to learn more <grin – I'm being droll>. By the way, Email me with further examples. Thanks in anticipation".

The <g> (or grin) insertion is particularly interesting – because we're communicating via Usenet, we do not have the advantage of facial expression, tone of voice and so forth to judge whether a statement is in jest, is serious or is abuse. The insertion of such an abbreviation is cloying, but prevents many unintentional conflicts. Smilies are sometimes used for a similar purpose. Also known as emoticons, all will be revealed if you turn this book by ninety degrees such that the colon is closer to the ceiling and parenthesis to the floor : -)

Too many smilies can be annoying > : - (enough to make you cry : ' - (

An AOLer?

You may come across a group of individuals upon whose heads is dumped a surprising amount of communal odium – subscribers to the proprietary service known as AOL (America Online). Although only a minority of AOL's subscribers are antisocial or act in a particularly unintelligent manner, a sufficient number have found their ways onto kill files to ensure that 'AOLer' is now a term of abuse.

There are several reasons why this has occurred. Some of it is intellectual snobbery, but AOL's expensive and condescending service is a partial cause – by policing and keeping a close observation of their subscribers in the closed-system area, some do not have the self-control to behave responsively in the non-regulated environment of the Internet. A lesson there for schools, perhaps?

Newsreader software

As with Email software, there are plenty of news browsers around to choose from. Some are more complicated than others, some are better at online reading (where the phoneline must be up as you read) others at offline reading (where your selected articles are downloaded and saved on disc for later perusal without incurring phone charges while reading).

FreeAgent (Free)

Sibling to commercial Agent, but still brimming with offline features.
Win3.1 Win95
www.forteinc.com/forte/

News Xpress (Free)

This popular browser boasts a good, intuitive interface and is quick.
Win3.1 Win95 Mac
http://www.awinc.com/cwsapps/

Newswatcher (Free)

Very popular Apple Macintosh newsreader
Mac
http://mothra.tamu.edu/netstuff/news.htm

Termite Internet Suite (Commercial)

The suite includes a newsreader, which is easy to use, but not as feature filled as those on some other machines.
Acorn
http://www.doggysoft.com/

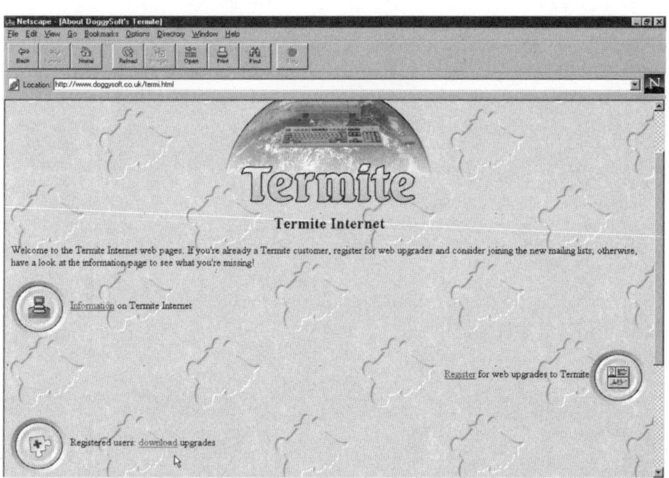

Left: The Termite Internet suite for Acorn machines contains newsreader software. Upgrades to the package can be downloaded straight from their world wide web site at *http://www.doggysoft.co.uk/*

Getting Files via FTP

FTP allows you to access and download files and programs from all over the Internet.

Getting resources from across the globe can be no more difficult than copying a file from a floppy.

Chapter 6

Another chapter, another three-letter acronym: FTP stands for File Transfer Protocol. As its name suggests, it is a standard way of transferring files between one machine on the Internet and another. In practice, a major use of this facility is for downloading documents and data from specific FTP archives, machines with large and secure storage areas set up specially for that purpose. These FTP sites are all over the world and contain many different types of data and information. Some sites are used as archives for Usenet News, others are receptacles of popular public domain programs for a variety of machines. An FTP server might have a wide range of information and data or be dedicated to a specific area of research or interest.

Many companies now place upgrades, additions, libraries and other resources for commercial packages online. Now, therefore, when bugs are fixed in new releases, or new features are added, you do not need to send out a mail-order to another country and hope for the best – you can connect to the Internet and download the patch you require immediately.

Although the FTP protocol is one of the oldest on the Internet, it is not complicated to use, and allows you to upgrade your software and collect new programs with little more difficulty than copying it off a floppy disc or CD – except the transfer isn't taking place between two drive-heads on your computer, but between mechanisms perhaps thousands of miles apart.

Anonymous FTP

Whatever the nature of the information on the FTP site, the method of attaching your computer to that site is standard. In order to connect to a remote FTP site, you are required to provide a user-name and password before you are granted access. Unless you have been issued explicitly with such a name and password by a specific network manager, you cannot access the FTP site in this manner.

Fortunately, most sites allow you to log on with the username 'anonymous'. When you are requested for a password, you simply type your standard Email address, after which you are allowed guest access to the FTP site. While you may not be given the same freedom as an actual account-holder, the restrictions on anonymous users (often little more than limiting the number of anonymous users logged in simultaneously) are minimal.

Not all FTP servers offer anonymous login, but if you're unsure, try logging in as such. If you are unsuccessful, it'll give you an error message. As well as downloading files, FTP also allows you to upload files. You will not need to, and will probably not be allowed to, upload files to anonymous sites. In circumstances where you are (for example, in publicly augmented archives), you will usually do so in one specific directory, usually labelled incoming.

Software through Anonymous FTP

There is a wide variety of software available for downloading. Some of it is public-domain (known as Freeware), which you can save and distribute as much as you want without cost. Other programs are distributed as Shareware, where you can download and distribute them, but are requested to send the author some small payment in cash or kind. You will usually receive upgrades, manuals or other goodies in exchange, as well as the removal of the annoying reminders which pop up in many unregistered copies of shareware software.

There is another category called the GNU Public Licence. The licence allows you to distribute, change, sell for profit, copy and do whatever you want with software, as long as you don't remove anyone else's rights to do the same, so that the software will never become proprietary. This philosophically libertarian licence is used for surprisingly large projects – like the Linux operating system, which can be downloaded from a number of FTP sites.

Machine address

This is a useful point to insert a reminder about the Internet's addressing system. Each FTP server machine on the Internet has a unique address. In order to access the FTP site, you need to know this address. You can use either form of Internet address – the IP number or the fully qualified domain.

The IP number will look like this:

```
192.135.191.128
```

These are also known as dotted quads, for obvious reasons. They are not easy for humans to remember, but they are the only form of address the computer can deal with. In order to make things easier for humans, each IP number has a textual equivalent, very much like the part of an Email address after the **@** symbol (which makes sense, because when you send Email, you're sending Email to a **`user@domain`**. Here's an example of a fully qualified domain name:

```
ftp.apple.com
```

This translation is achieved by a Domain Name Server (DNS), a dedicated machine with a database at your ISP. You don't need to know the mechanism of the name server – it all happens behind the scenes. Your ISP will provide you with the IP number of their DNS machine, which may be required during installation of the *dialup* software, after which, you will never have to think twice about it again.

Keep in mind, though, that there are rare occasions when you will be given the IP number instead of the fully qualified domain name. This number can be used in exactly the same context you'd usually use the textual address.

Finding FTP resources

Because there are so many machines containing FTP areas, it can be difficult to find the information or program you want, or even to know whether it exists. Nevertheless, there are several ways of tracking down what you want.

The simplest method is asking in a relevant Usenet newsgroup. This can be effective for specific requests (like "Does anyone know of an FTP site containing Blah v2.24") or more general enquiries ("Are there any public domain programs available via FTP which will help in teaching Quadratic Equations"). If you are looking for a particular program, it makes sense to focus your attention on newsgroups dealing with your particular type of computer system (eg: **comp.sys.ibmpc.applications**).

If you are looking for some information or data that is not system specific, like images or text files, you should ask questions in groups related to the information for which you're searching. If you were looking for an online archive of Mediaeval Madrigals, you would ask the question in **rec.music.early**. Remember, it pays to read any relevant FAQ files before asking questions which may have been posed many times before.

Archie

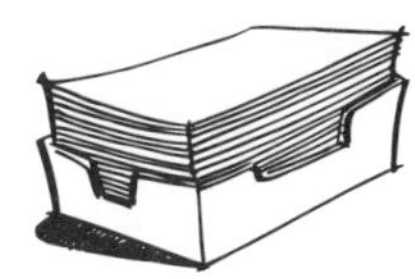

There are automated ways of finding information. A common way is via a service called *Archie*. Archie is a large, publicly accessible database containing information about files in thousands of FTP sites. The system allows you to search for files using keywords, and the database will then return the addresses of all the FTP sites on which a file related to the keywords is found.

Email access

If Email is the only Internet service you have, the Archie database can still be accessed. If you are not limited to Email, do not use the Archie mailserver – the methods for access listed below are more convenient for you and the server machine. Nevertheless, accessing Archie via Email is relatively painless – you mail request commands to one of the following addresses:

archie@archie.doc.ic.ac.uk
archie@archie.hensa.ac.uk

In order to find out what the available search options are, send a completely blank message to one of the above addresses with just the word **help** in the subject line.

Command line access

Archie can be accessed in many ways. A clean and simple method is by attaching yourself to an Archie server via Telnet (see below). This will give you command line access to the server, where various typed instructions can be issued. Type 'help' once online for comprehensive information on searching. At the core of the search, though, is the **prog** command. For example:

```
prog Bach
```

will return information on all FTP sites with filenames containing "Bach".

There are Archie databases all over the world. The UK has two alternative addresses, so if one is down, the other should be available:

archie.doc.ic.ac.uk
archie.hensa.ac.uk

Once you have connected, and are asked to log on, you simply type 'archie' as a username, which requires no password.

Fancy access

These days, there are far easier ways to access Archie (and most other Internet services) than the command line. There are Archie "clients" available for most computer systems which give Archie a friendly graphical interface. These programs are usually in the public domain, and so can be downloaded from an FTP site. Therefore, your Archie search for an online Archie client may well be the first and last time you access the service via the command line!

Alternatively, you can access Archie through the world wide web. There are "gateways", where you insert your keywords into a fill-in form, click on search and have the results presented to you, all within your normal web browser.

There are many all over the web. Here are two to try out:

http://www.legend.co.uk/cgi-bin/archie1
http://www.bblink.com/ut/archieform.html

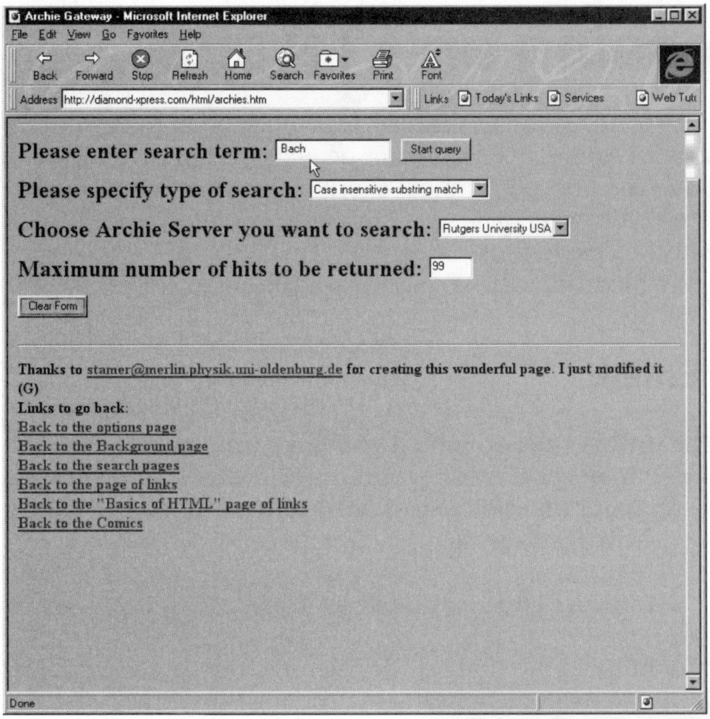

Left: Searching for filenames through the world wide web using an "Archie Gateway". The keyword "Bach" is typed and the "Start Query" button is clicked upon. Not all web gateways to Archie will look like this, but they are never more complicated.

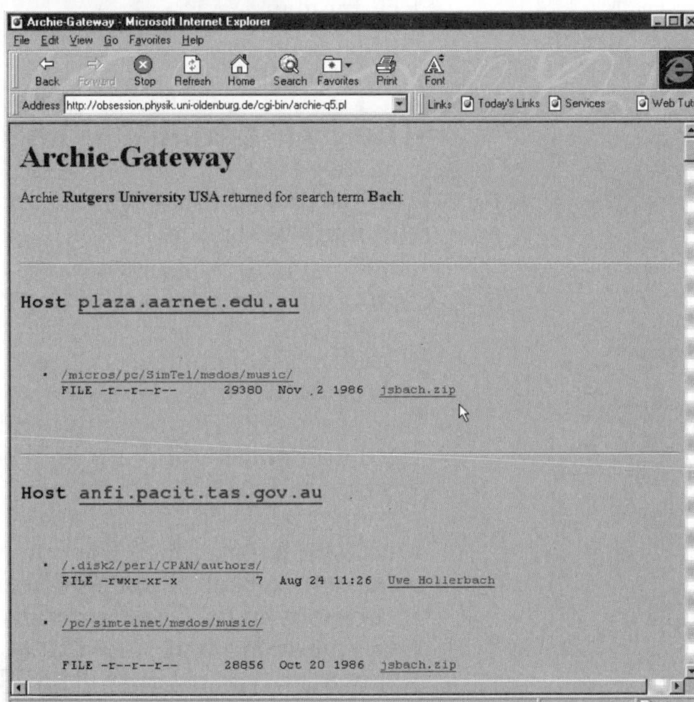

Right: Moments later, a list of file names and the servers upon which they can be found appears. Notice that both "jsbach.zip" as well as "UWE Hollerbach" have been found.

Accessing an FTP site

A popular way to access an FTP site is directly, with an FTP program or client. As with Archie, FTP sites can be accessed in several ways, with the command line, a graphical client program and even with a world wide web browser. The latter in particular allows point-and-click integrated access to these sites, which makes it easy enough for any user to download exactly what he or she requires.

FTP by Email

If Email is the only service to which you have access, you can mail requests to FTP mail servers for programs or data, which will then be sent back to your mailbox in a suitably encoded form. Send an Email to the following address:

`ftpmail@grasp.insa-lyon.fr`

Put the world 'help' in the first line of the message (not the subject line). The help file will give you full instructions on how to use the FTP-by-mail service.

The FTP command line

This used to be the only real way to access an FTP site, but today it shouldn't be the first choice in a school environment. There are so many free, mouse-operated clients available that the command line is, in most case, redundant in this area.

Nevertheless, familiarisation with basic FTP commands is useful, especially for pupils whose tertiary institutions may rely on command line operated FTP programs (often simply because the university's system administrator is an old hand at using command line operating systems and so can't comprehend why any student might not be).

Once you have connected to the FTP site, you have to log in. At the request for a user-id, simply type the word 'anonymous'. If you log in as anonymous, no password is really necessary, but you will still be requested to type one in. It is customary, polite, and sometimes required, to type in your full Email address at this stage.

If your log in has been successful, you will see something similar to "guest login ok", with some other information. Once this has happened, you will be at the FTP command line. This is where you type your instructions.

FTP Commands

The format of these commands may vary, depending on the operating system running on the FTP site's machine. Type "help" at the command line.

`ascii`

Type this before downloading a simple text file (ie: a file in ASCII text which contains only characters and symbols, but no extra computer data). Often, you will only use this option for files with the suffix **`.txt`** and in other cases when text you download appears garbled without it.

`binary`

If you are downloading anything other than a simple text document, type "binary" before downloading it, or you will receive a corrupt file, because it will be formatted internally as if it were plain text. You only need to type this once per session, though.

`cd` ***`directory`***

Where *directory* is the name of a directory. This command is similar to the MS-DOS command, and will place you in the indicated directory. Most FTP and data information for the public is kept in the **`pub`** directory, which lives in the root directory, so you would type

```
cd /pub
```

At this point, the **`ls`** command will reveal you are now in the **`pub`** directory and will show you all the files and directories accessible. Say, for example, there is a directory entitled "education". To access it, you'd type

```
cd education
```

You'd be placed in the **`education`** directory.

To move back to the **`pub`** directory, you'd type

```
cd ..
```

The double full stop means "take me back one directory in the hierarchy" which, in this case, will take you back to the **pub** directory. Repeating the command would place you back in the root directory, which, as it suggests, is at the bottom of the hierarchy.

You can jump to specific directories up the hierarchies by separating each one with a / so, if you were in the root directory, typing the following would teleport you to the education directory (which, in turn, lives in the **pub** directory):

```
cd /pub/education/
```

get *filename*

Where *filename* is the name of a file, this command will download filename and save it in the currently selected directory on your local computer. You can select which directory you'd like this to be with the **lcd** (local change directory) command, typing the path afterwards.

ls

This command will display a list of the current directory, (or another directory, if it is specified after the **ls**) which will include the titles of files or other directories within it. If you are used to using a mouse-run desktop, a directory is simply the command-line word for the folder (or drawer) you see on the desktop. The actual format of the list will vary from site to site and depending on the options you have selected to display the list. Typing "help" will provide further information.

mget *filename1 filename2 ...*

This command has a similar function to the "get" command, but allows you to download whole groups of files with just one command. The filenames can contain wildcards. On most systems, the symbol for the wildcard is the asterisk. Their operation is best illustrated by example:

```
mget maths*
```

This will download all files in the current directory containing the string "maths". It would download a file called **maths1, maths_CGSE, mathsoft.exe** or even just plain **maths**).

The actual format varies, so its best to type "help" once online.

mput *filename1 filename2 ...*

Like the **mget** command, but in reverse. It allows you to upload files from your local computer to an FTP site, assuming the site allows you to do such a thing.

help

This command should provide you with a list of all the available FTP commands. Some are more obscure than others.

lcd *directory*

Will change your local directory (usually on your local hard disc) to what you specify. This is the directory to which programs will be downloaded and from which files will be uploaded.

put *filename*

The opposite of the "get" command. It allows you to upload a file from your local computer to an FTP site, should the site allow you to do so.

```
Connect  Edit  Terminal  Help
ftp> ls *.zip
227 Entering Passive Mode (158,152,1,44,10,55)
150 Opening ASCII mode data connection for /bin/ls.
-r--rw-r--   1 root     archives    10500 Nov 20  1994 amt.zip
-r--rw-r--   1 root     archives     1348 Dec  4  1994 checklst.zip
-r--rw-r--   1 root     archives     7854 Oct 29  1994 dbl_crsh.zip
-r--rw-r--   1 root     archives     2361 Feb 11  1995 disabled.zip
-r--rw-r--   1 root     archives     5399 Nov 20  1994 emacs.zip
-r--rw-r--   1 root     archives     3476 Nov 20  1994 hse.zip
-r--rw-r--   1 root     archives     4466 Oct 29  1994 indepart.zip
-r--rw-r--   1 root     archives     3849 Dec  4  1994 manufact.zip
-r--rw-r--   1 root     archives     1704 Nov 20  1994 ms-kbd.zip
-r--rw-r--   1 root     archives    10392 Feb 11  1995 pointers.zip
-r--rw-r--   1 root     archives     3978 Oct 29  1994 qigong.zip
-r--rw-r--   1 root     archives     1315 Oct 29  1994 rsi-dbl.zip
-r--rw-r--   1 root     archives      709 Oct 29  1994 rsi-uk.zip
-r--rw-r--   1 root     archives     3728 Oct 29  1994 rsitreat.zip
226 Transfer complete.
ftp> get rsi-uk.zip
local: rsi-uk.zip remote: rsi-uk.zip
227 Entering Passive Mode (158,152,1,44,10,72)
150 Opening BINARY mode data connection for rsi-uk.zip (709 bytes).
226 Transfer complete.
709 bytes received in 0.0107 seconds (66385 bytes/s)
ftp>
```

Left: Getting a file through FTP via the command line. As is Unix's way, things look much more complicated than they really are, and the art of becoming proficient with the operating system is knowing what of its output you can ignore.

The only two commands issued in the above example have been delineated with a black background.

Fancy FTP Clients

While it is useful to be *au fait* with the basic command-line FTP access, it is no longer essential. There are many excellent FTP clients available which are mouse-driven – you simply select the remote file you require with the mouse, dragging them between the local and remote system. In a school, such a client is invaluable. Most of them are free (or shareware), and they are available for every system.

As well as dedicated FTP clients, virtually all web browsers now allow access to FTP sites – they log in anonymously automatically. To access an FTP site, type its address with a prefix of **`ftp://`** (rather than the usual **`http://`**) in the location field of your browser. For example, if you wanted to access the **`pub`** directory of the Apple FTP site, you'd point your browser to

```
ftp://ftp.apple.com/pub/
```

A list of the files and directories will appear, which can be accessed with the click of the mouse.

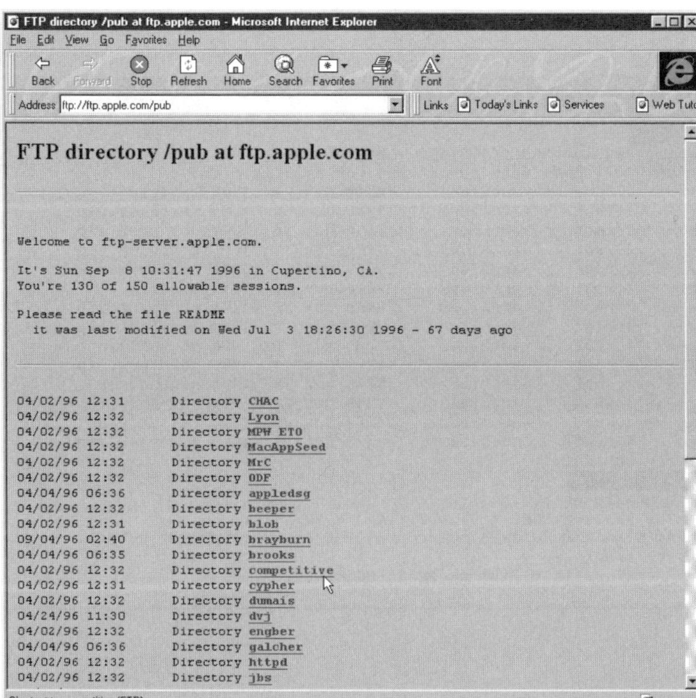

Right: Accessing an FTP site through a web browser is just as easy as accessing any normal web page. The files available for downloading can be selected with the mouse, at which point the browser saves it on local disk.

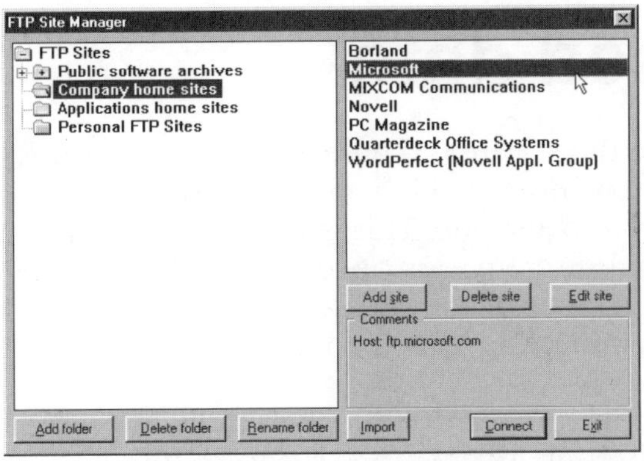

Top: With the modern FTP client, it is very easy to set up a collection of your favourite sites, which may be accessed thereafter with the simple click of the mouse. Here we're connecting to the Microsoft FTP site.

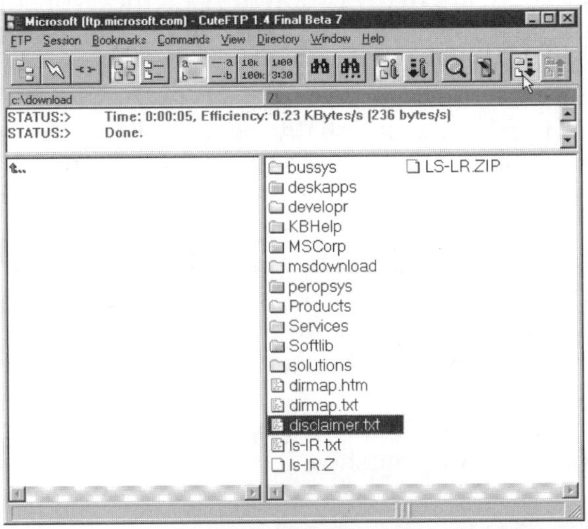

Middle: The window is divided into two. The right-hand "pane" contains the currently selected remote directory, the left-hand contains the currently selected local directory. We select a file with the mouse. To download it, we can simply drag the file from right to left, or, as in the illustration, click on the "Download" button.

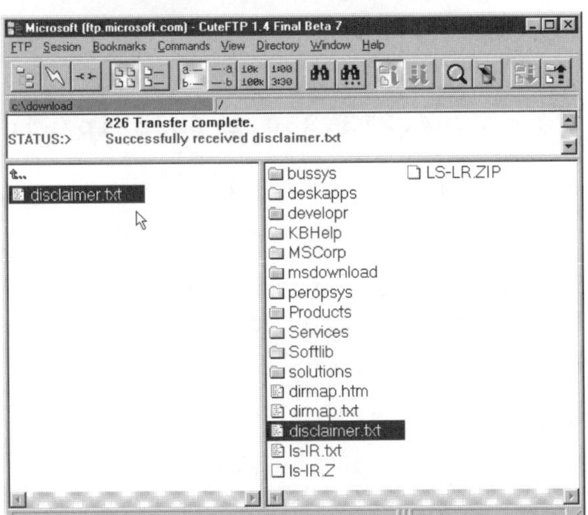

Bottom: The file has now been downloaded and appears in the left-hand pane.

Compressed data

In order to save space on the server and time when downloading, most files in FTP sites are compressed in some way. Sometimes, a group of files is squashed into just one. This is known as archiving, and extracting the original discrete files once again is termed de-archiving. A file which is archived or compressed will have a suffixed filename, with the suffix indicating which compressor was used.

All this means is that once you have downloaded the compressed file, you need to run it through a decompressor to restore it to its original state. There are many proprietary methods of compressing and encoding data for each computer. Often, the **`readme`** file in the **`pub`** directory on the FTP site will give you some information on what programs are required to decode the online files. The relevant decompressor will usually be in a directory on the FTP site, in a format that decompresses itself without the need for an external program.

Fortunately, new FTP packages have the ability to read and decode programs automatically. The school's Internet administrator should ensure that there is a directory on the local hard disc or network containing an assortment of the latest decompressors, though.

Two comprehensive tools are *Winzip* for Windows machines and *Stuffit Expander* for Macintoshes:

Winzip for Windows95:
`ftp://204.213.250.17/winzip/winzip95.exe`

Winzip for Windows3.1:
`ftp://204.213.250.17/winzip/wz16v61.exe`

Stuffit Expander for Macintosh:
`ftp://wuarchive.wustl.edu/systems/mac/info-mac/`

FTP etiquette

On searching for information, there are a few things to keep in mind. Having anonymous access to a resource like FTP for no charge is extraordinary. If philanthropic individuals are going to continue offering such services, it is important to be considerate. If you can, always try to use FTP sites in or close to your country. If you live in the UK, don't download a file from Australia if it is available in England. Many popular international FTP servers have mirror sites in many parts of the world. Mirror sites are FTP servers which contain the same information and programs as the "mother" site. This information is updated regularly. Usually, simply logging on to an FTP site will inform you whether a closer mirror site is available.

When you log on anonymously, you are requested for a password. Although you may be allowed in to the site if you do not provide one, it is considered courteous to leave your full Email address so that the system manager at the site can monitor from where people log in. Most FTP clients will allow you to save this as your default password, so you don't need to type it in each time.

Downloading a file increases the burden on the host machine. Therefore, it makes sense to try and download files "after hours". Remember to take into account time differences. Not only is it considerate to keep your downloading time to after-hours, but the machine will serve you more quickly. In addition, many FTP servers have a quota on the number of anonymous users online at one time.

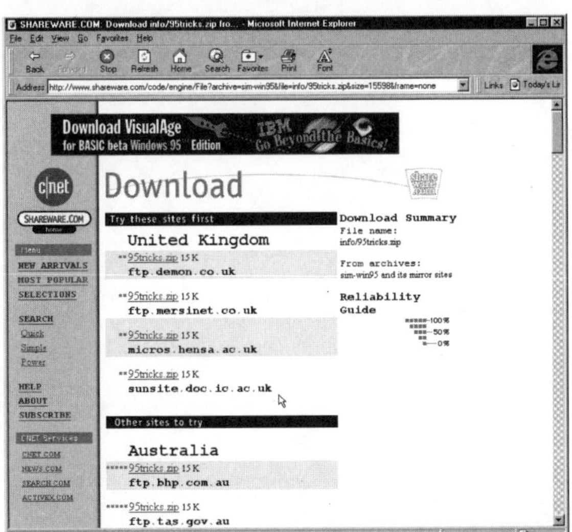

Left:

http://www.shareware.com/

is a site that provides a searchable web frontend to thousands of files from hundreds of locations. When it finds the file for which you're searching, it provides a number of locations from which it may be downloaded – so you can choose one closest to you.

Internet Tools

There are a number of tools and utilities which help in roaming the Internet. Some are for browsing information, others help in diagnosing problems.

Chapter 7

There are several standard Internet tools which help you access and monitor services. Many of them had their origins as Unix programs, but are now available on most systems. Originally, they were activated by typing complicated commands one after another but there are now good mouse-run programs for more user-friendly access.

Some of these tools are for accessing Internet services. Others are for diagnosing problems, checking routings, examining logs and so forth. Some are useful only for network managers and system technicians. Others have a broader appeal, and can be used for creative tasks not originally envisioned for these particular tools.

As long as you have a full connection to the Internet, you will be able to download these tools from FTP sites and run them on your computer without having to worry about whether they are compatible with your particular service provider. Your ISP may not support all the features of a particular tool, but the great majority are standard for all Internet connections, regardless of the provider through whom they are achieved.

Port numbers

Before describing any particular services, it's worthwhile understanding a few concepts which will be of use. The first of these is the *port number*. By now, you're probably familiar with each machine on the Internet having an address – for example:

```
banana.easynet.co.uk
```

which has a corresponding IP number:

```
193.131.248.224
```

But what if the machine is running more than one service? How do you access the particular service you want? The solution is similar to a telephone switchboard – you have a phone number which gets you to the right address (the IP number) and, to get to the right department, you dial an extension (the port number).

The port number is like the specific telephone extension number, taking you exactly where you want on a particular Internet machine. The port number will be between two and four digits, and each different Internet service the machine is running will be allocated a port number.

For example, a POP-3 server-program might be running on port 110 with a news server running on port 119 of the same machine. When a user checks his or her mail, his or her mail software knows it should connect to the POP-3 port, while someone browsing news will have his or her news package connecting to port 119. As long as the machine isn't too overburdened, port numbers are a cost effective way for an ISP to get one machine to do more than one completely different thing at once.

Often, you will not need to know about what service is running on what port – your software will know where the defaults are. Nevertheless, your ISP may be running a special service on a non-default port, so you may need to plug the number into your program's configuration section.

Often, MUDs (online games) will run on a specific port, which you will need to specify in the program you use to access them.

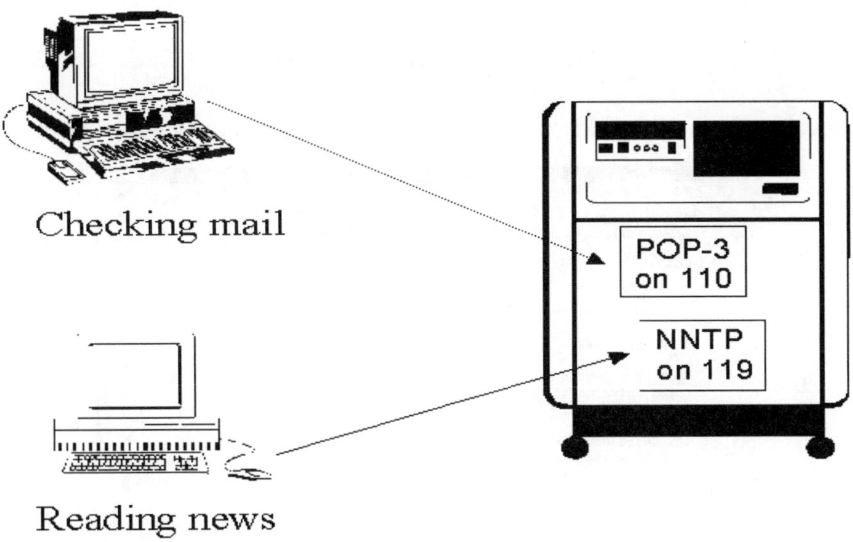

Standard Internet Ports

Most of the time, you'll find the following services on the following ports of your ISP's server machines. Programs will usually use these values by default:

ftp
(File transfer)
21

telnet
(Remote login)
23

smtp
(Email)
25

finger
(status checks)
79

http
(web)
80

pop-3
(Mailboxes)
110

nntp
(Usenet News)
119

Telnet

Telnet is the standard Internet way of logging in to a remote computer's command line and, perhaps, accessing a remote line-text based service. Telnet software usually has the ability to emulate various "dumb terminals" (those green screens and keyboards you see connected to mainframes in photographs from the 1970s). The software allows the logging of text and data.

To access a remote machine, you need the machine's Internet domain name (or IP number), a user ID and password. Some publicly accessible services, including online library catalogues, Archie Servers (see the FTP chapter) and MUDs (chatlines with game content), either allow you to become a registered user, or allow immediate access without an individual user ID.

Sometimes, as well as a machine name, you might be required to specify a port number – the same machine could serve a library catalogue and a chatline on different ports. If you are using Telnet from the command-line (it is, for example, built into the MS-DOS which comes with Windows95, as well as all versions of Unix), you'd be able to access services by typing:

```
telnet servername portnumber
```

For example, to try the French Minitel service over Telnet, you'd type

```
telnet minitel.fr 23
```

Because 23 is the standard Telnet port number you could leave it out.

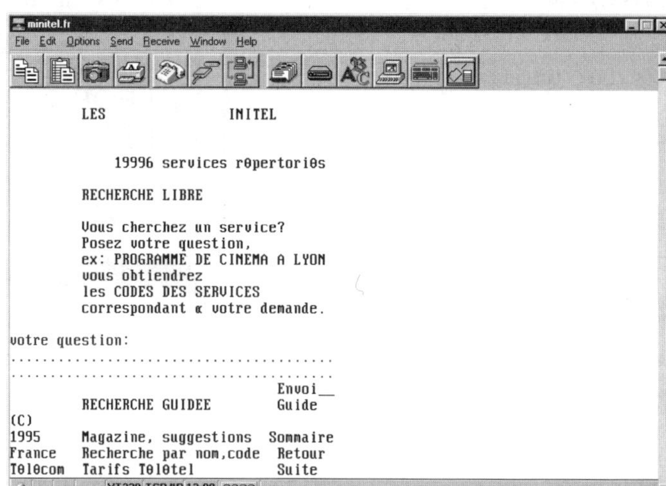

There are also some Telnet access programs which offer some modicum of mouse-driven support. The service is still text-based, but you can run multiple Telnet sessions in windows, set up address books and so forth.

A good place to get information on useful Telnet resources is the Scott Yanoff Internet Services List, available at

`http://www.spectracom.com/islist/`

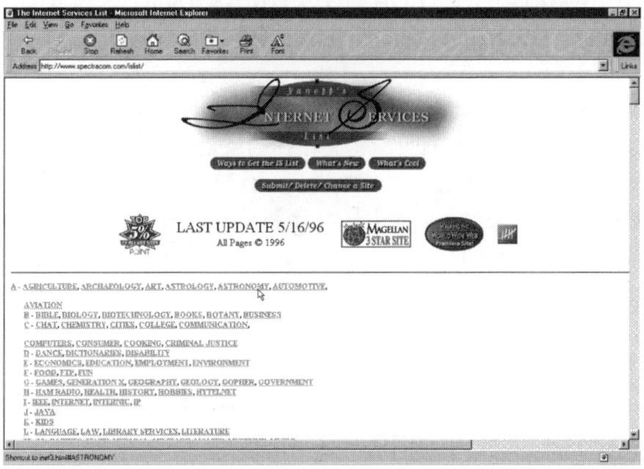

A major remaining use of Telnet is for browsing online library catalogues. A web page linking to these and many other library resources is at

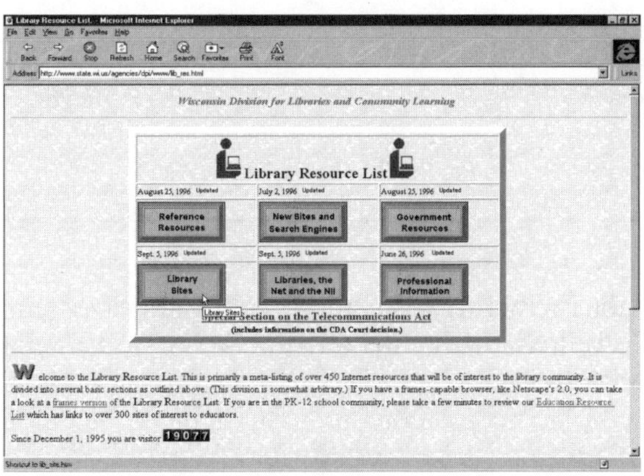

`http://www.state.wi.us/agencies/dpi/www/`

Note that this is one of the few occasions when America's "us" domain is actually used.

Finger

This little program will allow you, amongst other things, to view who is currently logged in to the Internet on any machine anywhere in the world. If you "point your finger" to an Email address, you may or may not be given further information about that person – his or her real name, when he or she last checked Email and so forth. The precise details will depend on how the person is connected to the Internet, and how their ISP configures each account.

Some people set up their accounts so that a little aphorism or thought-for-the-day appears upon fingering. Sometimes sports results. Sometimes more obscure information – for example, an American student built an interface to the University's cold-drink dispenser, such that when its "address" is fingered, it reports automatically the number of drinks left in the machine!

In practice, if you are accessing Finger through the command line (through DOS or Unix, for example), and it was installed on your system, you'd type something like

```
finger koekie@mail.easynet.co.uk
```

With this particular provider, the following results:

```
Login: koekie                          Name: Nicholas Mailer
No Mail.
Last read on Tue Aug  6 23:36 1996 (BST)
```

Some Internet providers also allow other services through Finger the example below brings up current service information for that particular provider:

```
finger status@gate.demon.co.uk
```

Which will bring up a list like the one on top of the following page.

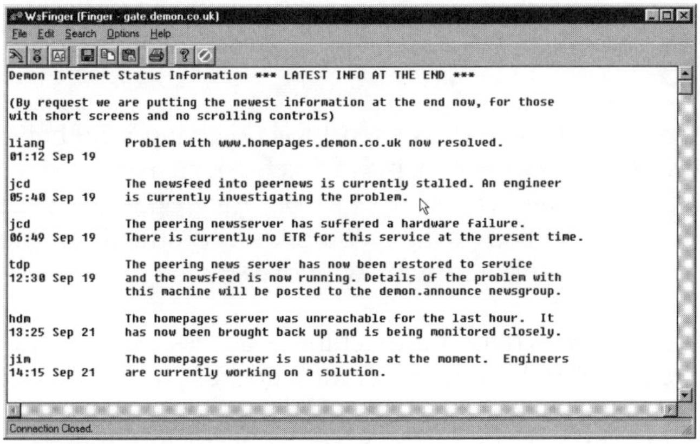

Left: An ISP's status message, produced courtesy of the Finger program. Finger, like other Internet tools, can now be found in friendly windowed and mouse-driven incarnations,

If you leave out the username to the left of the **@** symbol, you may get information about the machine as a whole – for example, the following provides information about a server machine at a University – who's connected, how long they've been connected and so forth.

```
finger@sun.leeds.ac.uk
```

This brings up the list of information:

Login	Name	TTY	Idle	When	Where
root	Operator	pe	1d	Mon 13:59	snst.leeds.ac.uk
chmmks	M K Sangun	q2		Wed 10:50	woolhouse_pc74.l
root	Operator	q3	6	Mon 15:37	ecusun1z
bmbjcy	J C Yang	q5	48	Wed 09:05	alf2.mrc-lmb.cam.ac.uk
menajf	A J Fenlon	q7	24	Wed 10:26	mensgi6.leeds.ac.uk
men5sk	S Koetniyom	q8	5	Wed 10:28	trib_pc40.leeds.ac.uk

Login is the login name, *Name* is the real name, *TTY* is the terminal they're using (each will have a different number in case they've logged in twice), *Idle* is the amount of time their computer has not been active on the network (for example, if they're connected but not doing anything), *When* was the time the user logged in and *Where* is the Internet address of the computer they're using.

As with other Internet services, you are no longer restricted to the command line. There are some mouse-run Finger clients which can be downloaded freely. You can then set up an address book of frequently fingered machines, so you can have easy access to your ISP's status, the amount of unread Email and so on at the click of a mouse button.

Ping

This curiously named tool is useful for detecting whether there is a problem with a connection or, indeed, whether a machine is connected to the Internet at all. There are lots of fancy options available with various versions of Ping – which comes as a command in Unix and the version of DOS distributed with Windows95.

If you want to see whether a machine is accessible over the Internet, just type **`ping`** and then the machine's address or IP number.

For example, if you want to check whether the ISP *Zynet's* mail server was up and running, you'd type

```
ping mail.zynet.co.uk
```

The response depends on what variant of Ping you're running. It will either respond with a message such as **`mail.zynet.co.uk is alive`** or it will show you its attempts at sending small "packets" of information to the remote machine, and its reply (if any). If the machine is not available, Ping will time-out, with no reply arriving.

Traceroute

This tool is similar to Ping, but more useful. It shows you the route you're taking across the Internet to reach a remote server. You may be surprised at the number of hops along the way, but that is the nature of the Internet. For example, from a London ISP to **`www.whitehouse.gov`** indicated 17 hops before arriving. Not only is this a marvellously illustrative command, but can show you where problems are occurring. If one hop is timing out or taking a very long time, it identifies the bottle-neck.

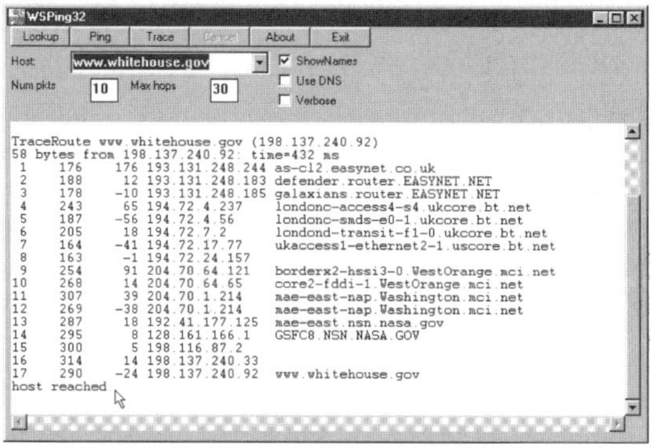

Right: Traceroute reveals a typical route over the Internet from London to the Whitehouse – it takes seventeen hops on different router machines before it finally arrives at its destination!

Gopher

Everyone has heard of the world wide web, but fewer realise that this was not the first attempt to give a friendly mouse-driven face to the Internet. A system which you might encounter is called Gopher. Although less versatile than the web, the system was popular for a while, and you may still encounter Gopher sites. It is an illustration of how quickly things in the Internet world evolve that, in the first edition of this book, Gopher was considered sufficiently important to merit half a chapter to itself. Now it remains little more than a footnote in the Net's frenetic development.

Although you can download special Gopher-browsing packages, it isn't necessary, because you can access Gopher sites through virtually all world wide web browsers. Instead of the web's usual **`http://`** prefix before the address, you will see **`gopher://`** – this indicates that the resource you're accessing is a Gopher site. The only way you'll notice any difference in the browser is that there'll be fewer graphics, and the information will be presented in a more linear fashion than the typical web site.

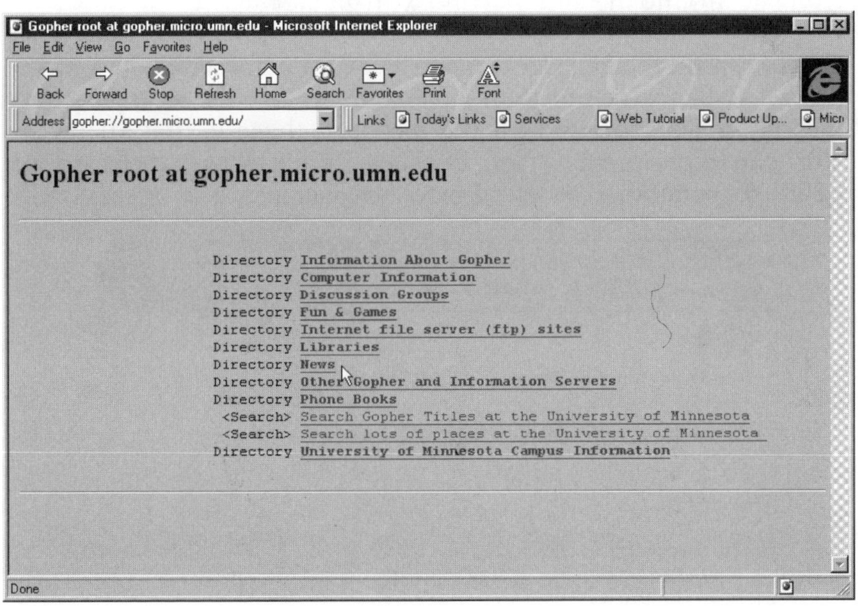

Left: Even modern web browsers remain compatible with Gopher sites. This is useful, because although these sites contain none of the razzmatazz of the web, they still remain repositories of useful textual information.

The gopher site illustrated here is the "home" of Gopher, the University of Minnesota, the "Gopher State" from which this Internet tool gained its punny name.

gopher://gopher.micro.umn.edu/

MUDs

A MUD allows you to chat (in text, of course) in "real time". This means that, as soon as you type something and press return, someone else on the Internet will see what you've typed. MUDs allow many people to connect to a machine and to talk to one another. The MUD will contain a world of rooms, with text descriptions and, sometimes, objects with which users can interact.

Many MUDs are set up as multi-user games. Indeed, MUD is sometimes said to stand for Multi-User Dungeon, because of the *Dungeons and Dragons* scenarios which are sometimes enacted through them. Others (sometimes called "talkers") are more environments for chatting. These can be fun, but some pupils find them so addictive, they run up large phonebills while chatting to people for hours on end.

MUDs can be accessed via Telnet – you simply Telnet to a MUD server at the correct port number, and follow the online instructions for setting up a character name and so forth. There are fancy MUD clients too, which give a friendly interface to a MUD, allowing you to navigate around the virtual world with greater clarity.

Currently at the cutting edge of interactive communication development are MUD-like systems, running in 3D environments, sometimes through a web browser. At the moment, these virtual MUDs are still at an experimental stage, but suggest that a "virtual classroom" could soon be an interesting place to visit.

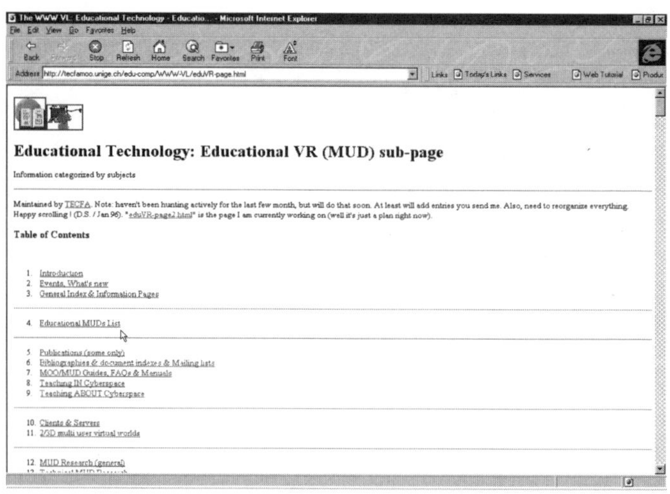

Right: MUDs are being looked at for educational purposes, this web page is a repository for a large amount of information, as well as links to many MUDs. Some, called MOOs (Mud: Object Oriented), are a particularly interactive variant, with rooms and objects which can be continually "built" by users.

http://tecfamoo.unige.ch/edu-comp/WWW-VL/eduVR-page.html

MUDs in education:

new environments, new pedagogies

This article on the educative potential of the MUD is by, and reprinted with the kind permission of, Tari Lin Fanderclai, University of Louisville.

Early in the spring of 1993, a small community of writing teachers who use computers in their classrooms discovered MediaMOO, a MUD operated at MIT and used by media researchers for real-time discussion and collaboration. The synchronous communication possible in a MUD, the immediacy of the exchange, the constant access to geographically distant colleagues, and the blending of work with play made MediaMOO uniquely appealing as a place for members of a professional community to come together. New collaborations arose; new projects were born; boundaries between established authorities and newcomers to the field seemed to blur; previously disenfranchised members of the academic community found audiences.

As we saw how the MUD benefited us, we began to ask how MUDs might be useful in our writing classes. The possibilities seemed endless. Students could have contact with people from cultures and subcultures outside their own. They could construct their own spaces and try on new personae, new ways of thinking, new ways of interacting. They would get immediate responses to their ideas and to the text objects they created, experiencing dynamically the effects their words have on others.

Perhaps most intriguing, MUDs could disrupt the hierarchy of the traditional classroom, giving students more power and responsibility and a chance to learn to use them wisely in order to accomplish their goals. Because students would be unseen and relatively anonymous, we hoped that they would feel more comfortable expressing themselves. Because everyone could talk at once and everyone would be heard, no one could dominate discussions. The teacher could not stand in front of the room and lecture and direct; students would have to be responsible for their own actions and develop their own methods for accomplishing their goals.

MUDs and the Traditional Classroom:

surprises and disappointments

So, since the fall of 1993, I have been bringing first-year composition students to MUDs. As we construct our characters and our workspaces and talk and interview people and collaborate with classes from other universities, many of those predictions about classes and MUDs come true. People who hesitate to speak up in class use their MUD characters to talk about their ideas. Students learn to describe strategies that they use to communicate in the MUD and to apply those strategies to other writing. They benefit from the exchange of ideas with experts and students from other locations. They mix work and play effectively, and they respond extremely well to having control over and responsibility for their own work.

In addition, there is a great deal of incidental learning, for many students log into the MUD on their own time, building spaces for their groups to work in, learning to program objects, discussing topics from our class and other courses they're taking – and, of course, generally playing around. Quite possibly they learn more from projects and activities they invent for themselves than from any I assign; certainly they learn things I could not teach them in our four-walled classroom.

And so I am surprised and disappointed, as I continue to use and explore MUDs that describe themselves as educational, to see many educators and MUD administrators working hard to bring elements of the traditional educational environment into these virtual spaces. This reduces the uses of MUDs for education to an attempt to inject simple novelty into old pedagogical techniques rather than to exploit the potential of MUDs to provide new learning experiences for students.

All too frequently I log onto an educational MUD to find myself in a virtual representation of a university campus. Separate buildings highlight the traditional divisions among disciplines, and within these buildings are elaborately programmed classrooms. Teachers can lock students in and others out; they have tools for delivering lectures, for silencing one or all members of a class, and controlling who speaks when. Some MUDs have separate character classes for teachers and students, allowing the teachers to control whether or not the students can build rooms or create objects, where they can go in the MUD, when they can leave the virtual classroom, and so on.

The unrealized potential of MUDspace

Whether or not a MUD requires teachers to use these kinds of tools, they obscure the unique possibilities of a MUD, predisposing teachers to think of the MUD as an extension of the real life classroom rather than as an alternative learning environment. Classes end up doing in the MUD what can be done more simply and perhaps more effectively in other environments; the MUD becomes a gadget, a gimmick; its potential goes unrealized; students and teachers become bored or frustrated.

For instance, the novelty of being in a virtual classroom will not last through an on-line lecture; MUDs are designed for interaction, and students will soon want to DO something. Yet the presence of programs designed to make lecturing on-line possible makes the practice seem appropriate. Programs for queuing speakers suggest that controlling the flow of a MUD conversation is desirable, and students are often forced to learn confusing commands for raising hands and receiving permission to speak. The teacher has an even more complicated task in queuing requests and directing who speaks when. Everyone is preoccupied by their frustration with the queuing program, and the group misses out on the rewards of a freely-flowing MUD conversation.

And, while commands for controlling students' behavior may seem efficient, they are also dehumanizing, robbing students of choices and suggesting to them that they cannot be trusted to behave appropriately on their own. The potential for empowering students is lost. Naturally, rightly, some students rebel against these controls. They may find more and more inventive ways to disrupt classes or disturb other users, and MUD administrators can find themselves programming in more and more controls to deal with problems that should never have come about. Even incidental learning is squelched under such conditions; even if the students are allowed to connect and socialize and create things on their own time, they've been given little reason to want to do so.

Questioning tradition: empowerment and innovation in classroom MUDs

The reasons for these conditions are rooted in traditional notions of what education is and is not. A university or other organization may feel forced to create a virtual representation of a "real" university in order to make their MUD appear a legitimate educational endeavor to those who do not understand its nature or purpose and yet control the funding.

Campus computing departments, some of whom already have problems with users of gaming MUDs taking up resources that others need for work, cannot understand why a teacher would want to encourage MUDding. Teachers are used to having control in their classrooms, and the chaotic and playful nature of MUD interaction can make them worry that no one is getting anything done. They may gratefully latch onto tools that allow them to make the environment imitate their real life classroom practices. MUD administrators, faced with large groups of newcomers with varying degrees of preparation descending on a MUD all at once, may feel forced to institute programming that they hope will provide a measure of social control. And such practices are self-perpetuating; change is difficult and innovation becomes more and more unlikely as the routines are passed along to each new teacher who brings in a new class.

But changes seem to be on the way. Recently, I have been pleased to read in various on-line forums debates in which those who use educational MUDs question the usefulness of practices that imitate elements of the traditional classroom. I have seen class groups in MUDs working under teachers who have explored the possibilities of the MUDs and used them to empower their students and give them learning experiences not available in the traditional classrooms. I have read of teachers able to negotiate with the most skeptical of campus computer departments to allow their students access to MUDs. I have even seen a few situations where administrators have granted funding for a MUD, and then stepped out of the way to let the teachers make of it what they will. Administrators of a few educational MUDs have recognized that well-prepared teachers can eliminate the need to control students with programming, and they are developing resources to help teachers learn to exploit the potential of MUDs.

I am hopeful, therefore, that the near future holds more of these changes. MUDs are places for self-directed learning, learning that blends work and play, that often looks chaotic but that is uniquely effective. A MUD is not an environment that can be controlled; to use MUDs effectively, educators must replace control with structure. Students need clear goals, and knowledge of the tools and methods they might use to accomplish those goals. And then they need for us to stand out of the way and let them learn. Perhaps as MUDs become more accepted in education and we make better uses of their potential as learning environments, we'll even take a few of those lessons about empowering students and staying out of the way of their learning back to our real life classrooms. And that, it seems to me, might be the most important thing any of us could learn from educational MUDding.

IRC

Internet Relay Chat is similar, in some respects, to MUDs, except it is a distributed chat system, not run on one server by one individual or group of individuals. If MUDs are separate kingdoms of chat, IRC represents a federation of chat. Individual users log in to local IRC servers, which communicate with the IRC system as a whole, bouncing messages around the world.

Each user can set up a "channel". This user then becomes the channel operator. Other users can then join the channel, but the operator has rights of banishing or even banning troublesome users. This is a useful facility for educational users, who can set up their online classrooms without fear of external disruption.

Below is an extract from an information area about KIDLINK IRC, an educational use of IRC, especially for children all around the world. This project has a reputation for making amongst the best use of online interactive technology.

Kidlink IRC

Some people have asked us: "What is KIDLINK IRC?"

Sometimes we take for granted that all the terms and parts of KIDLINK which are familiar to most of us, are familiar to everyone on KIDLINK. We should always take into account the new kidlinker, and especially someone who is entering the world of cyberspace for the first time.

Therefore, although these things are well-documented in many KIDLINK files, I will provide a few words of explanation of what IRC is, and especially why KIDLINK IRC is so different from GLOBAL IRC.

IRC (Internet Relay Chat) is a method by which we can "talk" on-line simultaneously with a number of other users (kids/ adults). Our computer screen is split into two parts. In the upper larger part, all of the messages written by the other users on the system appear, together with the nickname of the person writing the message.

For example:

```
Sarah: Where are you from, A-Hannah?
A-Hannah: I am from Israel.
```

(on KIDLINK IRC, adults put an A- before their nickname. Only real names are used as nicknames)

At the bottom part of the screen there is a small area where you write your own message. After you press return, your message also appears in the upper part of the screen.

```
> I am from England.
```

The other people will see your nickname beside what you wrote.

When you begin, you join a specific channel. On KIDLINK IRC, the main channel is **#kidlink**. Sometimes there are many users, and the screen becomes crowded, so someone decides to create another channel with a specific topic where people who want to talk about this topic can "go". Sometimes this topic is created at the very beginning because of a special "talk".

Anyone with an IRC client can get into GLOBAL IRC. The problem with GLOBAL IRC is that it contains a huge number of users from all different ages discussing many topics to which we would never want to expose our children. Thus KIDLINK IRC provides an excellent alternative, and I believe it provides a unique IRC environment which is not matched anywhere else in the world. If you do not have an IRC client, you can also reach KIDLINK IRC by Telnet.

Mark Hunnibell set up KIDLINK IRC, and over the years has devised a system in which kids and adult educators from around the world can talk together, without fear of negative influences and harmful disturbances from the outside. In order to do this, a registration system was set up by which only KIDLINKERS can register. The registration system also enables us to cut off troublesome users (although usually a warning is enough) and thus ensure that KIDLINK IRC is being used properly and beneficially for all.

KIDLINK IRC can serve as a place where kids come together and chat. It can also serve as a learning tool for "distance education" and special "talks" about certain topics. Once a week there is the KIDCLUB talk, where kids from around the world discuss a specific different topic each week. KIDCLUB is an exciting development which is run by kids for kids, evolving as the result of the vision of Patti Weeg.

We hope this has given a wider picture for those of you who didn't have this information at your fingertips before.

For more information, you can retrieve a number of IRCHELP files from the KIDLINK listserv. In order to do so, pull down the first IRCHELP file in the following manner:

Send a message to: **`listserv@vm1.nodak.edu`** Leave the subject area blank. In the message area, write: **`GET KIDLINK IRCHELP`**

This file will then provide you with information as to how to retrieve other relevant files.

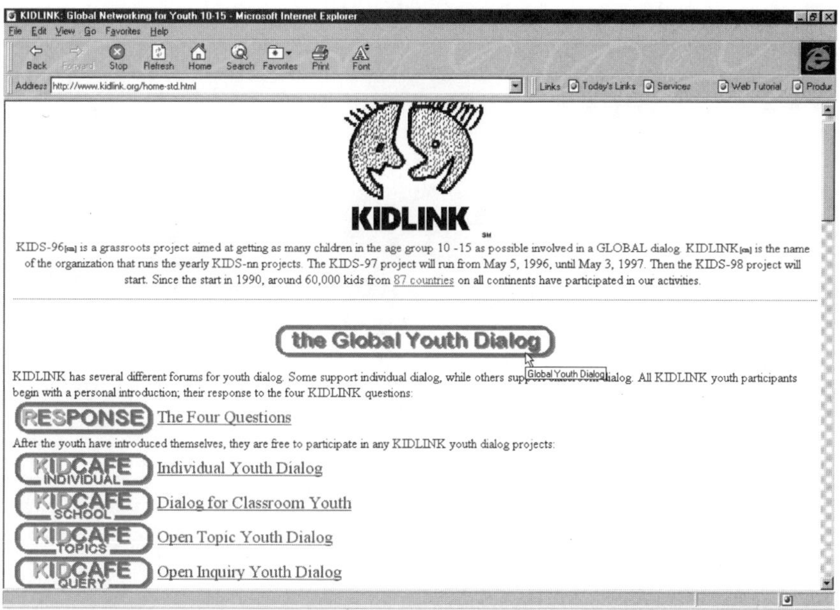

Left: Kidlink's Website at `http://www.kidlink.org`

World Wide Web

A look at the most popular way to browse the Internet – the world wide web.

Including example sites, Java, VRML, plug-ins and HTML.

Chapter 8

Theworld wide web is, by far, the most popular Internet service. In fact, when some people talk of the Internet, they mean the worldwide web. The web is directly responsible for the Internet's burgeoning popularity: it placed a unified and friendly face on existing Internet services while introducing a range of unique attractive interactive services of its own.

As with the rest of the Internet, the web (often referred to as WWW or even W3) has no centre and is owned by no-one. It consists of millions of online documents on differently-owned machines scattered around the world. These documents can be almost infinitely varied, and are connected to one another via hypertext. In practical terms, hypertext (or, in todays multimedia world, hypermedia) links mean that pertinent words, phrases, or even images within one document lead, when clicked upon, to another document related to it. This allows you to click your way through masses of information without worrying about machine names, directory hierarchies and so on.

Describing hypertext in abstract is difficult, but in reality, we use similar methods in traditional publishing when we use footnotes, except with the web, you're not simply pointed to an annotation, but another page, and, perhaps, another "book" in another country. For example, a pupil might be browsing a web page about 20th Century drama, and you come across the phrase

After the 2nd World War, simple Agit-Prop evolved into a more sophisticated workers' theatre, typified by Joan Littlewood's Theatre Workshop.

The pupil isn't sure what Agit-Prop is. Fortunately, the web page's designer has provided a link from this page to someone else's agit-prop pages. The pupil can tell, because the word is underlined and in a different colour. He selects it with his mouse-pointer and clicks the mouse button. The welcome page for a set of Agit-prop pages somewhere on the other side of the world is displayed, containing explanations and further links to playscripts and other websites. The pupil *bookmarks* the page, deciding to come back to it later. From now on, it will appear on his personal mousse-clickable list of favourite places He goes back to the original page and notices a picture of some clowns dressed in army uniform. He clicks on the picture and is transported to a gallery of pictures and sounds from *"Oh! What a Lovely War"*.

History of the web

For those who comment on the great American influence upon the web, it comes as a surprise that the system was invented by a British person in Europe. Tim Berners-Lee, was employed by CERN, the scientific particle physics establishment in Geneva. He was interested in distributing information in a way more akin to the human thought process, over a multitude of computer systems. In March 1989, he posted his proposal, and began constructing the *protocols* required for the Web.

CERN was quick to see the benefit of this approach in disseminating scientific papers over the local network, and the idea spread slowly through the scientific community. The real breakthrough occurred in 1993, with the release of Mosaic by NCSA in America (The National Center for Supercomputing Applications, based in the University of Illinois), the first easy-to-use mouse-run Web browser. By the end of the year, versions were available for all popular machines, and the Web began to catch on like wild-fire.

Mid 1994, one of the students who helped to program Mosaic started a new company, which was to become Netscape Communications. The Netscape Navigator proved even more popular than Mosaic, with millions of home users downloading the software. As the software developed, more and more fancy effects were added, with web browsing becoming an ever increasingly multimedia experience, culminating in the integration of a Java, a programming language produced by Sun, which allows programs to be downloaded and run immediately through the web browser on any machine.

Bill Gates, CEO of the behermoth of a software company, Microsoft, in an about-turn that astounded the industry in its celerity, suddenly decided that the Internet was important, and began developing Internet tools in earnest - in particular the Microsoft Internet Explorer, the company's web browser. Netscape and Explorer are continually leapfrogging one another in features, with both companies committed to integrating the web browser ever further into the operating system of the computer running it, such that a user will be able to browse his or her local hard disc in the same way he or she would browse outside links.

Accessing the web

The only practical way to access the Web is on a mouse-run system, capable of displaying colour. You require a Web client, which is a program known as a web browser, which will display the information and allow you to interact with your mouse. There are, as ever, available via FTP or from your Internet Service Provider. The world's most popular browser is Netscape Navigator, a comprehensive package available free to education establishments. Another increasingly popular browser is Microsoft's Internet Explorer, which is being integrated into its Windows95 operating system. This, too, is available freely. Both packages can be downloaded from the Internet. Netscape's homepage is at `http://www.netscape.com/` with Microsoft's at `http://www.microsoft.com/`

Even with today's fast modems, graphics within the body of a document (known as inlined images), sounds and animations can take quite a while to display. Fortunately, web browsers allow you to turn off the graphics, or download the text before the graphics, so you can read the document while its illustrations arrive.

Web services

There are many specialised web sites, set up as pretty alternatives to the text-only sites - the Web is the first widely used Internet service which allows multi type-sizes, columns, tables and colourful images within documents in real time. This has allowed for a proliferation of virtual museums, art galleries and even shop windows.

The real beauty of the Web is that, in addition to the aforementioned specialised services, it offers access to other Internet services, like Usenet, Gopher and FTP sites, all in the same browsing environment. So, in one session, you could visit the Louvre, download a picture and post your opinions of the postimpressionists to a Usenet newsgroup.

With its colourful, intuitive interface, the World Wide Web is the most attractive and popular use of the Internet yet. Its growth remains exponential, its absolute size impossible to judge.

URL names

Each document on the web has what is known as a *URL address*. This stands for *Uniform Resource Locator*. As its name suggests, the URL is a standardised Internet "filename", which contains information on where and what the document is. Every web page has its own URL address. Most of the time, you won't need them – you'll be travelling through the web in the way it was designed to be browsed – by intuitive clicking. Nevertheless, in magazines and books (including this one), Internet resources can be pointed to through their URL. You type the URL into a specific location requester on your web browser software, and you are transported to that page.

This is a typical URL:

`http://www.bbc.co.uk/index/schedules.html`

The URL is divided into four parts.

The service (`http://`)

What appears before the colon and the two slashes depends on the type of resource you are accessing. Most of the time, this prefix will be **`http`**, which denotes those documents specifically designed for the world wide web and its protocols. URLs can point to other resources too, though – if the prefix is **`ftp`**, for example, you will be accessing an FTP site, effectively using your web browser as an FTP client. For example, **`ftp://ftp.demon.co.uk/`** will facilitate an anonymous-ftp login to Demon Internet's FTP site.

The server (`www.bbc.co.uk`)

After the prefix, until the next slash, will be the name of the Internet server machine to which you wish to connect. If these machines are web servers, they will often have **www** as the first domain (as in the above example, which is the BBC's web site – curiously, for a public, non commercial corporation, they now use **`co.uk`** instead of the **`org.uk`** domain – are they trying to tell us something about their future direction)?

The path (`/index/`)

These are directories (you might know them as folders if you use Macintoshes or Windows95). The hierarchy is separated with slashes. In this example, we are directed to a directory called **`index`**. If the example was **`games/arcade/`** then we'd be pointed to the arcade directory, itself in the games directory.

HTTP

You may well have noticed that web pages have the prefix http:// attached to their URLs. This stands for the HyperText Transport Protocol. This is the "mechanism" by which pages are transported from the server to your browser, managing connections, security and so forth.

The actual web pages are written in HTML, the HyperText Markup Langauge. So, one would describe the process of browsing the web as the transferral of HTML pages from a Web Server machine to your web browser via the HTTP protocol. You will never have to know what happens "under the bonnet" at the HTTP level.

The page (`schedules.html`)

Most web pages will end **`.html`** or **`.htm`**. This indicates that these documents are written in the "language" of the web (hypertext markup language) and are proper web pages. Web browsers will also display text files and some types of graphics. What your web browser does with other sorts of files depends on its setup. You can usually instruct the browser to do particular things with particular files – load up external graphics viewers, for example, or a sound package, so the data can be accessed. An even more up to date method of dealing with different types of files is to use a "plug-in" – an extension to your web browser you can download and install, which allows a particular data format (for example, an animation file) to be displayed within your web browser's window, just like normal a web page.

Sometimes you'll see a URL with no apparent indicated page or document. For example, **`http://www.koekie.org.uk/`**. What happens in such examples is that your web browser will try to access a default page (usually **`index.html or index.htm`**) in the specified directory. If such a file does not exist, an error will be displayed.

Navigating the web

The web is an enormous resource. It has an unimaginably eclectic collection of information scattered all over the globe. To new users, this can be intimidating. Fortunately, finding useful information is no longer just a case of fortuitously stumbling over it - there are an increasing number of online catalogues which help you in your research.

Virtually all the catalogues now allow you to type in a word, group of words or phrase for which to search. The "search engine" will then begin to search an index of a large proportion of the web - some of the larger engines catalogue over 20 million pages - for your keywords, producing a list of successful "hits" for you to select. Astonishingly, the search usually takes just a few seconds to complete!

There are an increasing number of catalogues pointing to a large number of web reviews. These are even better than the search engine, in that they give a précis of the site and its content, sometimes giving it a rating. For schools who wish to start with a pre-reviewed group of well-designed resources, these review catalogues are invaluable.

We have a catalogue of academically reviewed web sites in an appendix of this book. You are welcome to try them out - simple type the listed URL into your web browser's "Address" or "Location" box and press return.

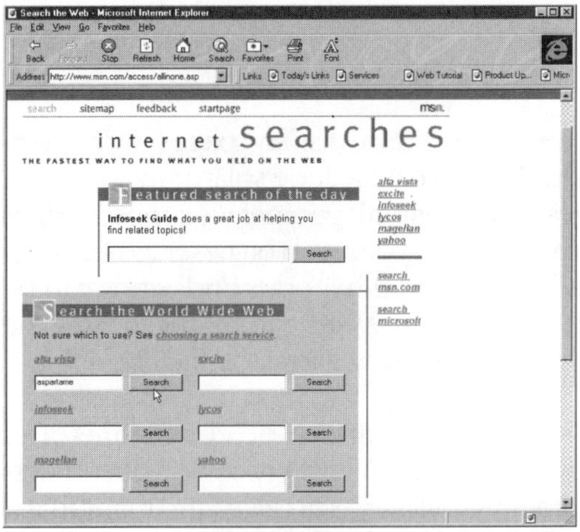

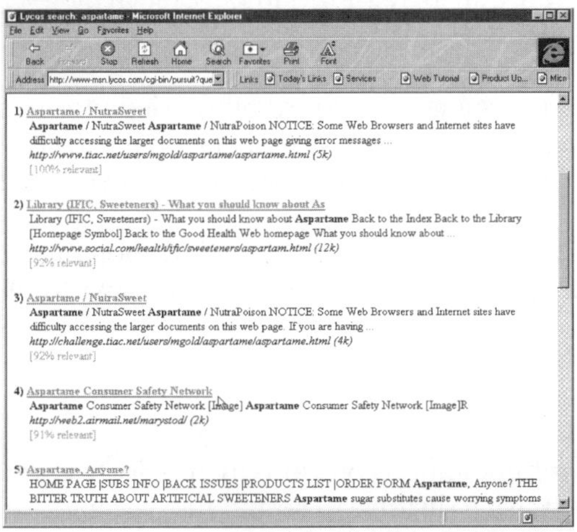

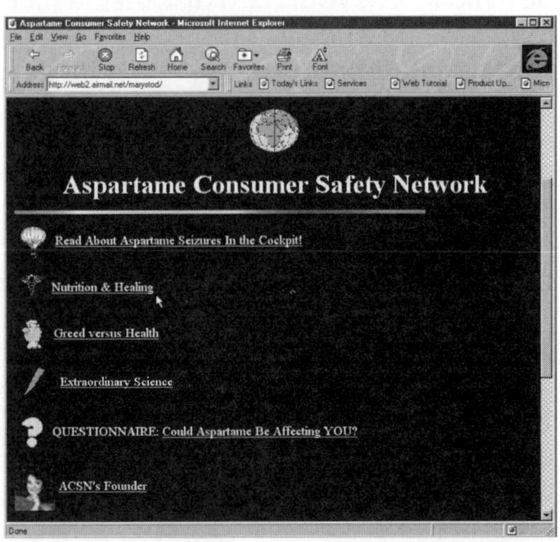

Left Top: First, we type the keyword `aspartame` into one of the search engines. This page represents a collection of six to try.

Left Middle: After clicking on search, an index of millions of web pages is searched for that keyword. A few seconds later, a list of "hits" is displayed – we click on one of them.

Left Bottom: We are transported to the web page, and we can browse through it.

Plug-ins

By default, world wide web browsers can display pages with ever-increasing typographical variety – pages can include split-frame displays, fill-in forms, background images, foreign-language typeface support, tables and columns and more. The capability of your web browser to deal with weird and wonderful sounds, images and other odds ands ends can be extended with web *plug-ins.* The first browser to use these was the Netscape browser, although most others now allow the facility.

Plug-ins are programmed by a wide variety of companies and organisations. One might allow you to view word processed documents directly in a web browser. Another will allow you to view and manipulate 3D images. There are an increasing number of such plug-ins now available for downloading.

A plug-in, as its name suggests, can be downloaded and, when installed, will integrate with your web browser. The operation is usually so seamless that an end-user will not realise a special plug-in has been installed.

Many plug-ins can be found at **`http://tucows.cableinet.net/plug95.html`** – this is for Windows95, but has links for Windows3.1 and Mac as well.

Audio

There are a number of audio plug-ins available. Without plug-ins, if you wish to listen to a sound file, you need to download it to your hard disc first, which can take a very long time indeed for a long piece. Plug-ins like RealAudio (**http://www.realaudio.com**) use "streaming" technology, which allows the file to play while it is being downloaded. Of course, the file is not the normal computer sound file – it is highly compressed, and the sound may not be CD quality, particularly over a modem connection. Nevertheless, it is now possible to listen to news programs from all over the world, and there is already a healthy repository of educational programming, which looks set to increase.

Video

Because video requires a quick connection, it is difficult to achieve quality video-conferencing and the like over a modem. Nevertheless, several products, like VDO-Live (**`http://www.vdolive.com`**)

allow streamed video over the Internet. With a modem, the picture will be small and jerky, but is an indication of future possibilities.

CU-SeeMee software was the first attempt at video conferencing over the Internet. If you don't expect full-screen full-motion video, the system can be quite impressive (**`http://www.wpine.com`**).

Telephone

Although some are separate programs, more and more Internet telephone software integrates with the web, including Netscape's Cool Talk (**`http://www.netscape.com/`**), which includes a web-based "address book". Internet Phones, as their names suggest, allow you to talk to another Internet user via a microphone connected to your computer.

Some products, like Microsoft's NetMeeting, allow you to interact with other users via a "virtual whiteboard" – collaborative scribbling as you talk. These products, as they grow in sophistication, will become more and more useful in distance learning.

Although the quality can be ropy, for Britain to be able to speak to New Zealand for the price of a local call is sufficiently impressive to cause some measure of concern with the major telecommunications companies.

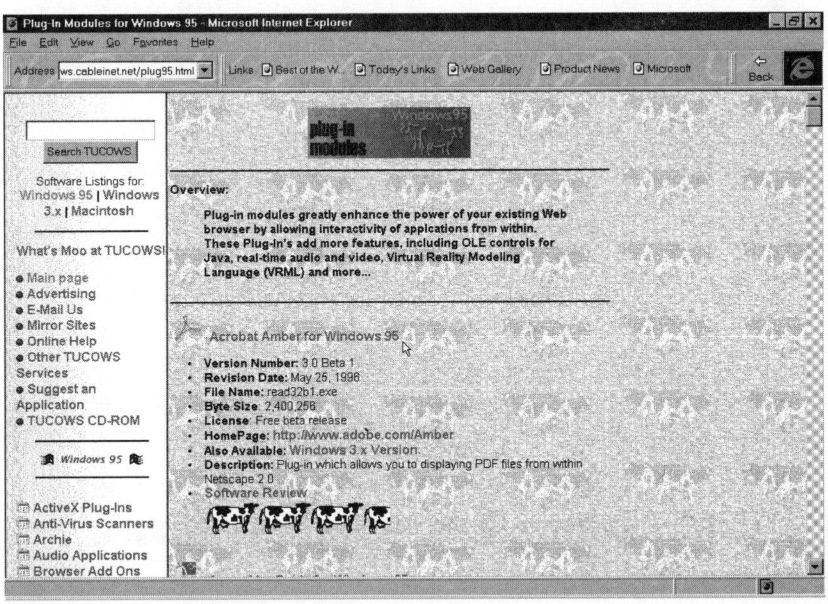

Left: The TUCOWS site contains a comprehensive collection of plug-ins, reviewed and available for immediate downloading.

http://www.tucows.com/

Multimedia

Currently, a popular multimedia plug-in is Shockwave. This allows scripted multimedia presentations to be displayed through your world wide web software. Software like this will, eventually, integrate the CD-ROM and Internet worlds. It is available for downloading at **`http://www.macromedia.com/Tools/Shockwave/`**

Microsoft is currently promoting a technology called ActiveX which allows plug-ins to be downloaded "on the fly" – if a page doesn't support a particular effect, the plug-in required to facilitate it is downloaded automatically. Some people are worried that this will give Microsoft too much of an advantage in the Internet realm, but they have given over the technological specifications to an independent organisation, so it remains to be seen whether it will develop as an open-platform standard.

VRML

Another development is VRML. This stands for "Virtual Reality Modelling Language", and allows 3D objects and worlds to be represented and interacted with over the Internet. Several plug-ins now built into popular web browsers allow for 3D environments integrated within the web browser's window. Information and examples are available from **`http://www.vrml.org/`** Links to thousands of VRML sites can be found at **`http://www.aereal.com/`**

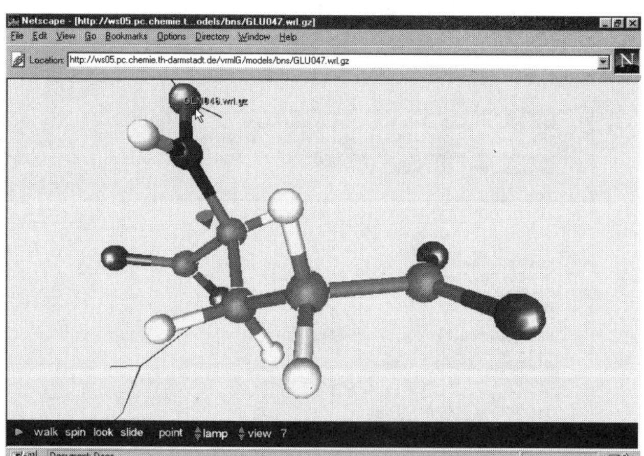

`http://darmstadt.de/vrmlG/`

Right: A VRML site – a rather sweet molecule is displayed in the web browser's window. Being VRML, it can be rotated, manipulated, zoomed in and out. VRML is one of the technologies which will, as it matures, become more and more useful.

Java

Currently, a most significant development in the Internet's evolution is Java, a programming language (based on C++) written by Sun Microsystems. Whatever Sun might say today, it was not originally constructed with the web in mind – it was designed for "embedding" into consumer devices and so forth – but they recognised a niche when they saw it.

The language allows completely interactive content throughout the web. The property of Java that makes it particularly suited to integrating into the web is the fact that the programs written in it (often termed "applets") can run on a wide variety of operating systems without re-writing for each. This is facilitated by a Java "virtual computer"(a program which translates the Java code into something the native computer, upon which it is running, can understand). Unfortunately, this continual translation can slow down the running of the program. Solutions to this include "Just in Time Compiling", where the program is pre-translated for the native computer before it is run, after which it can be executed at top speed.

Below: This site includes a number of games, written in Java, which help in language learning.

http://www.bahasa.com/

Those who are hopeful about Java's future sometimes have the overzealous enthusiasm and motivation of those who believed Esperanto represented the future of human language. Nevertheless, although Java's current implementations can be quite slow and buggy, software developers are beginning to realise its significance. It remains clear that Java or its descendants will continue to make the Internet more than an interesting addition to your local computer, but an integral part of your computing experience.

With truly interactive networking, the possibilities for education are boundless. There is the glimmer of the possibility that quality educational applets could be the medium through which many youngsters, in the developing nations, who crave to learn, might finally become a part of a global pedagogical culture.

A good repository of thousands of Java web sites is located at **http://www.gamelan.com/**

Your school's web pages

It is now not uncommon for a connected school to have its own web pages. Many ISPs now allocate a certain amount of free or inexpensive webspace to each subscriber, whereby users can create pages, and graphics, uploading them to the provider's web server, where they will be accessible to the world as with any other web pages. For example, the *Internet For Learning* service provider is schools specific, helping the school set up its web page, and placing it in a national online schools' directory. Another ISP, Easynet, now provides unlimited amounts of webspace free to each subscriber.

You can create the pages locally, previewing them on your hard disc with your web browser. You can then upload them to your webspace using an FTP program (see FTP chapter). This is one of the few occasions where you will not be using anonymous FTP, but actually logging in to your space with a username and password. This means you, and you alone, have full control of what appears on your web space.

Schools often place a version of their prospectus on the web. "Prospectus schools" will find their interactions with the Net more rewarding if they also put up some creative content – pupils' essays and artwork, outing reports, local history and even pupil homepages.

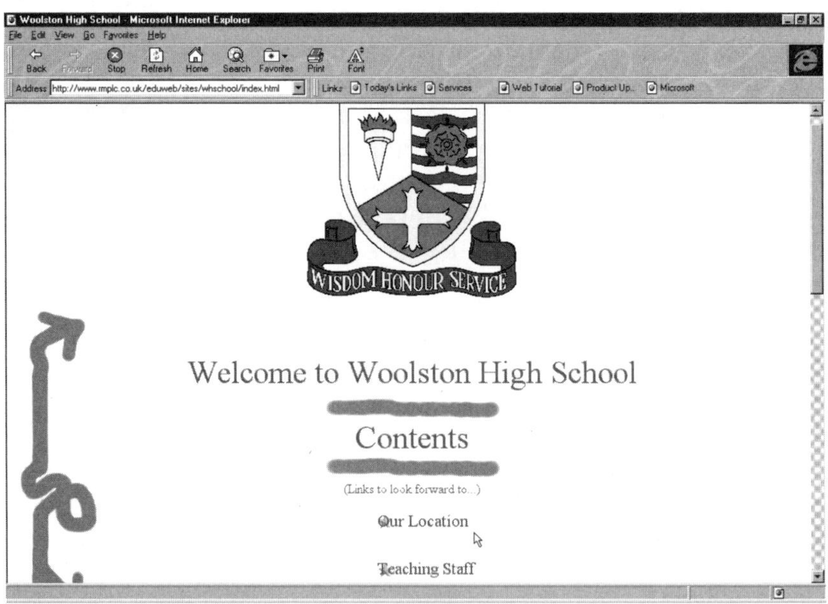

Right: UK Schools are currently blooming on the web – children and teachers are learning basic HTML, and using their combined skills to create vibrant home pages.

`http://www.rmplc.co.uk/eduweb/sites/whschool/`

Editing web pages

Web pages are written in HTML (hypertext markup language). These are simply text documents with control commands inserted, instructing the Web browser to do a number of things with the graphics or text on the page. These commands are inserted in between chevroned brackets like **<this>**.

For example: If you wanted some text to be displayed in italics, you'd do it like this:

This <i>word</i> is in italics.

Which would display this when loaded with a Web browser:

This *word* **is in italics.**

The slash indicates where the previous command should be terminated. That's the basis of HTML – a command in chevron brackets at the beginning of some text, terminated with a slashed command in chevron brackets.

Because HTML pages are just text, you can write them in the simplest text-editor on any machine and preview them locally with your browser. Alternatively, there are pieces of software which help in producing the web pages. Some of them just provide a menu of HTML commands which you select and paste into your text. Others are even easier to use, hiding the commands and producing a *WYSIWYG* (what you see is what you get) display of what your text should look like in a web browser – you can insert pictures, change typefaces and so on, almost like a word processor.

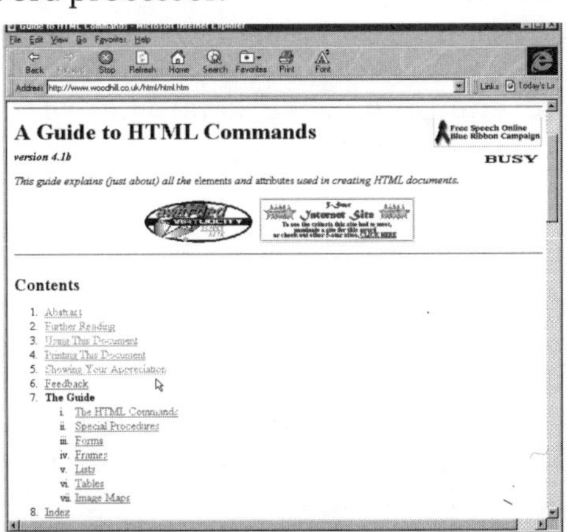

Below Left: With the hundreds of tutorials and online manuals available, learning HTML is very easy when you have the Internet as a resource. This British tutorial is an example of the enduring spirit of the Internet – it is an impressive work, its contents superior or equal to many expensive books on the subject – but it is available to all for free. It is no wonder that several traditional publishers are beginning to worry.

http://www.woodhill.co.uk/html/html.htm

A selection of web sites

The following is a sample of the variety of educational web sites available. It is not in any sense an exhaustive survey, barely scratching the surface of what is out there. Nevertheless, it gives some idea of the different ways in which the web is currently being used. A number of syllabus subjects have been picked, in each of which six example web sites have been selected.

For a much more comprehensive catalogue of web sites, see Appendix 2.

Note

Each example's URL should take you to the site described. Nevertheless, you may find that the design has changed, the content is different, the page has moved or, perhaps, is no longer available. Web resources are in constant flux, so this should come as little surprise. If the address appears to have changed, and there is no indication of the site's location, try using a web search engine to find it.

Mathematics

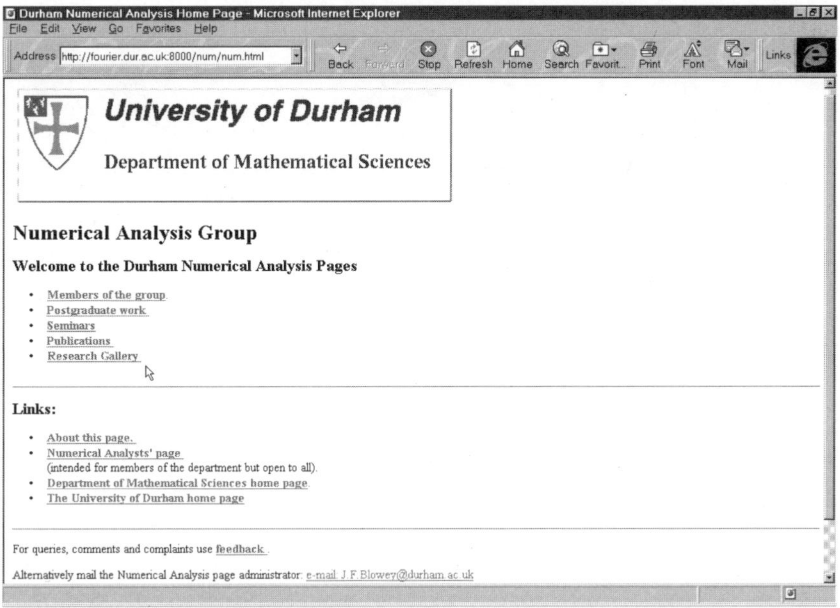

http://fourier.dur.ac.uk:8000/num/num.html

There is a large pool of creative mathematics and mathematicians on the Net. Some of it is high powered, high level research, like the British site left.

A-Level students will be able to get a flavour of university maths by browsing such sites, and perhaps corresponding with the authors.

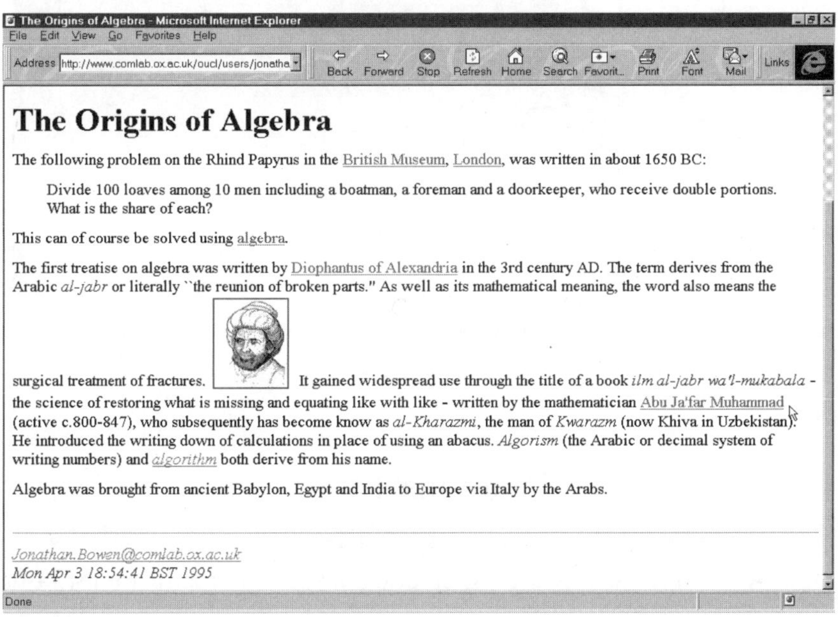

http://www.comlab.ox.ac.uk/oucl/users/jonathan.bowen/algebra/

This site is an example of a resource specifically for lower-level learners. It is an entertaining multimedia introduction to algebra by an Oxford professor.

There are several interactive inter-classroom projects on the web. As the name suggests, MathMagic is run in America, but teachers from all over the world contribute. It is difficult to interest some children with mathematics, but projects like these are beginning to bear fruit.

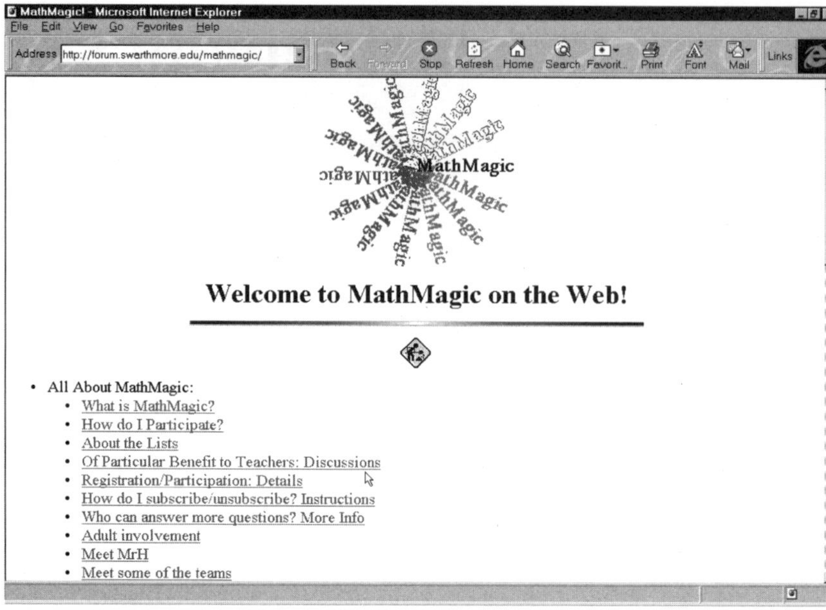

http://forum.swarthmore.edu/mathmagic/

There are quite a few lesson-planning resources, as well as banks of detailed and illustrated questions. This is one of them.

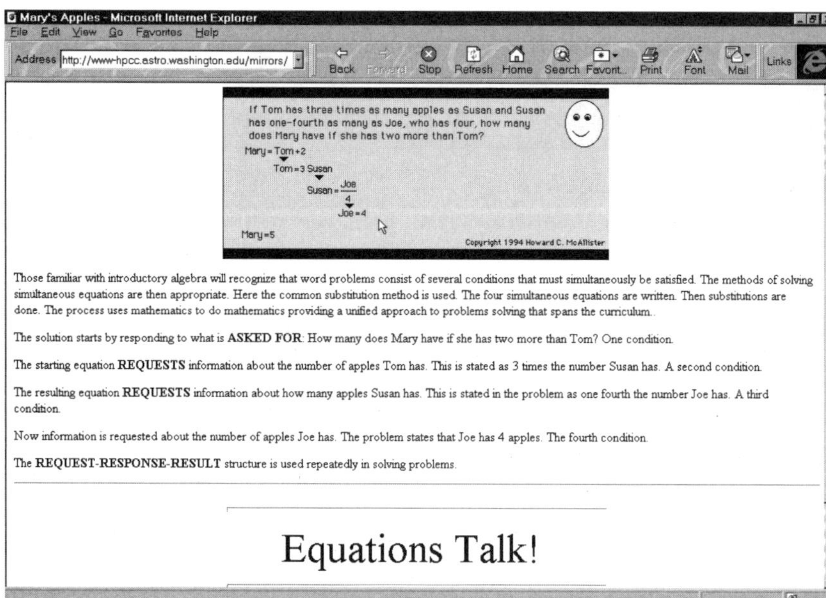

http://www-hpcc.astro.washington.edu/mirrors/suremath/home1.html

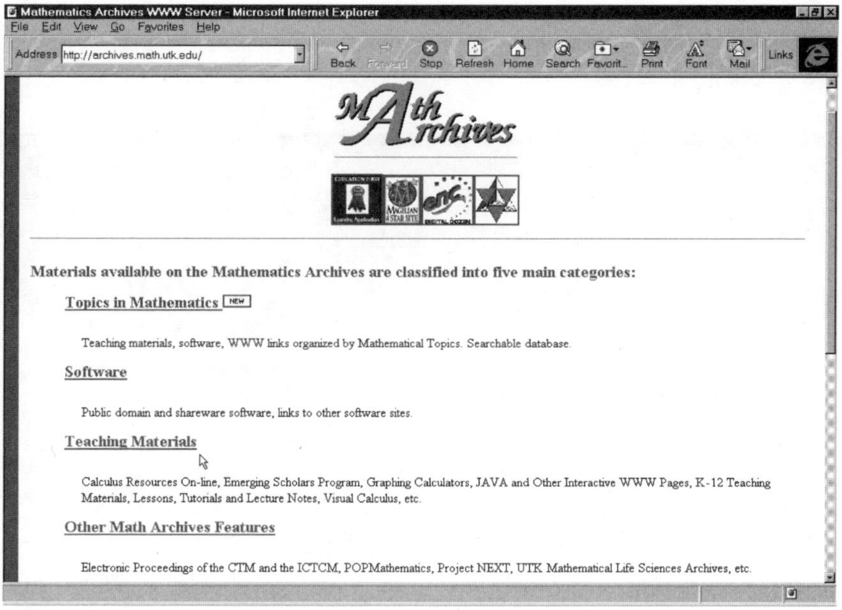

http://archives.math.utk.edu/

There is much public domain mathematics software and teaching material online, and archives like this help you get hold of it.

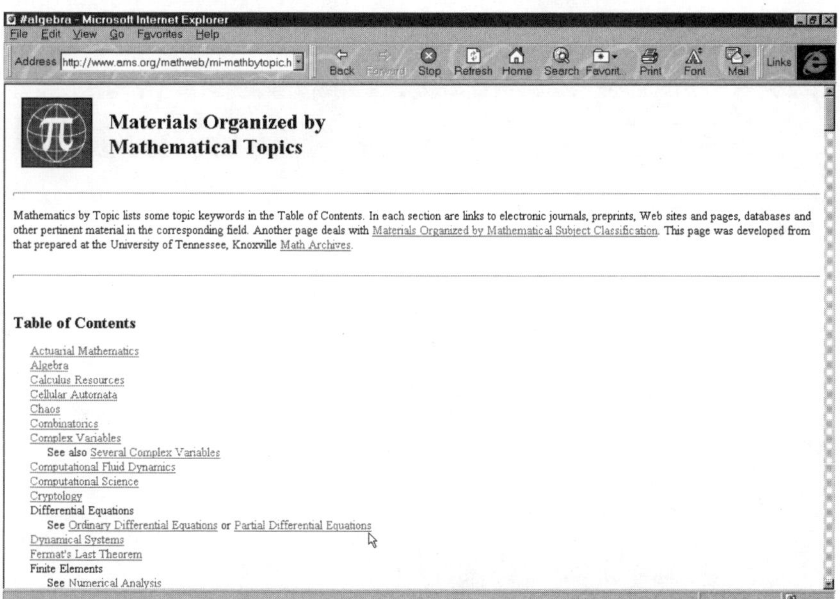

http://www2.hawaii.edu/suremath/jmarysApples1.html

With catalogues of resources like this one, it seems that there is no topic in any curriculum which is not represented in some form online.

Physics

Every branch and every level of physics has its presence on the Internet. This is the introductory page to an online multimedia course.

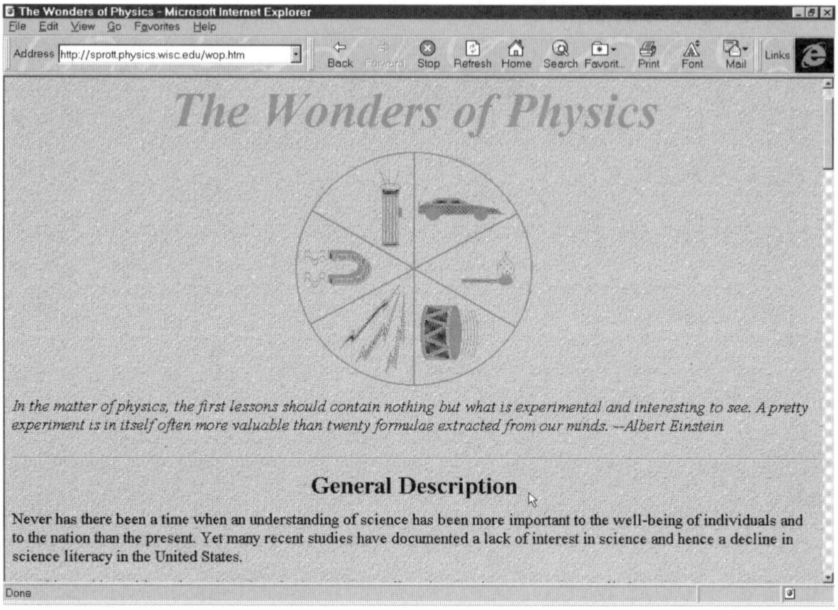

http://sprott.physics.wisc.edu/wop.htm

For those who wish to know what's happening at the pinnacle of the discipline, institutions like CERN are online. Indeed, the web was invented by CERN to share highly-detailed scientific data.

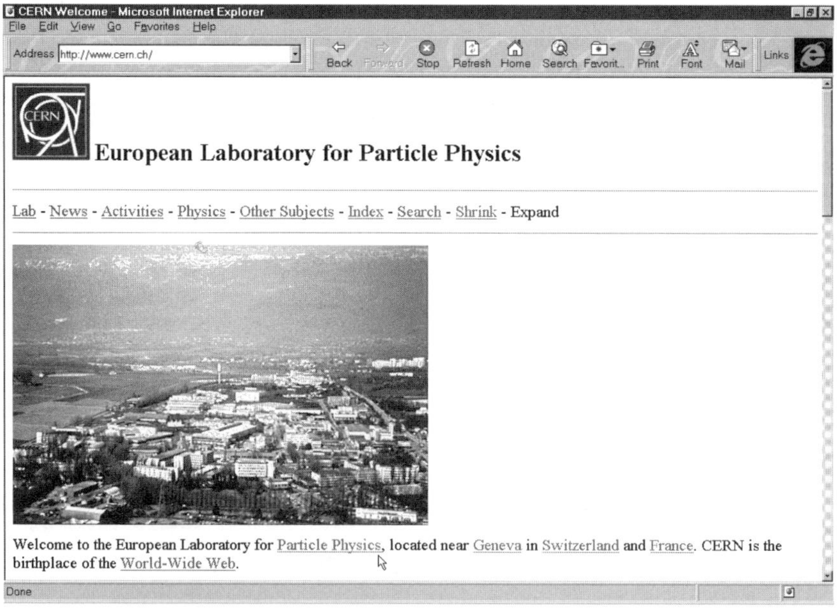

http://www.cern.ch/

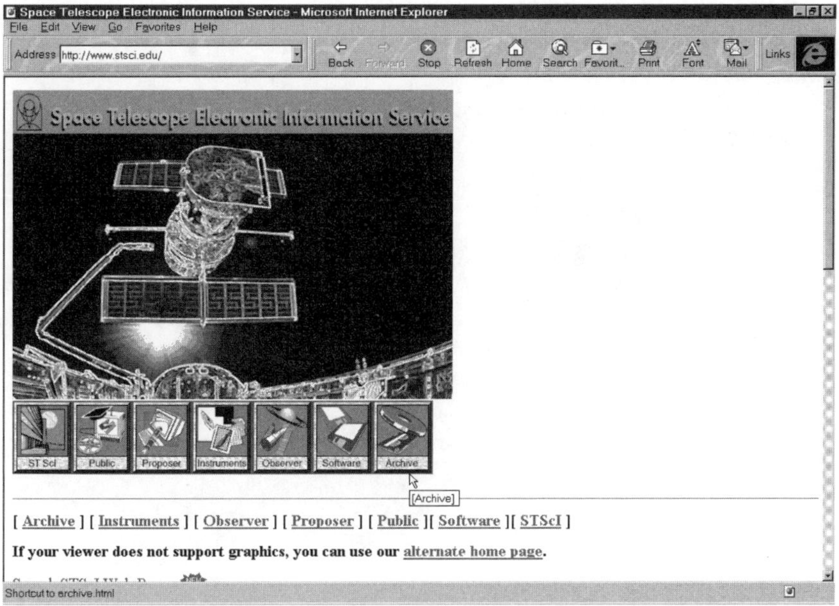

http://www.stsci.edu/

The Internet has always excelled in the quantity and quality of its astronomy resources. There are demonstrations hosted by the major institutions, including NASA and the Hubble Space Telecope (left), which downloads its spectacular images straight to the Net. Now, there are even real telescopes available, whose tracking and imaging programs can be controlled by anyone on the Internet!

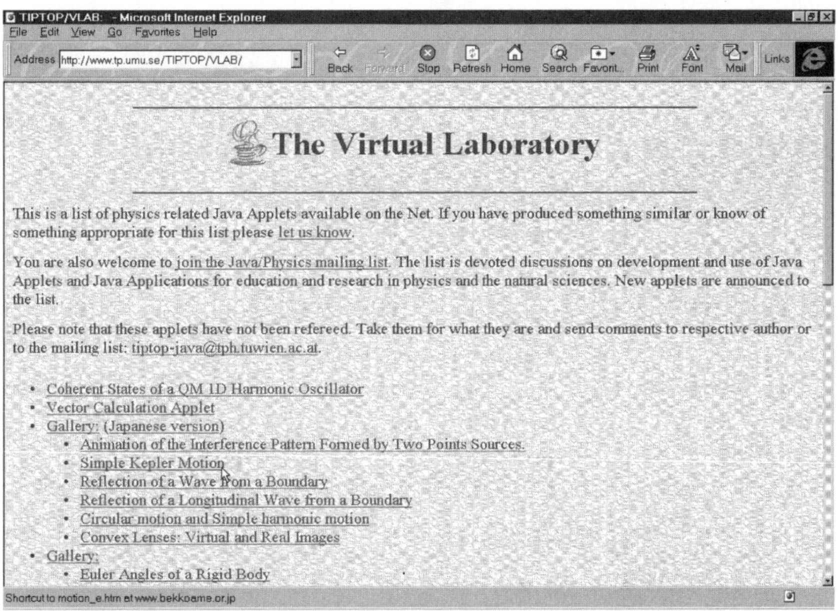

http://www.tp.umu.se/TIPTOP/VLAB/

With Java, animated interaction becomes possible. Several virtual laboratories have been established, with active on-screen scientific instruments, gauges and equipment. In cost and safety conscious days, such experiments become particularly useful.

An example of a Java applet. It is a lucky school which can afford a laser for one experiment. With a free web browser, you can have the next best thing.

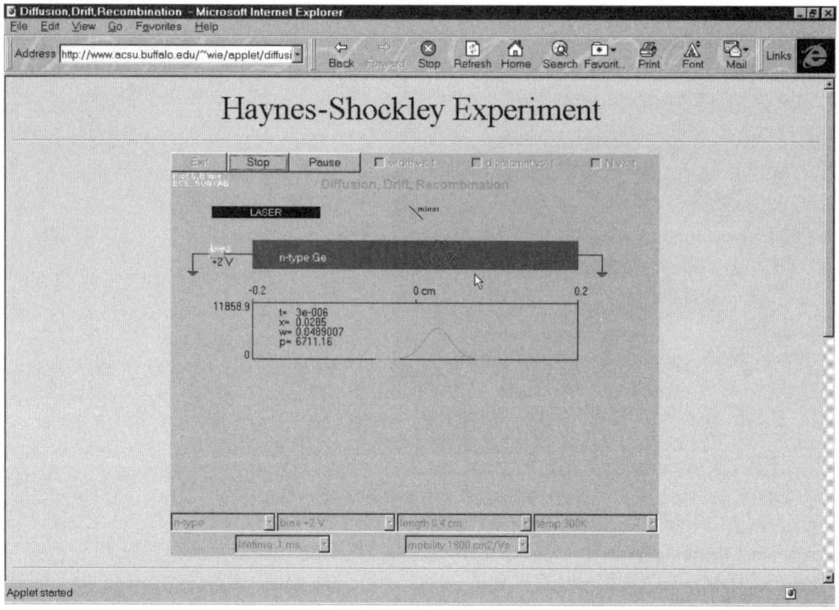

http://www2.ari.net/home/odenwald/qadir/qanda.html

It's not all laboratory science. Social and ethical science is represented at all levels, with alternative energy resources particularly well catered for.

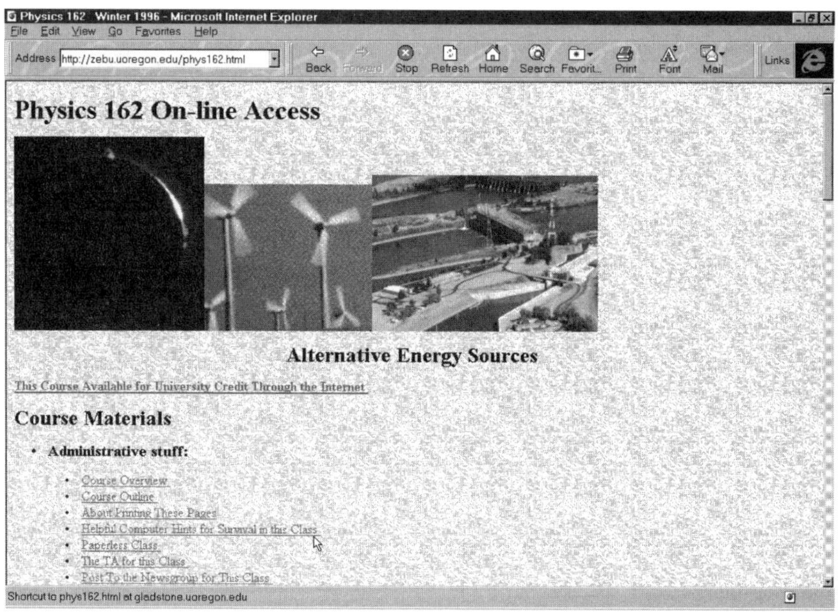

http://www-hpcc.astro.washington.edu/scied/physics/physcourse.html

Chemistry

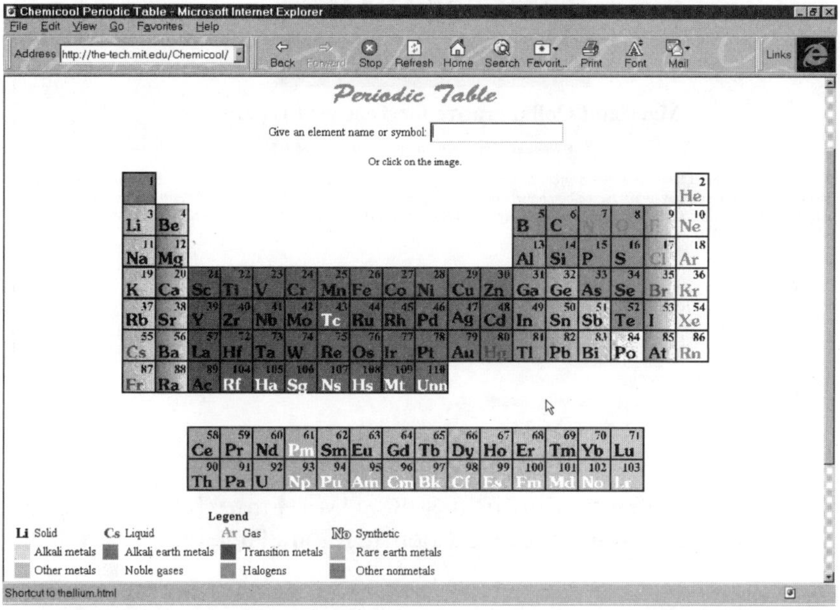

http://the-tech.mit.edu/Chemicool/

Chemistry is inherently a dramatic subject, and the online chemistry resources back this up with information to shame even the most comprehensive school data-books. In the example left, clicking on an element reveals pages and pages of data and information.

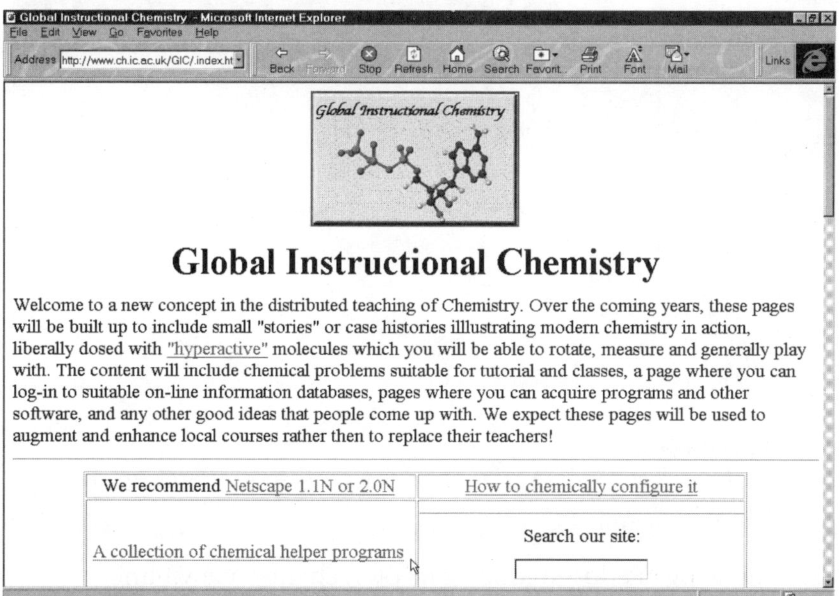

http://www.ch.ic.ac.uk/GIC/.index.html

This is the beginning of an online chemistry course for pupils, run by a professor at Imperial College. Notice the interactive nature of the Net always makes itself present in his request for ideas and information for his continually evolving course for classroom teachers.

This site is another such example, this time from America. This course was especially developed for beginners in Chemistry, and includes links to many related Internet resources.

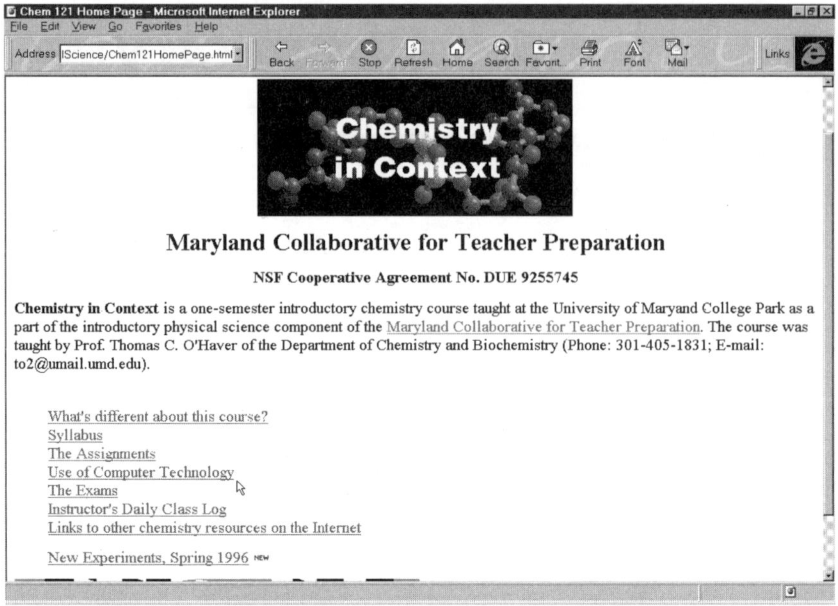

http://www.inform.umd.edu:8080/UMS+State/UMD-Projects/MCTP/Courses/PhysicalScience/Chem121HomePage.html

The nice thing about online textbooks is that the author is always an Email-message away if you have a problem understanding something!

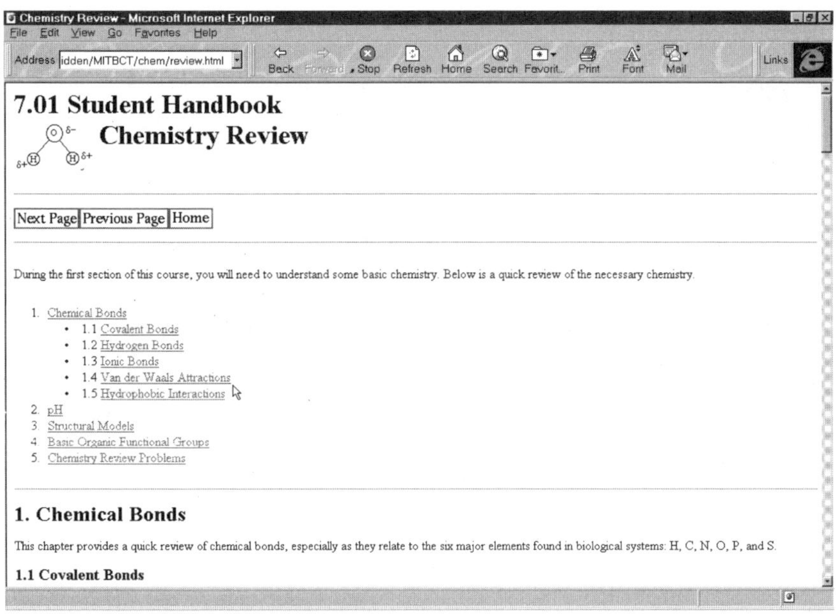

http://ernie.bgsu.edu/~midden/MITBCT/chem/review.html

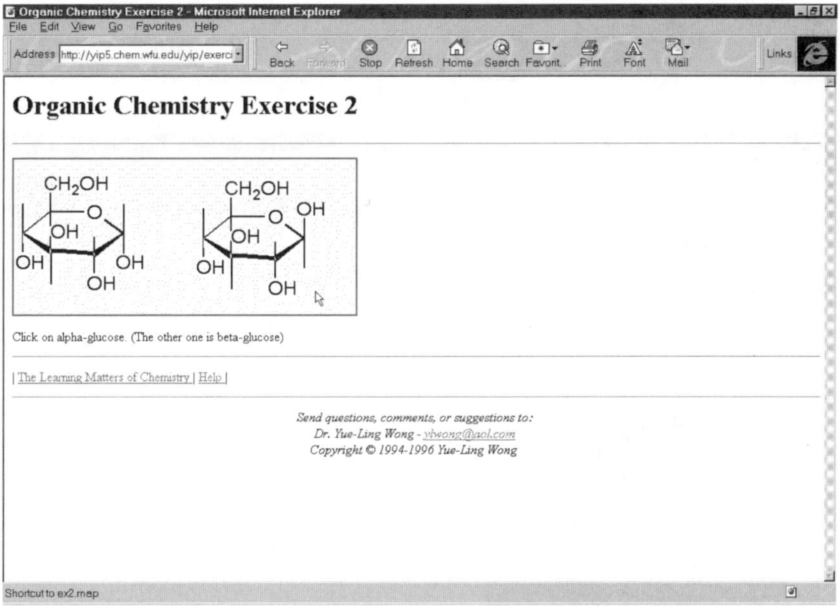

http://yip5.chem.wfu.edu/yip/organic/org-home.html

As the web becomes more interactive, we can expect to see more exercises like this one – an online multiple choice quiz.

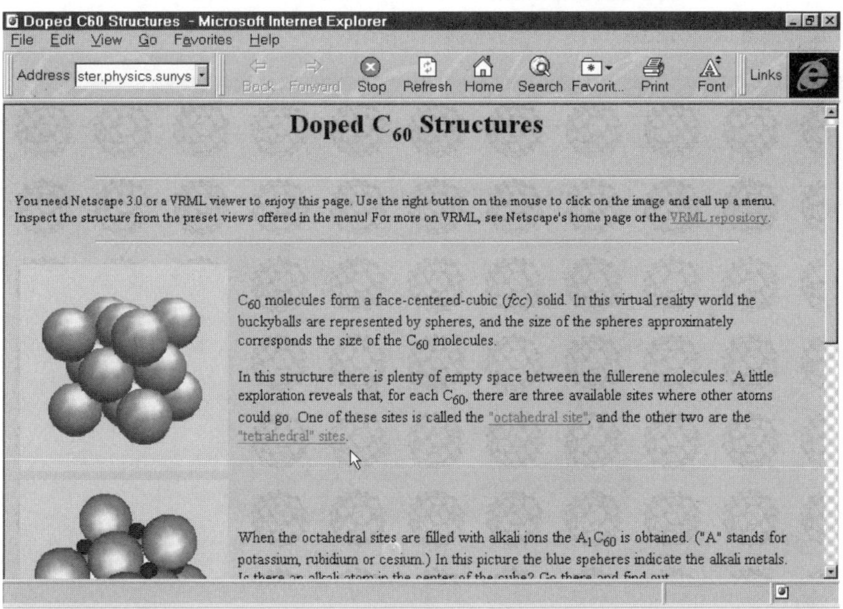

http://buckminster.physics.sunysb.edu/solids/c60str.htm

Carbon-60 has interested a large proportion of the scientific establishment. This site is particularly special in that the molecule fragments (left) are VRML, and are therefore fully animated, and can be manipulated within the browser.

Biology

There are many innovative biology and natural science resources on the Internet. The Tree of Life is such a project, which intends to develop into a knowledge-sharing forum, concerning every aspect of life, for researchers, teachers and pupils.

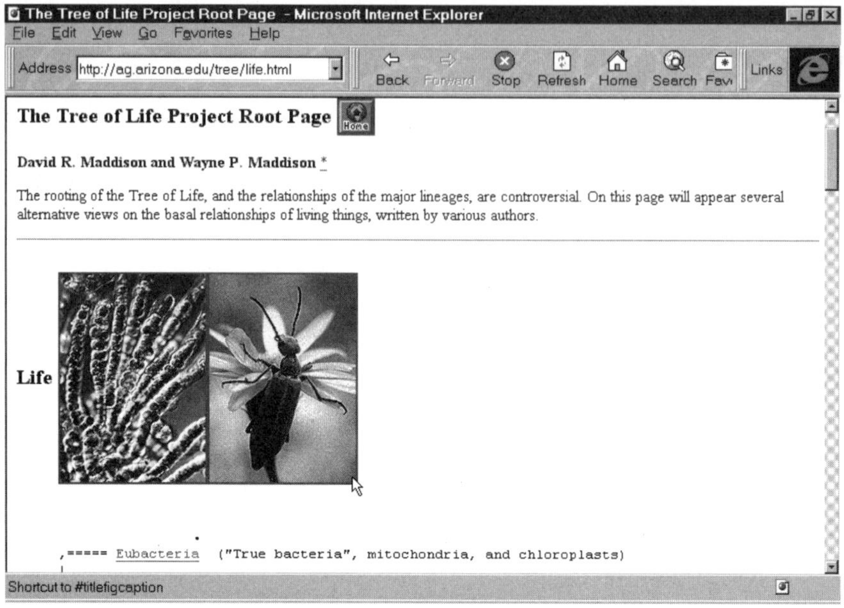

http://ag.arizona.edu/tree/phylogeny.html

With each animal having its home on the web, school projects on any topic can include research and interviews with experts on the animal in question.

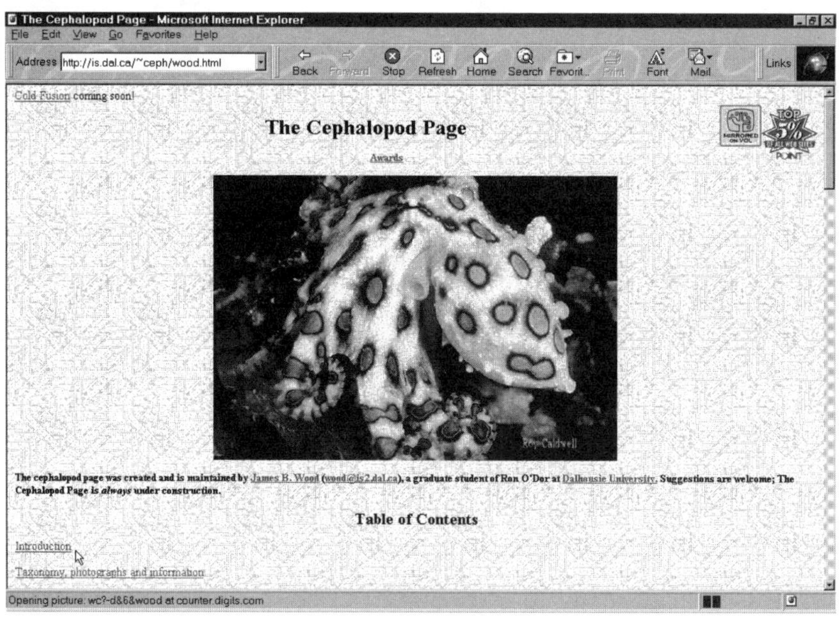

http://is.dal.ca/~ceph/wood.html

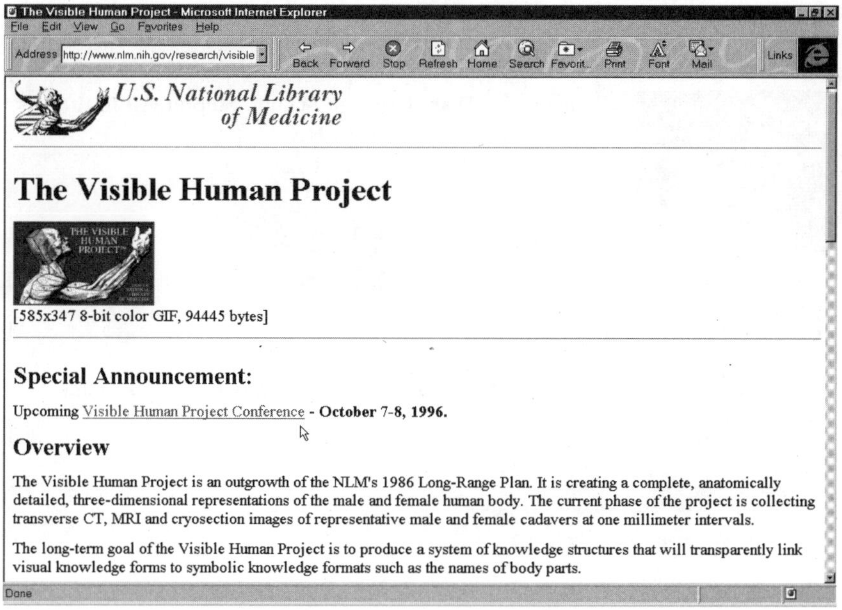

http://www.nlm.nih.gov/research/visible/visible_human.html

The American government's Visible Human Project provides a unique resource for anatomy studies. Other pages include a virtual frog dissection. As resources like these become ever more detailed, it becomes less necessary to put children through the trauma of genuine dissection before they are ready.

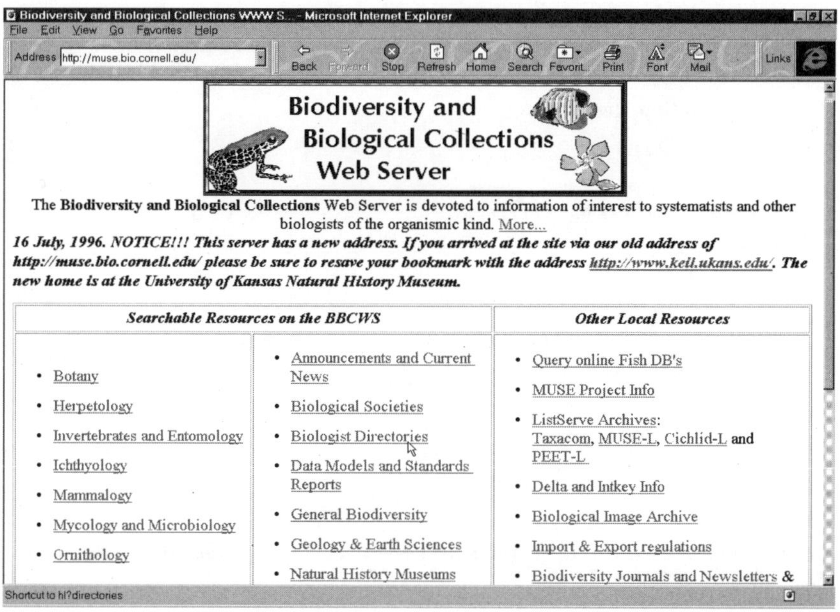

http://muse.bio.cornell.edu/

Biodiversity and ecology is well represented on the Internet, with academic organisations and pressure groups including databases, discussion forums and contacts.

Schools are beginning to put their biology lab and field-trip reports online, for the world to read and comment upon.

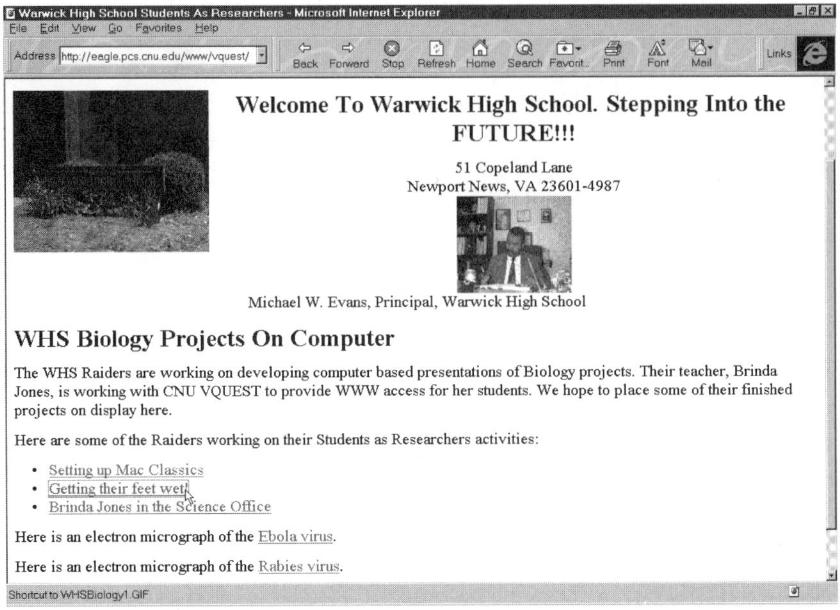

http://eagle.pcs.cnu.edu/www/vquest/CNU-STARS/SAR/schools/warwick/warwick.html

With exhibits, games and online museums, this site dealing with evolution includes links for children of all ages.

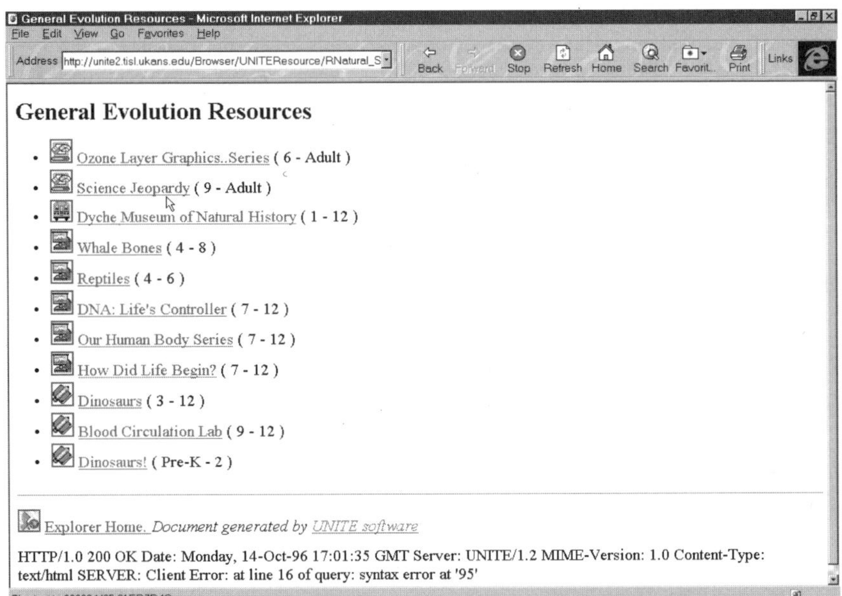

http://unite2.tisl.ukans.edu/

Geography

Because the Internet is global, it is ideally suited to the study of Geography. Sites like "The Virtual Tourist" allow you to click on a map, which zooms you in to a more detailed map, from which you select countries of interest. Many country and regionally relevant sites contain information, displays and exhibits.

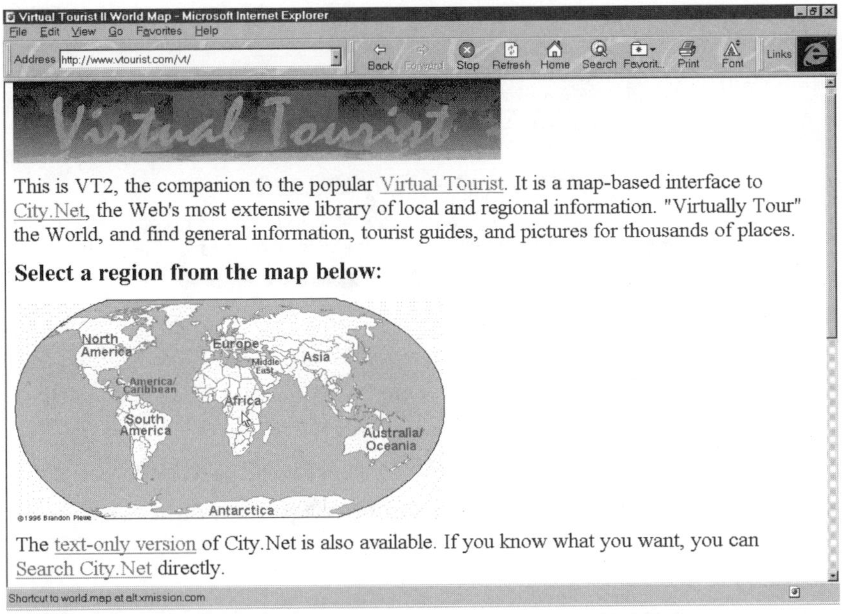

http://www.vtourist.com/vt/

Here, for example, is a homepage for Australia, which includes links to information sites, maps, virtual tours, geophysical and environmental data as well as many cultural and political areas.

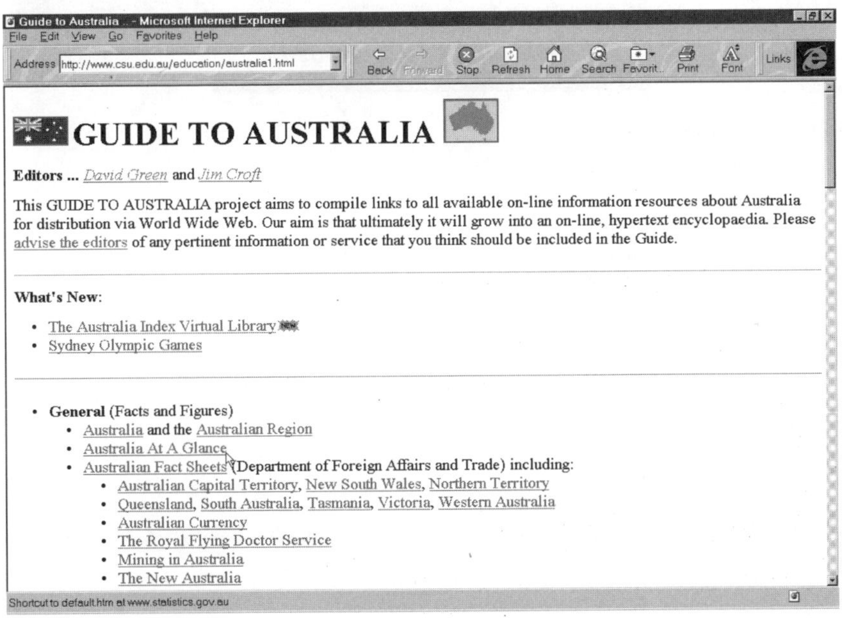

http://www.csu.edu.au/education/australia1.html

Geology and petrology sites abound, with this site a particular gem.

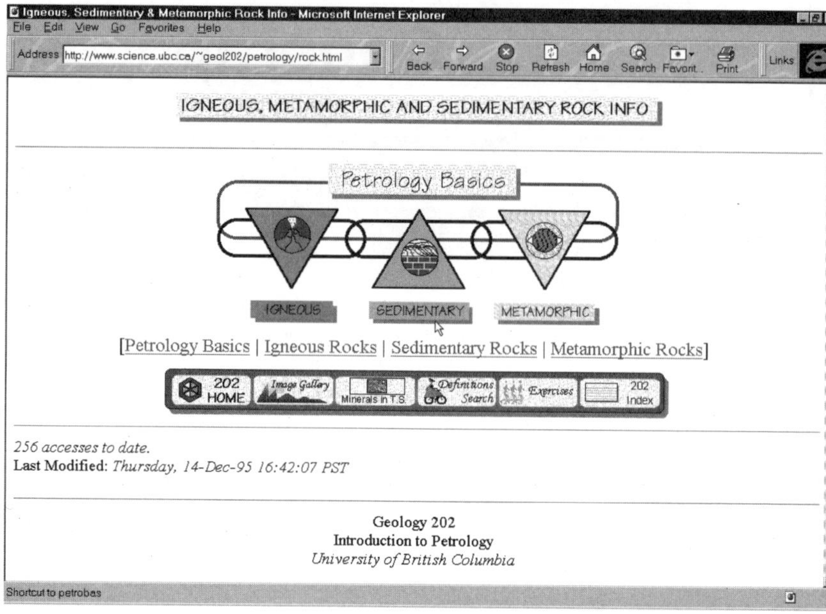

http://www.science.ubc.ca/~geol202/petrology/rock.html

The Net provides an up-to-date source for geophysical information. This is the Earthquake update. Clicking on an on-screen map will reveal information and photographs about any quakes there, as well as providing live contacts with people in the area. There is a similar resource for volcano information.

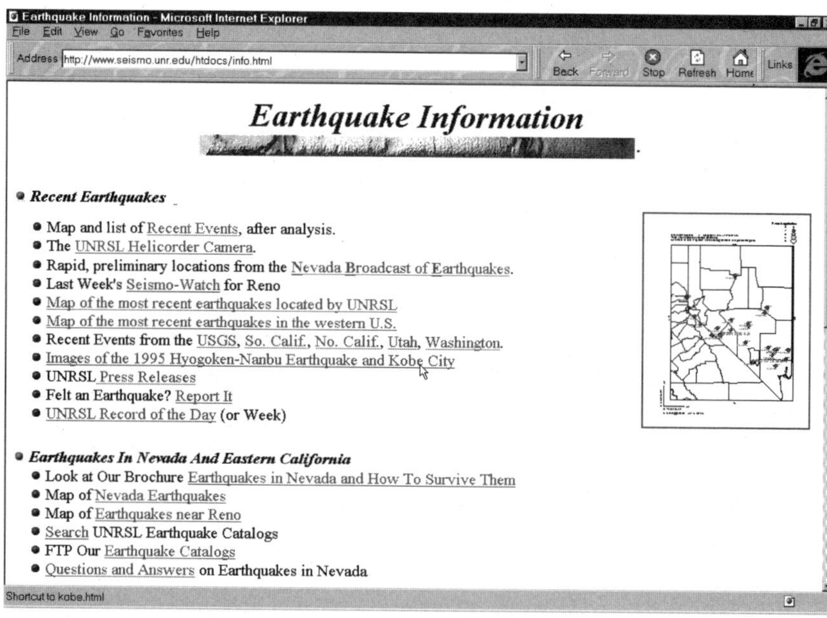

http://www.seismo.unr.edu/htdocs/info.html

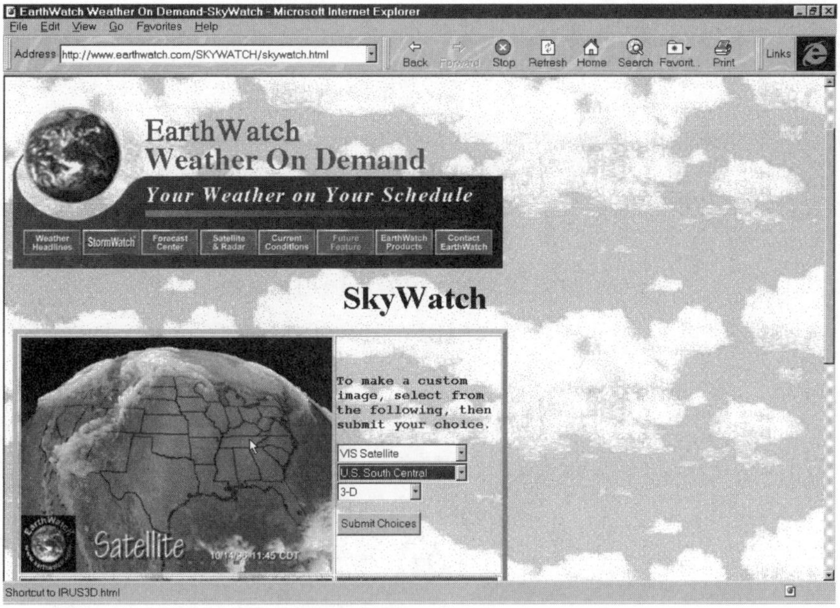

http://www.earthwatch.com/SKYWATCH/skywatch.html

Global weather and climate information is abundant, including up-to-date satellite images, in all wavelengths, which are readily available for any global position.

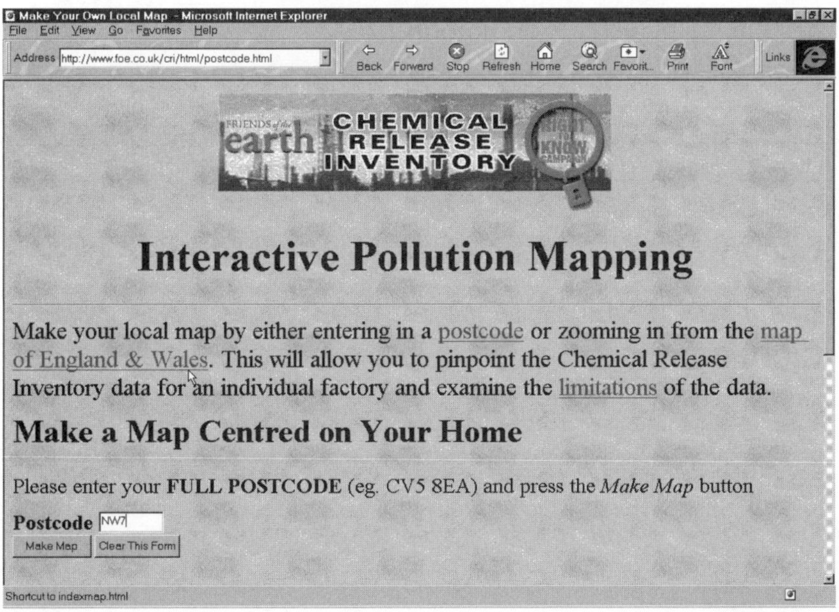

http://www.foe.co.uk/cri/html/postcode.html

Local social geography is complemented by sites like this one hosted by Friends of the Earth. It allows you to monitor any possible polluting industries and current hot-spots in your local area.

History

The humanities are just as well provided for as the sciences. Rare primary documents can be downloaded, sometimes as clear transcripts, and sometimes the images of the documents themselves.

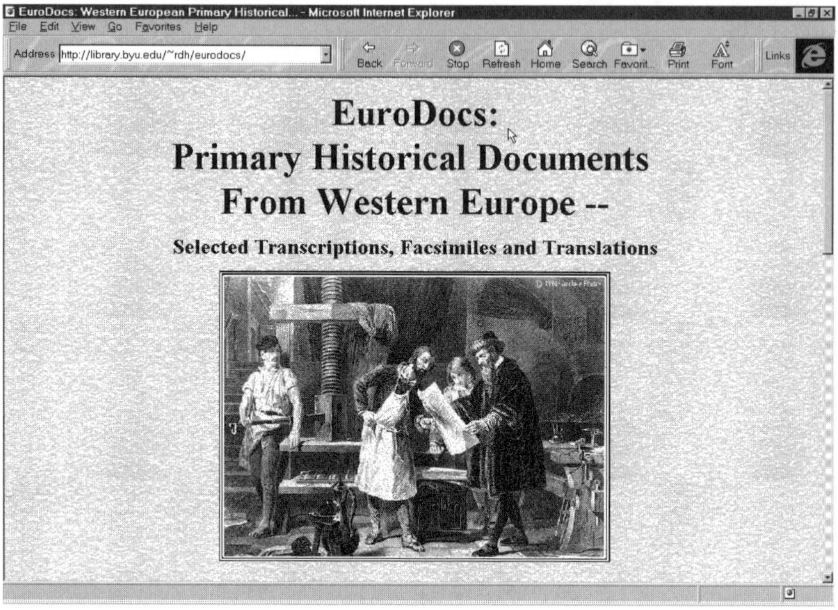

http://library.byu.edu/~rdh/eurodocs/

There is a large amount of quality textual information, which can be downloaded and printed out. The relevant areas can be found through keyword searches.

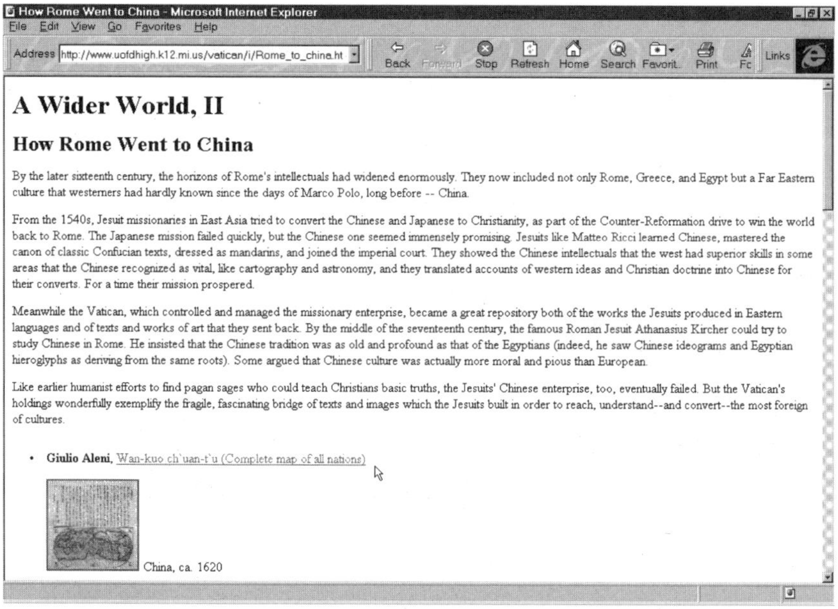

http://www.uofdhigh.k12.mi.us/vatican/i/Rome_to_china.html

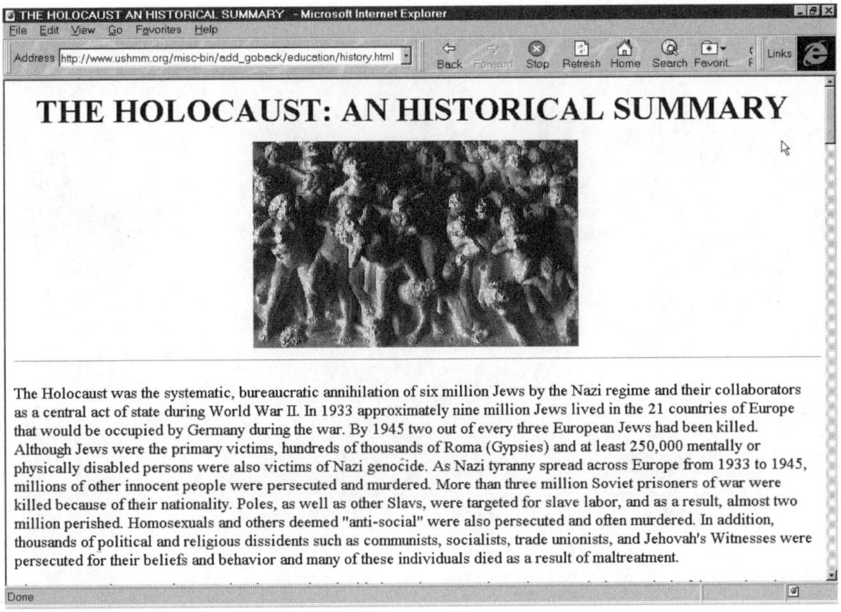

http://www.ushmm.org/

Many historical museums and archives have their presence on the Internet. This is from Holocaust Museum in America. It provides links to rare photographs, testimonies, sounds and even full motion video resources.

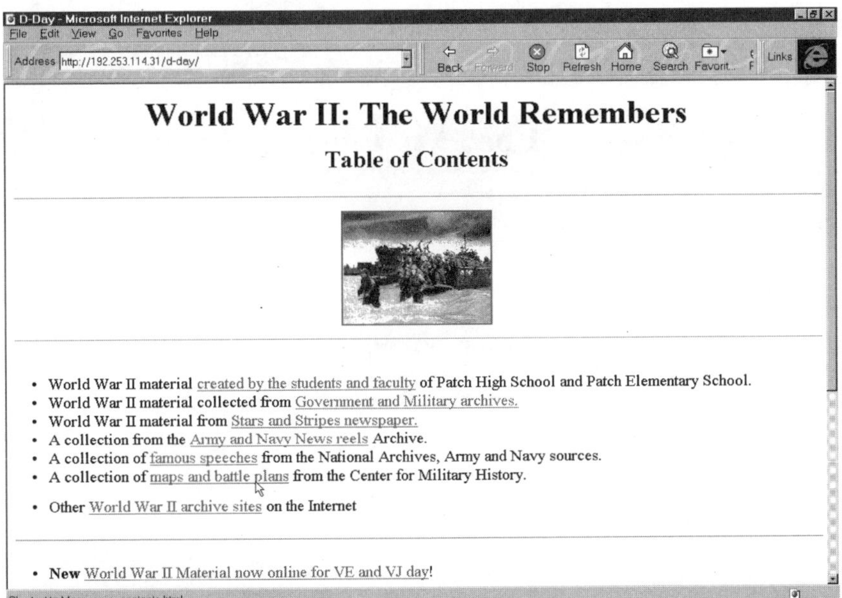

http://192.253.114.31/-d-day/

This D-Day site combines work by high-school pupils and official government documents, maps, diagrams, interviews and photographs. Web sites are increasingly offering a global audience for good quality school work.

British historical resources are popular, particularly well-designed and colourful sites, like this Anglo Saxon history exhibit (right)

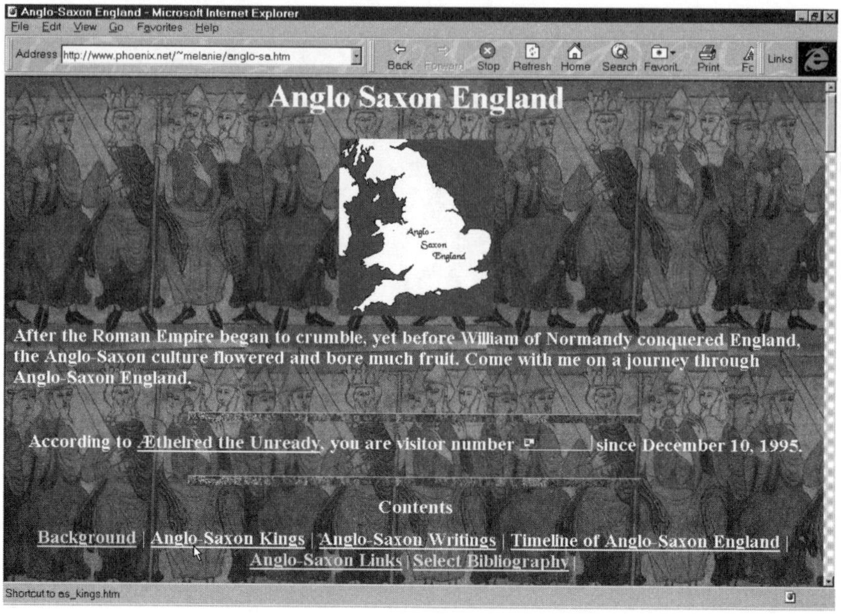

http://www.phoenix.net/~melanie/anglo-sa.htm

As well as current artists and collaborative groups putting their original work online, the History of Art is well catered for. This site takes the browser through the origins and development of modern art in a clear and non-pretentious manner.

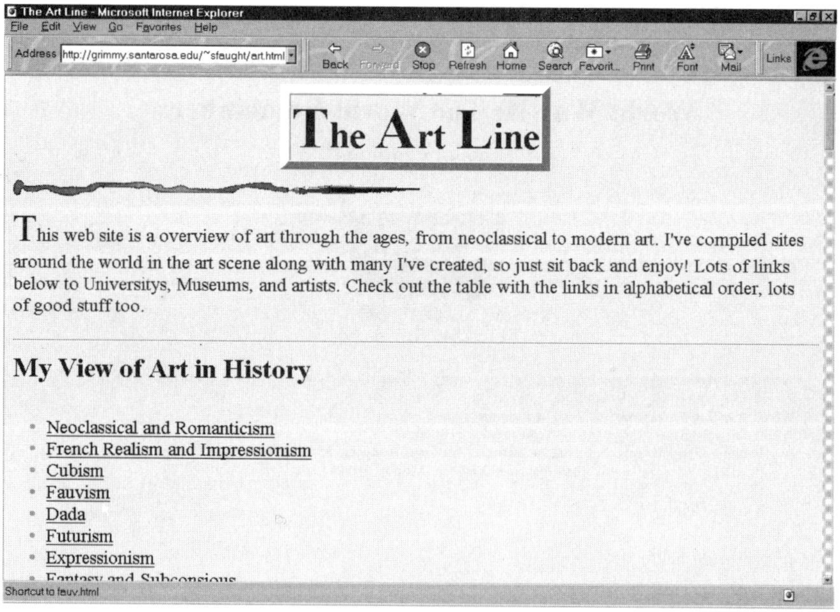

http://grimmy.santarosa.edu/~sfaught/art.html

English Language and Literature

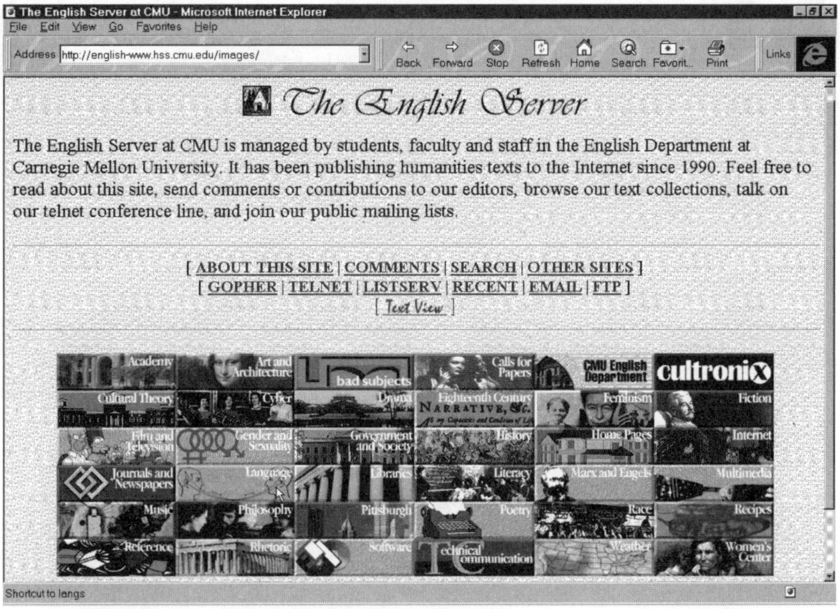

http://english-www.hss.cmu.edu/images/

There are resources spanning the whole range of English language and literature. The English Server provides a convenient clearinghouse to many of the popular documents, displays and discussion areas.

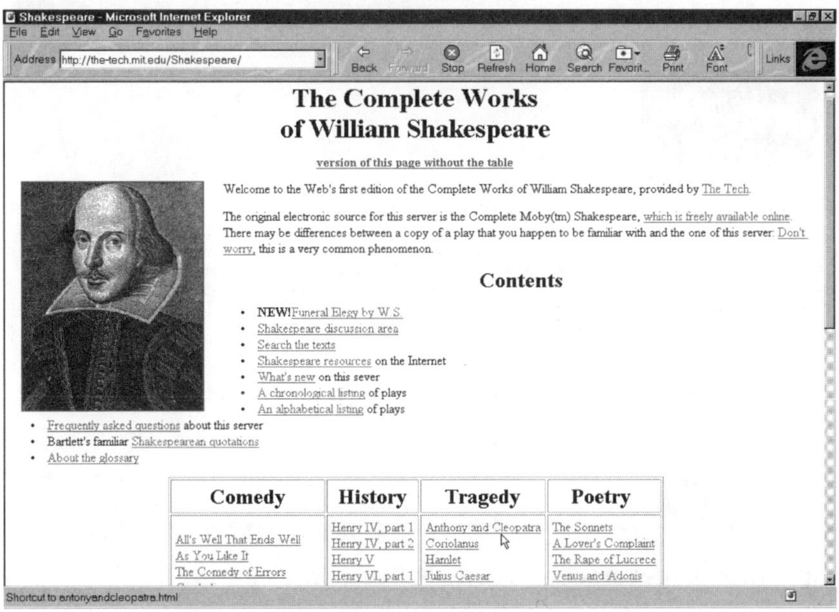

http://the-tech.mit.edu/Shakespeare/

There is a vast amount of literary material online. If it's out of copyright, it's there! The Bible, historical documents, novels, plays, criticisms, dictionaries and all the great philophical works are online. This site is a keyword-searchable "Complete Works of Shakespeare", fully annotated.

This site provides backup, accessible to all, to the Usenet newsgroup dealing with all aspects of English usage. This web site provides links to language puzzles, online dictionaries, archives of frequently asked questions and so forth.

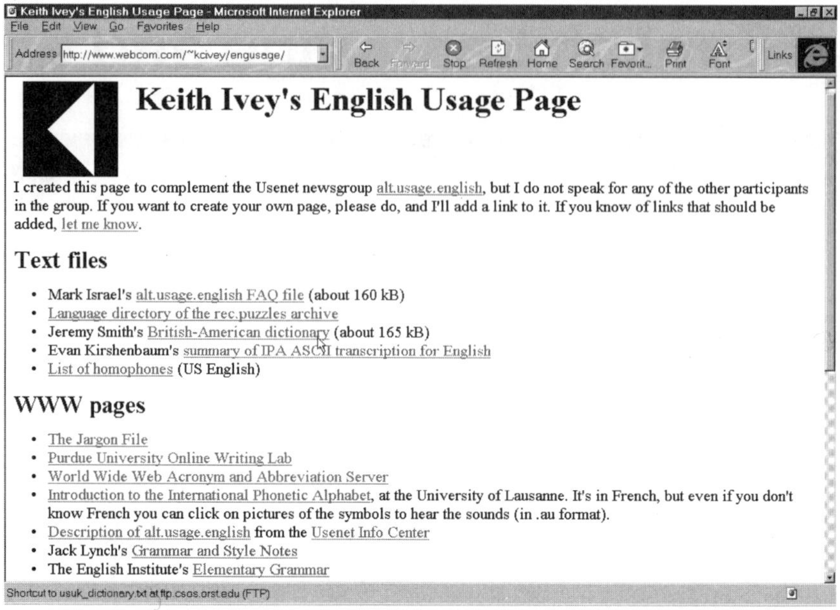

http://www.webcom.com/~kcivey/engusage/

Online literary magazines are good places to contribute creative writing pieces, and teachers and lecturers are running popular interactive online creative writing courses, like the one right.

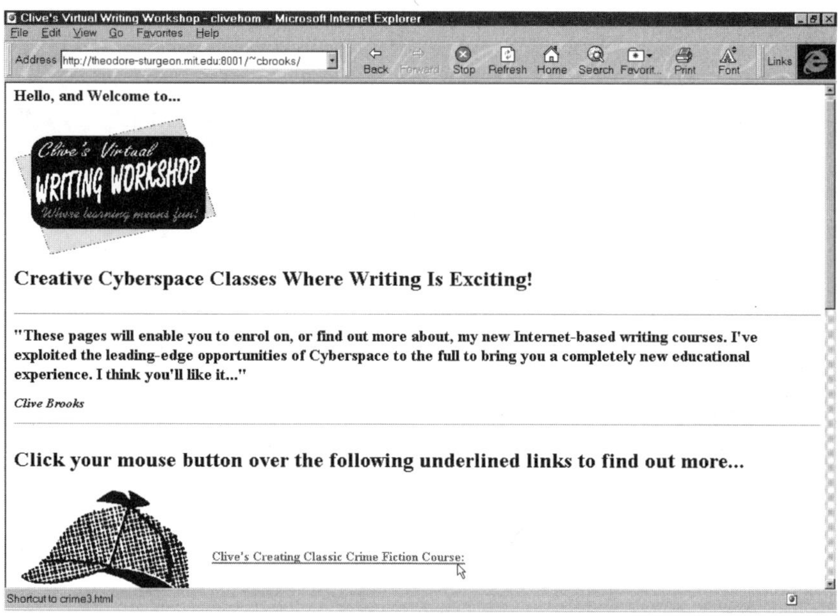

http://theodore-sturgeon.mit.edu:8001/~cbrooks/

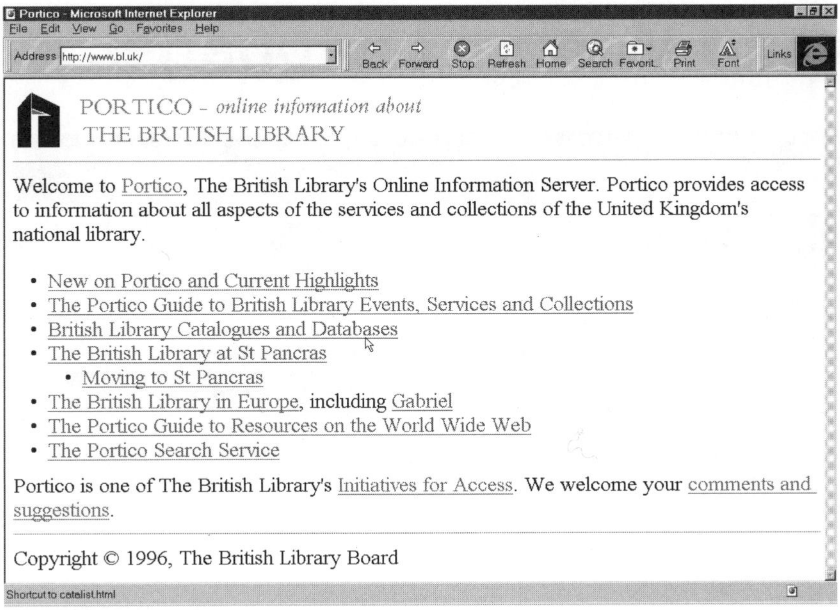

http://www.bl.uk/

Any major world institution's library now has its full catalogue available for searching online. Several, like the Library of Congress and the British Library (left), provide much more as well, including online texts, multimedia cultural exhibitions and discussion documents.

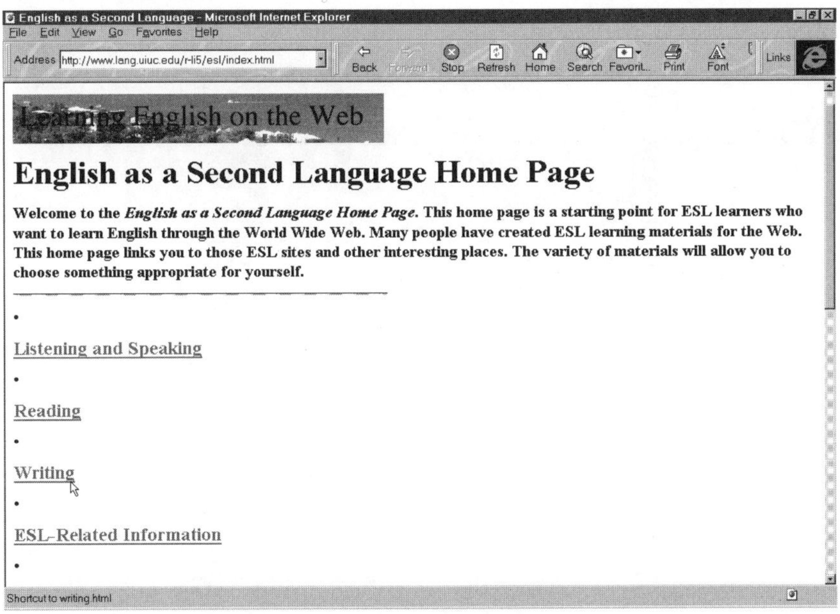

http://www.lang.uiuc.edu/r-li5/esl/index.html

There are an increasing number of "English as a Foreign Language" resources on the web, including online courses for beginners, as well as interactive sessions for those who wish to practise their skills.

Foreign and Modern Languages

Once again, the Net's global scope makes it ideal for learning and studying foreign languages, ancient and modern. This site provides links to materials for almost any language you could name, including online courses, literature, exhibitions and access to native speakers.

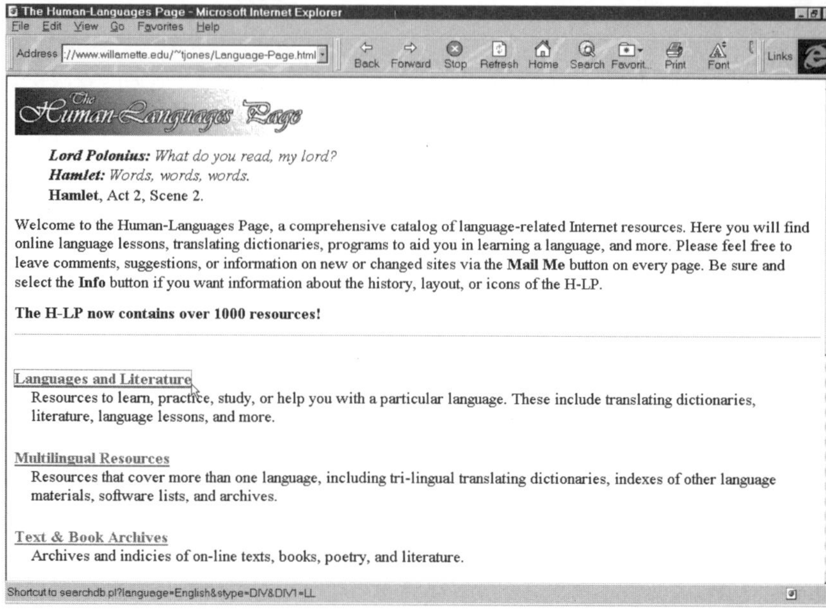

http://www.willamette.edu/~tjones/Language-Page.html

This is an example of an online language lab – a French tutorial. What makes such courses special is their interactivity. As the tutor says, "feel free to send me an email ... I hope we'll have the opportunity to exchange some email in French".

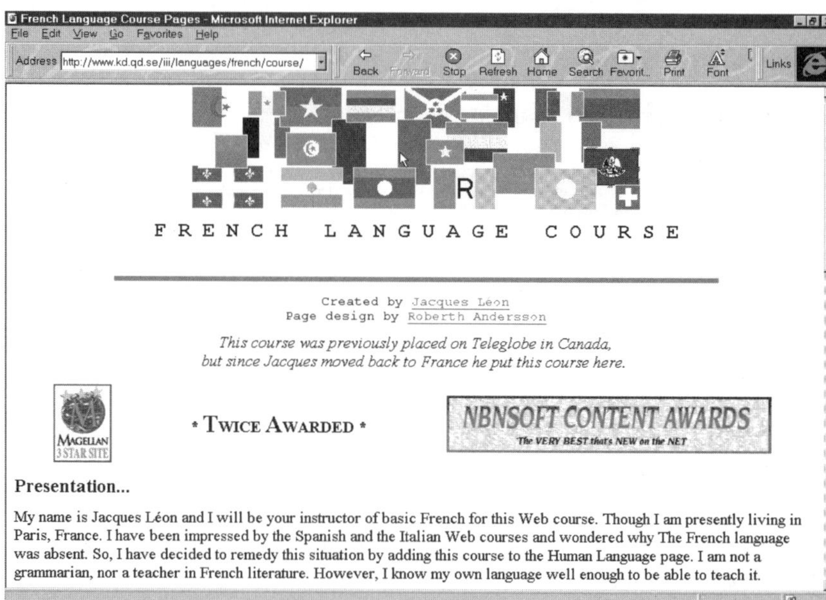

http://www.kd.qd.se/iii/languages/french/course/

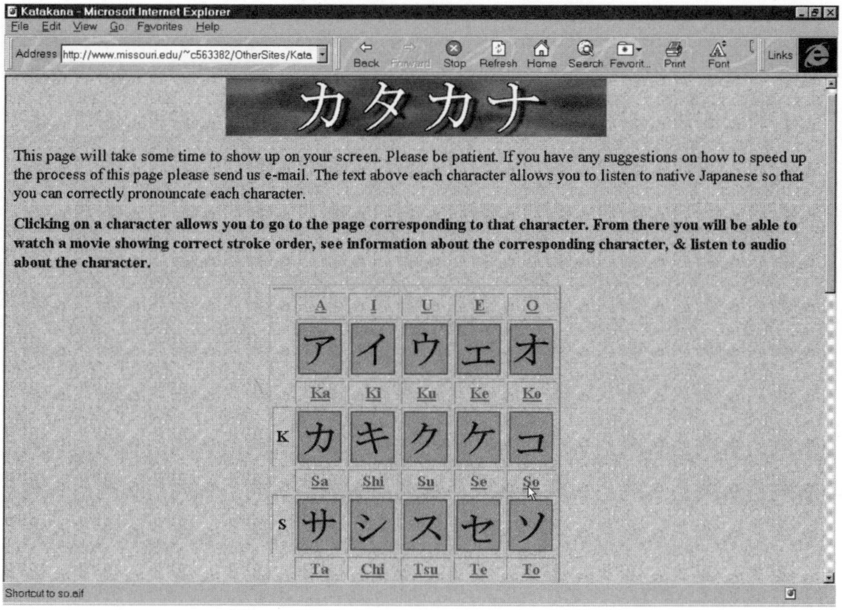

http://www.missouri.edu/~c563382/

Because of the web's graphical nature, even languages requiring non-Latin alphabets can be taught and learned. This site is a multimedia Japanese course.

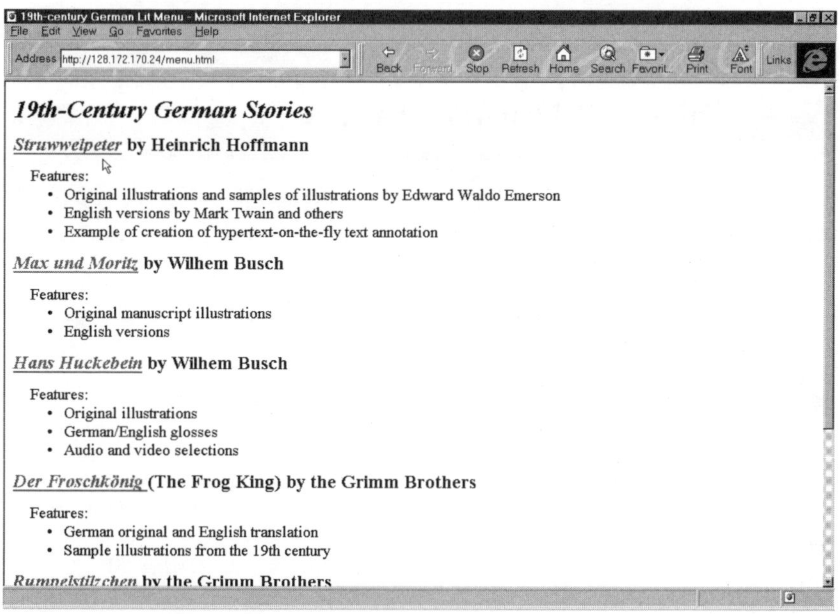

http://128.172.170.24/menu.html

As with English, there is a large amount of online literature in foreign languages. This site includes links to illustrated German works, including audio and illustrations.

Many languages have their own keyword-searchable multilingual dictionaries. Selected here is the English/ Spanish translator.

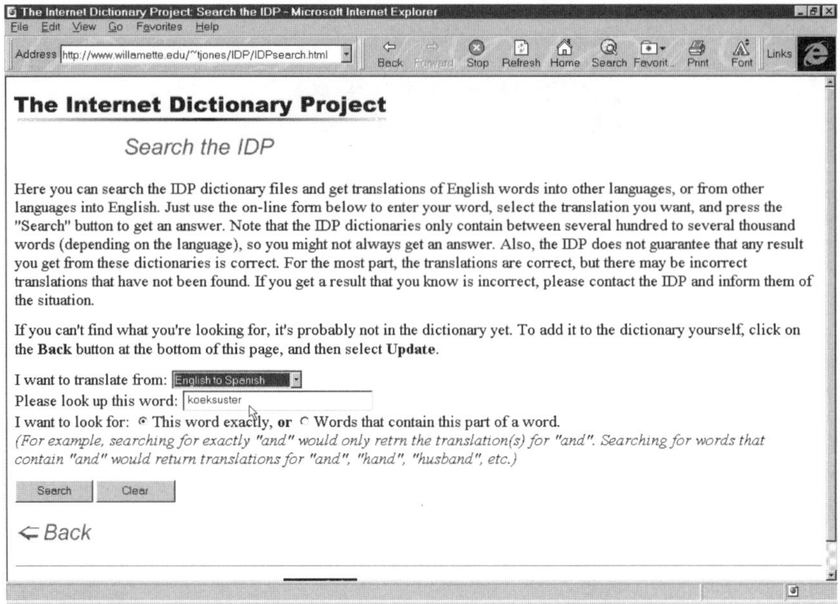

http://www.wiliamette.edu/~tjones/IDP/IDPsearch.html

There are resources for ancient and minority languages, including Latin, Ancient Greek, Aramaic, Sanskrit and Yiddish. This is a Gaelic site.

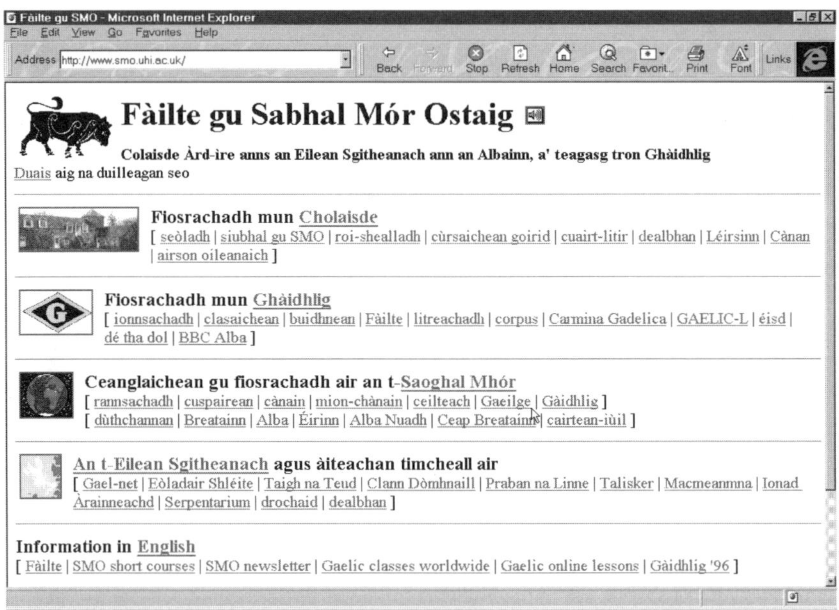

http://www.smo.uhi.ac.uk/

Internet and the School

A potpourri of tips, ideas and arguments for connecting a school to the Internet.

Includes INSET, Acceptable Use Policies and integrating the Internet in a school network.

Chapter 9

Schools work best when filled with happy pupils and teachers. The curriculum, administration, timetable, cultural, sporting, and other extramural activities support this aim, as do pastoral areas, parental involvement, and relations with the public. Social engineers among the school sponsors rejoice in it.

The greatest aid to happiness in the school community is the quality of work and achievement in it. Any system like the Internet that gives pupils and teachers an academic handle is bound to be attractive. Two groups in particular can get a more rounded perspective on the world: high fliers, and the many children with reading and communication skills who become strongly motivated in dealings with electronically found pen-pals.

Schools' brainstorm

There is a gaping divide between old class-style learning and the individually responsive and responsible targets of today. Most teachers have taken fairly comfortably to the GCSE enquiry-based methods and standards, now spreading both to the A-level senior years and beyond, and through the early years, and are finding the Key Stage concepts of the National Curriculum sensible, if unwieldy at times. The well-endowed schools proud of their positions in the national ratings are enhancing the curricular minima, partly so their wide range of candidates will feel comfortable in the examination room, partly to give additional motivation for future courses and careers. The few problem schools are under increasing scrutiny from a sympathetic but cost-driven inspectorate, government, and taxpayer.

The middle majority are keen both to move up a grade, and to benefit from the feeling of success in tackling change, providing education that the pupils enjoy, and to direct ambition towards the higher education now seen as universally valuable for both earner, state and future pensioner. Changing discipline structures force teachers to negotiate harder than ever for pupil attention, particularly for reaching the larger numbers of pupils from disadvantaged backgrounds in every type of school; and tragically, many senior teachers now retire early from a profession originally chosen for ideals and interest. Finally, education in the UK can also be seen as a major spender for the supply industry, two major export industries in its own right, a boon to journalists in the silly season and at crisis time, and a political football at election platform-planning.

In sensitive and confident hands, the Internet can offer partial solutions to all of these challenges. It will slot in easily anywhere because, while ultimately the most democratic of all educational tools, it can also be demanding on rigour and accurate expression.

The academics who answer Physics questions online may be intolerant of loose wording and grey thinking, while encouragingly blind to the linguistic errors of those working outside their native language. For schools whose target is National Curriculum Plus, the self-service aspect of the Plus could start here.

Internet for research

Central to classroom use of the Internet is high quality research. The electronic libraries of the world never close, silence is not the rule, and there are neither guarded reference sections nor age rules on access. Files of data can be downloaded, some directly from the authors' computers, and research is limited only by the searching-skills of the pupil and the electronic tools he or she can handle. Lessons in searching, and selecting or designing appropriate search engines, are available on-line:
`http://www.yahooligans.com/`

History is not bunk

During the first computer revolution, one in a classroom became one per class, complementing the developing class-set in an IT room over ten years, while with the Internet, teachers and pupils will be much faster to use research and interaction facilities out of hours and build critical mass for general acceptance. Much has also been learnt from hand-held calculators: opinions vary from invaluable tool to despoiler of fundamental skills. Internet enthusiasts will, of course, trumpet the upsides; the professional educator will be aware of the problems, from the initial press reaction to this new "devil's tool". Happy the school whose Information Technology co-ordinator is also Deputy Head. The socialising power of today's computer-club room allows a patch of privacy as well as the opportunity for public achievement and status for both the community-challenged and even the future Bill Gates', unlike the original computer club, which had little attraction for normal males and less for girls and women.

The two communities standing to benefit most from the Internet are the high percentage of girls who need the informative power of the Internet to bring academic tone to their coursework, and of course the teachers who succeeded in their own studies through use of books and libraries. While in the past only a future IT co-ordinator could become a computer expert and perhaps guru, the Internet has had so much press coverage and INSET build-up that in many schools, several departments have been experimenting with phone-line, modem and provider. Teachers are rapidly adding the Net to their teaching skills, even if only in discussing its potential and problems in staff room and class. The staff room terminal gives lunchtime and free-period INSET. The easiest whole-school research method allows pupils to use a school Internet account at home or in the library. Other enthusiasts at the school will be ready to share successes and suggest learner-friendly ways of delivering curriculum ideas.

If all goes well, these ideas will be used to enhance worksheet check-boxes and give pupils freedom to explore beyond narrow syllabus constraints. If nothing else, effective access to information, to the people who are creating it and to the distribution methods will, for many of us, bring back some of our bright-eyed student-day interest in subjects we have been teaching for years: direct contact with live researchers at PhD time and at professorial level is the high point of single-degree academe, and the Internet offers this daily, on a lifelong basis, and in as many fields as we choose. The humblest learner on a newsgroup can read directly the discoveries of research institutes and the commissioners of new computer systems, and any educator can survey and share in finding solutions to teaching or timetabling problems worldwide without leaving a desk.

All universities are interested in attracting quality students: what better way of doing so than by making their expertise available to every school pupil and to every subject teacher, with opportunities to ask questions, to help with data-gathering, to stimulate school research, to find holiday jobs, to plan visits for bringing virtual friends to full life, and to get career guidance from experts.

INSET

The problem of preventing established teachers from becoming inflexible has traditionally been solved by velvet gloves of varying thickness: by patience, by promotion, by delegation, by combining subjects or introducing new ones. Teachers and their associations tend to accept redundancy with unease but applaud INSET. The top-down or Bakerday method of INSET opens different channels for the new information to flow: across faculties, a head of English can reach out to an historian, or between faculties. A computer scientist can pass ideas to arts teachers and vice versa.

A problem faced by arrangers of these training events is both quality of presenter and appropriateness of material. We have all been inspired by good ones and sat through the others, glancing at our watches. The internet offers a choice of presentations on almost every topic, but unlike video on demand, one can get back to the producer of the material during or after the current session, and for as long as the group or individual inquirer wishes. Within departments, a list of relevant sites visited can be printed or left bookmarked on the departmental computer, so that followup visits by other teachers give shared experiences of the issue the site covers. Printouts of relevant pages can be photocopied for class use by the teacher or by supply cover.

An extension of this is the research project commissioned by anyone in a school, in which the researcher prints a pack of relevant material as it is turned up by the online searches. The file is then passed back to the commissioner. Major advantages are that no appointments or visits are needed, and that quick, short prototypes can be delivered for redirection of effort without big investment by the searcher. Perhaps the biggest gains for the whole community are the bonds of gratitude and friendship that develop between all involved, leading to increased confidence for further collaborations.

Some topics for school INSET

In the curriculum: Usenet groups of schools' curriculum planners can share problems and solutions as they arise: "the time-tabler starts tomorrow and we don't know how much PE/RE is compulsory next year. Does Balanced Science really need all the lessons they are demanding? Which technology options have the right amount of electronics or materials science?" A recent debate by Directors of Studies on the old chestnut of how widening options for some pupils means overloading others stopped just short of suggesting that the abler pupils should be given Internet access and be told to get on with it, freeing teachers and lessons to help the needier. The members of supportive Email mailing lists can readily share ways of easing constraints or ways of pacifying the displaced and the outraged, and can seek alternatives.

In administration: "Is there a standard letter for an unusual outing? The county advisor recommends a database, our in-school head of department insists on a spreadsheet – let's get opinions from people who have used both." Examples are: lesson cover, absences and routine changes (Internet mail can be as quick as fax, and is always cheaper). Internal administrative web pages can be set up in any school through an "Intranet", with information available to all on the local computer network.
The development of management and legal skills in senior staff and

Governors is likely to come on line as the supervisory organisations start appreciating the ease, power and cost-effectiveness of regular instant contact with the best minds in the business, and set up simple systems for two-way daily contact. All Headteachers' Unions take note, especially of the reduction in telephone time for the Secretary.

In general for the above, use the Internet to explore and hone management skills without actually carrying the can. The timetabling, relief and examination officer years need not be the worst! Maybe they can be the best years of your life, if the extra time you get from the increased efficiency is well invested. Some heads we know are exploring developments in their academic subjects or the History of Education, some are writing serious pieces about the new problems pupils face, or the big issues facing educators. Hopefully the Internet will offer collaborative public writing by some of the most powerful benign social engineers we have produced.

In cultural activities: the soc.culture newsgroups host a wealth of ideas on most of the planet's cultures; users of alt.politics will win any debate by entering the motion and riding the resultant brainstorm; no composer is without his community and critics, a ready pool of which can be found throughout the collaborative composition projects on the web and through mailing lists.

In sport, nothing is excluded. Training tips, club contacts, problems answered, facts and opinions at all levels. The computer room wallflowers' chance to share a skill, develop an interest and help the coach and the first team: good for all parties. Recently UK outdoor activities ranging from angling, archaeology and football to walking and wildlife have appeared in the newsgroups, joining the predominantly American sports. Web pages for football clubs, cricket associations and the rest are hives of activity, and are an excellent way to introduce the most technically wary pupils to the online world.

In other extramural activities: Through its connection of active groups, the Internet presents community service opportunities, clearing-houses for skills needed and offered for the Duke of Edinburgh Award, for example; club assistance from willing experts without the need for travel or the expense that keeps so many of these out of our schools (chess, photography, film making, programming, philosophy, patisserie). The opportunity for newcomers to a field, looking for a project, to correspond with sympathetic experts will profit all involved. And a golden opportunity for the housebound or wheelchair-restricted to be of use to those out in the physical world. Please alert all therapists and carers.

In class meetings with form teachers and other pastoral areas: The Internet can be a golden incentive for those whose homework is done; GCSE year – indeed any year – study skill lists and revision timetables; access to appropriate distance learning materials for those wishing to take a subject further but not getting on with a teacher; regular private Email by staff or pupil to special needs advisor, counsellor or high level therapist about dips in progress; a private and anonymous Helpline for any child feeling threatened or compromised in the school situation – often better than the telephone because the child doesn't have to speak in real time, and the computer terminal is neutral and non-threatening.

In parent involvement: PTA drive-group meetings can be briefed about changing needs and decisions; parent problems can be Emailed to the secretary and answered or passed on. Better for the school to lead the parent community into Internet than to follow.

In public relations: the prospectus can be permanently on-line at the school's website for people moving to the area; enquiries can be logged for follow-up; school news can go direct to the local press.

In staff selection: teaching posts can be advertised as soon as the job description is ready, using newspapers as the slow lane, a short step behind those companies that only advertise their jobs on the Internet, reasoning that workers without the skills to use it need not apply. Teaching and technical candidates will also use it to circulate CVs, modifying presentations to catch eye, ear and full attention of potential employer: the quick virtual interview, by flicking through or being given a tour of the candidate's teaching website and worksheet collection and electronic mark book, perhaps watching a lesson, and interacting with the pupils in a class, is much cheaper and more effective than the all too rare visit to the candidate's school by a member of the interviewing panel. We hope no one is suggesting sole interview by Internet, but even just one less day-trip per year will save large sums of money. This electronic head-hunting approach may be novel and to many appear distasteful, but several schools have been piloting such schemes.

In "delivering" **moral and ethical education** and in the invaluable work being done for many types of underprivileged people, an Internet connection in any school would be a strong support for under-achievers at all levels in the scale by *inter alia* offering:

Opportunities for serving the school community by Email delivery

and teaching beginners. A withdrawal group for achievement and encouragement – an extension of the quiet corners in the library and the computer room.
Distance learning to those with unusual interests and offering open learning to those who discover they learn better on their own. For the very able, whose minds could stretch to it, repeated live contact with serious academics at university level. A transcript of one such meeting suggests that the Nobel laureate was gaining as much as the pupils.

The authors have seen all of these work at first hand.

Many schools are currently using modems for career guidance, higher education course searches and application with selection to follow, and for examination board contact for list exchanges, and passing on changes. A few foul-ups are inevitable, partly because the 'Internet' and 'Intranet' systems are so attractive that there is little incentive for full parallel running (a good old computer science principle observed more in the breach). This fits in with the "prototype now and get the user to beta-test" tenet of modern computing philosophy, and while individuals are stressed by errors, and the press has a field day, there is much to be said for trying out a system, even if it has not yet been fully tested.

From 1995 faster modems speeded up effective transmission, but the popularity of the Net often led to delays, failures, and a (media fed?) desire for more "bandwidth". The range of University courses advertised on line widened, and many reply forms became more effective and personal. Searchers could, perhaps, be forgiven for judging an institution by the quality of access they enjoy to admissions tutors, subject advisors, and departmental secretaries, and by the nature of the replies. Fortunately the frequently asked question list on the campus website can take much of the strain off staff, and contact via Email and local newsgroups with students gives an inside, if sometimes erratic, impression. No wonder quick courses in effective Email and website-building techniques for academics are becoming *de rigueur*. Increasingly, departmental open days are demonstrating Internet facilities, and *ad hoc* career conferences by the standard Internet services should soon extend to Inter Relay Chat and realtime audio visual conferencing where, say, a practising GP and a medical school lecturer could be questioned by prospective students. Perhaps bandwidth does need addressing after all.
Can lessons from these projects be learned for the general pupil-teacher relationship? A surprisingly traumatic problem occurs every day in every form tutor period: it is hard for the tutor, first thing in a busy day, bombarded by notes and questions, to spot and remember to deliver all the bits of help needed by thirty sensitive professional bluffers in a goldfish bowl; requests

made electronically from home to the staff room terminal would add healthy dollops of privacy, honesty, immediacy, planning, record if needed and even dignity to the process.

The key areas of this wide-ranging section have been some of the interactive, eclectic, opportunistic and enabling points surrounding the Internet. We have been indicative, not definitive, predictive rather than prescriptive. Future editions will encapsulate more results and perhaps fewer new suggestions. But we predict that for many years, the increasingly pervasive Internet with its growing range of tools will keep the hypothesis to accepted practice ratio comfortingly high in all of planning, personal interaction, and curriculum.

Homework exercises

The reader could be invited to select three topics from the following list of standard school situations and write short suggestions for using the Internet to improve their effectiveness-cost ratio; but we would rather see the newsgroups with their FAQ lists or range of interactive websites become a repository of good practice and a forum for mooting improvements. Valuable to beginner teacher and fledged professional alike.

- Role models for computer co-ordinator librarian.
- Internet as private tutor
- Internet as surrogate/replacement for missing teachers
- Disseminating, monitoring and revising
- Remote school security via Internetted cameras
- Balancing the CD-ROM/Internet ratio (For the mathematically challenged, this is the third and last ratio in the book.)
- The scrolling demonstration
- List, for budgeting purposes, the stages between solo terminal and class set for a teacher who could show educational reason for installing Internet in a classroom.
- Predict when this will be universally available in the UK.
- Internet as a teaching aid
- Internet as a self-teaching aid
- Internet as an instructor
- Distance learning vs distance instruction

Internet for classroom teachers

For the classroom teacher wondering like Aladdin if the genie is real, there is a well-used path: First contact is often a newspaper article, a friend or salesman's terminal, or an INSET day. Deliberate first meetings in a cybercafe situation often follow, where uncontrolled website visits can give a hollow feel: if we as responsible adults so easily cybersurf pointlessly, how can our charges hope to avoid the time-wasting and the unacceptable faces of Internet? No caring teacher would give all pupils uncontrolled access. We have met several robust teachers whose first impulse was to seek out "adult" material. These same good people have often hesitated to introduce Internet constructively into their pupils' learning lives. The pressure is particularly intense if one is IT co-ordinator, responsible for selecting the best of the computer world for classroom use, but confronted with an unpredictable "monster" threatening to do more harm than good. Not a few schools have left Internet exploration to the way-out boffins in Computer Science or to academically adventurous teachers in strong departments. This allows the benefits to be analysed while the risks are localised: the pioneers can be commissioned to run pilot projects as part of their normal academic study.

Once a critical mass of enough interested teachers has built up, a full INSET day will be useful: to outline facilities, to report on projects, to answer questions and relate their own research experiences, to give confidence in the buttons and the tools, and to build the shared skills of the school Internet-using team. The high-point of the writers' first Q&A demonstrations to groups of teachers has been helping as many as possible to search on a personal academic interest, and then following that interest through a chain of "hits". It is for the guide and the audience of peers both enlightening and humbling to share the thought patterns of the professional academic as the ski-lift takes them over training slopes and home ground, visiting mainstream areas of teaching, then pausing at side runs and finally venturing off-piste into unknown territory. Seeing decades of study being overviewed in a few seconds is an indicator of what motivated pupils might achieve.

Access to a tame terminal, one with a friendly technician around, to help with the first Email and the first web search, with as many repeats as are needed to build confidence, leads to one's first solo uses for research and sharing useful ideas within a department or wider community. This gives ground skills in Email, listserv, newsgroup, and the web. The older you are, the longer this takes.

Bookmarking is an art to learn early: these home-made signposts shorten learning paths dramatically. Printing out useful web pages to digest later gives ideas for other visits, teaching and class use, and for people to contact. After reading into a newsgroup and its FAQ list for a few days or weeks, one may feel ready to ask other questions or contribute ideas.

A useful next step is class demonstrations. The first class demonstrations can be entirely teacher driven, but the best experiences are with teacher voice-over while a pupil drives the mouse. Much depends on the teacher-pupil relation. Be ready to support the half-experienced pupil operator if the system collapses. A nice idea is for the teacher to challenge the class to convince a doubter that the Internet can be used for learning a specified topic, and to continue with a genuine discussion and investigation.

Pupils with their own Internetted computers at home can be at an advantage, not being under pressure to make contact within school hours. This is especially the case if families and friends are involved in school projects. To balance this, there is the disadvantage of undone homework or lost sleep and worse if the terminal is unsupervised at home. Much depends on family personality, making home Internet a very hard question for class teachers to advise on. This is besides the point of costs to the enthusiasm of many busy parents.

Primary education

A friendly, enthusiastic computer advisor is likely to be the greatest asset, motivation and finance the first hurdles.

Three early primary school ventures in the UK were the *Chatback Trust*, supervised IRC around the world, and Doug Weller's newsgroup **`uk.education.teachers`**. Through *Chatback*, pupils could contact Charles Dickens online, or a real live alien, or a London child coping with the blitz. In *Kidlink IRC*, typed conversations between pupils on all continents enable facts and opinions to ping-pong around the globe. The adult monitors are volunteers at home in the different time zones, working invisibly and almost never needing to intervene. In the first three years of the project only one character needed discipline.

The newsgroup `uk.education.teachers` in its early years carried reports of electronic exchanges, requests for information and help, and has given many hundreds of teachers a flavour of the generosity of the Internet world and its open-handed encouragement of constructive educational ventures. There have been lessons too: some good people have put too much into their public service, to the loss and distress of their immediate environment. It is very easy to take one's global responsibility more seriously than our evolutionary stage encourages. Ask any vicar's wife and kids.

Some of the current projects are clearly driven by enthusiasts, but this can lead to split loyalties, not always in the childrens' interest. At the other end of the scale is the teacher whose initial but considered and determined reaction to early media publicity was that the Internet would never be used by any children while she was teaching them. At least one prep school advisor has wheel-clamped freedom by believing that his pupils would never be able to resist showing off to each other.

Overall the return to the 3Rs movement may well find the Net to be a way of circulating material like exercises and tests, in an approach complimentary to the Kumon schools mathematics venture, and one foresees national electronic competitions, perhaps even inter-school, regional and national testing, being used to encourage successful practice.

At primary level, with no official curricular requirement to use the Net, and pupils too young reliably to police access, the busy class teacher who sees educational value in collaborative uses will be breaking new ground and laying foundations. Many schools start with a celebratory meeting, perhaps an open evening, inviting Email greetings from well-wishers. Other opportunities for exchanges are comparing celebrations like the hundred-day festival, Valentine's day, Halloween, Independence day, and so forth – simple cultural exchanges that pupils of all ages can appreciate. Where newer computers are available, web pages are a delight to create, especially now that "what you see is what they get" editing is common and free. They have the advantage that no connected terminal is needed in the classroom, as the floppy disc version can be checked and uploaded later.

Inverse ageism

How early can children start using the Internet? As early as the guiding parent or teacher can entrance the child is the lay answer. Be aware that the child will very early on overtake and start leading the adult into areas the senior partner in this learning process never even noticed or knew existed, and certainly has no skills in. From here on the trust and love and mutual respect developed in the first part of the process will bear full fruit to the advantage of all parties and the community.

Homework exercises for primary Internet

These are favourite topics, which have been tried before in successful early-years Internet projects:

- Mutual poems on agreed topics
- Ping-pong stories – each player adds a sentence
- My home and family pictures
- My favourite food
- The bean race – swap bean seeds with a school in another country. Both schools grow, observe and record details of progress.

Secondary subjects

There may have been some value in focusing in upon the value of the Internet to the various curricular subjects, but each teacher will find for him or herself the value by experimentation – one can take it as read that the eclectic, vast Internet does have something out there for one's subject. Below is a summary of how the Internet may be able to help in that most divisive and vital of school subjects – mathematics.

The mathematical problem

The Internet is another opportunity for mathematics teachers to use computers to delight pupils and inspire good thinking. To date, progress has been uneven, possibly because of the successive take-overs of computing by programming and then IT, both of which are at best peripheral and sometimes inimical to the activities of a cerebral maths department. National press reviews of Internet education may be partly to blame here: journalists may hesitate to tangle with mathematics teachers, perhaps from their own days of algebra and geometry in a maths classroom. The cavalry is at hand, however; the *Ask Dr Math* site has long produced a stream of pupil-friendly answers to maths problems, in the best sense: they won't do your homework for you, but they will put you on course for discovering the solution. And the new UK specific maths newsgroup looks to help both teachers and pupils cross the Great Divide between those with engineering potential and those without the maths to feel comfortable in an engineer's company.

Emerging learning

Just as the Fabians were enabled to tackle social revolution, and the Bloomsbury group led into politics through literature, Internet skills are likely to emancipate vulnerable learners, like dyslexics and children with non-mathematical mothers, from restrictive influences.

This cultural revolution is going to be an area of particular interest in the development of the future of the first-world economy, because of its significance in the gender education debate. Girls in the 10 to 25 age range are said to make up over 30% of Internet users, and if this includes those who are denied technical careers because of the difficulty they face in early teenage years of coping with a predominantly male maths-for-engineering teaching environment, the privacy offered to a dedicated hardworking student by online at-home study may well make up for lack of inspiring personal contact in the classroom. There can be few schools with only one maths teacher whose classroom would not be enhanced by allowing pupils Internet access to teach themselves.

The potential of Java for delivering short animated repeatable lessons at a level selected by the learner, and at a speed controlled by her growth of understanding as measured by questions she asks and answers, is already attracting publishers and will soon be seen as a vehicle for allowing corporations to advertise in the classroom as extensively as the oil internationals have in the chemistry laboratory. Heads of Mathematics in a school are then likely to build their own school's mathematical web site, selecting the approaches to each topic – such as trigonometry, or algebra, or statistics – the bane of those taught in over-formal environments – that favour their pupils' needs.

Pupils will be able to log in to the school mathsite for initial teaching and be referred elsewhere without noticing the transfer, and then do controlled graduated exercises and tests of increasing complexity, with a judicious mixture of self-marking and teacher assessment until they feel ready to tackle terminal tests and the next topic. Pupils not making progress will be clearly flagged for extra time with the most approachable members of the department, by Email if desired by the pupil, or repeats of unthreatening video and TV-style remedial presentations.

One unpalatable truth not generally recognised by professionals, pundits, or the public is that our national failure to produce a sufficient number of scientists and engineers stems from our children's lack of joy in science. One root of this is our ignorance of the beauty of elegance and an aversion for the process of gaining mathematical insights. Another is that teachers, often efficient practitioners of the subject who could be earning accountants' salaries, are openly derided by their erstwhile colleagues for accepting both the conditions of service and the rudeness of the pupils longing to escape from the tedium of a compulsory subject. Just one year with an unhappy teacher is enough to destroy confidence and ambition in the subject: and if the damage done can be lessened or even turned around by letting them and the same teacher use the Internet in that same classroom, we have enough reason for fund raising and putting up with all the pinpricks that Internet installation takes today.

This is perhaps the single area of greatest urgency, to start to reverse the dulling of the generation of pupils moving through a system that year by year denies all but the most resilient a career using the mathematics seen by all schools as a core subject.

Below: If one begins to revel in its sheer abstractness, one can begin to re-discover that kernel of magic that attracts the lucky few to mathematics. Perhaps sites like this will encourage the rest.
http://mars.superlink.net/abogom/

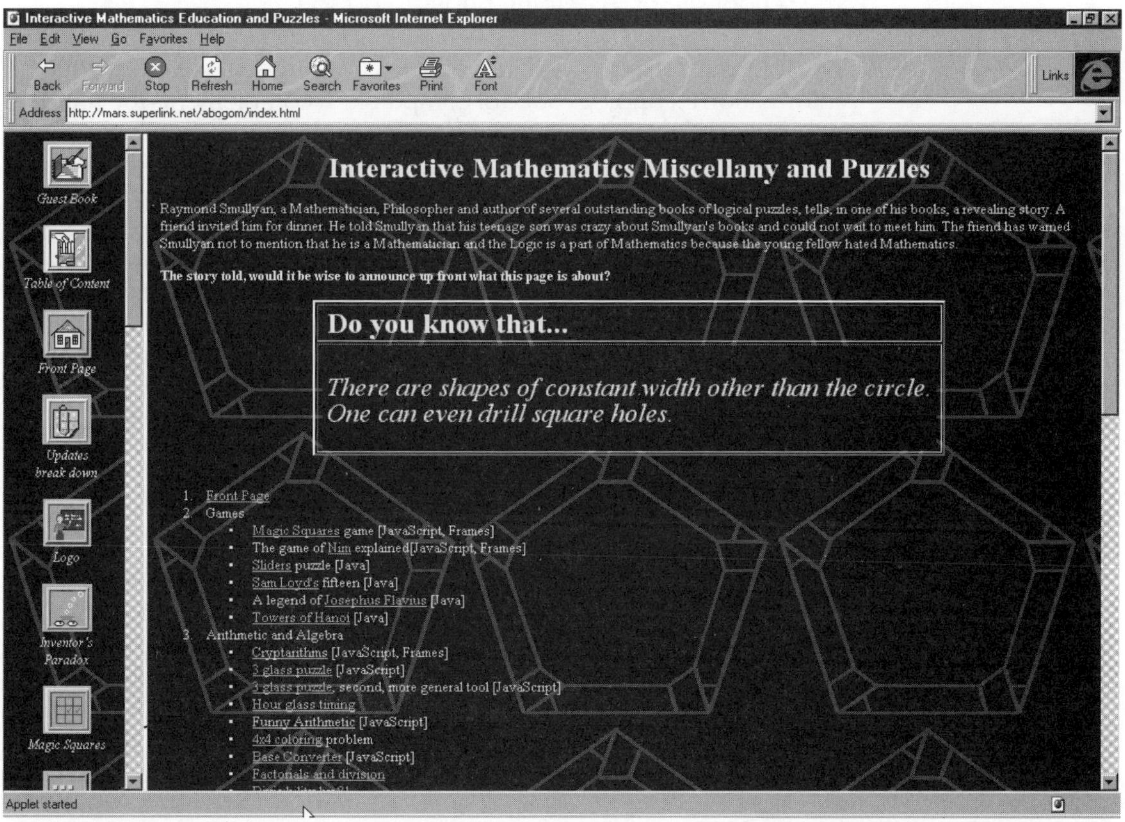

Hints for Heads and Governors

The computer advisors' adage still holds: if the Head uses it, the staff will follow. But unlike the first computer keyboards, a working Internet terminal gives instant rewards: for example a web page with pictures can be printed for a subject teacher to pass on to pupils for comment. No technical expertise is needed by any party in the chain, and all can feel good about their contributions. Curiosity and ambition should do the rest.

A Head used to using a word-processor would be well advised to take a three minute lesson in making a web page. The result could be a list of departments and teachers known to have educational Internet experience. Copying this to each, with a request for summaries of what they think the school could usefully do on the Internet, might bring out useful website display-making skills that could be tapped in building the school site or in helping pupils to do so.

An Internet terminal will happily exist alongside the conventional information technology suite of computers. It complements the standard computer education in a school. Compared to the normal integration of a new technology, there is little disruption. If the system administrator is careful, there will be no loss of user confidence.

Most new computer systems need a guru and a champion, often the same person. The guru is the idea provider, the wise old owl, and the fallback for support in times of problems; always available for consulting, for advising, and for warning, unruffled if you ignore his advice and it goes wrong. Gurus foresee and solve problems, they stay cool in hot kitchens, the more they know about the school and its people the better. A useful test of this book's long term value is how it complements your guru.

The champion, as opposed to the guru, is high profile and often on-site: he or she will sell the idea to the users, enthuse the doubters by example, set the system up, train beginners, and with luck, provide permanent monitoring and policing. In an ideal world, he or she will also estimate and then stay within budget. Proper champions neither become stale nor sidetrack onto new interests. This can be turned to advantage, allowing a first champion to build the system, others to run it: builders need broad shoulders, while runners are long on tact and foresight.

Ideas for system managers

The startup cost need not be exorbitant: any newish computer with a hard drive will do. Your Internet Service Provider will advise on cost-effective modems and cable and software – a good test of the quality of their customer support – and should say clearly what they offer, how much it costs to join, to take extra services, what protection levels they use, and how long it will take to set up. They will, of course, need to know what computer you have. Get the technical supporter's name, and drop an Email line to the manager if the service you get is good or bad. This will both improve the service for all of us, and give you a reputation as a caring customer.

Installing an Internet terminal has two advantages over most new systems:

- ✔ An expensive computer terminal is not needed, so long as it has a hard disc drive and printer.
- ✔ The machine can be left unsupervised, provided the phone connection is broken and locked away.

Disadvantages of doing this are:

- ✔ The modem plugs may be flimsy and are not designed for repeated insertion.
- ✔ The modem needs to be secured: they are as portable as a pack of cards.

Some straight talking

You clearly need to work well with both guru and champion. A good start is a meeting with an agenda for a full discussion of possible problems like cost including location, security and insurance, definition of unsuitable material, pornography, pupil addiction, time and paper waste, unauthorised pupil access: the Internet is so powerful that the best pupils – and many adults – will push up the phone bill looking at trivia instead of remembering to save material for reading off-line.

Compile a list of events that would force the school to pull the plug permanently, or close it for a rethink. Explore the attitude to a phoneline with bill paid by the champion personally. A club, paying an itemised bill, might be possible. A lock on the system is less good: keys wander, the duplicate duplicates itself, passwords unsurprisingly spread like news of a mishap – the escape is the mishap. Or the champion lacks the time, charm and patience needed for encouraging the general user – too often in his book every pupil is a mini-hacker set on sabotaging the system. He's often right too: "Sorry Miss, I couldn't do my homework, the Internet was down."

Pupils involved in exploring the Internet should be encouraged to focus on positive uses. The teacher in charge will need to blend gentle direction with discipline. The logical "love it or lose it" approach doesn't work long with folk adept at pushing their own mothers around for a third helping of ice-cream.

There are genuinely useful attempts by several companies to get education-friendly Internet service into UK schools at present. Most current service providers are professional, but there is no financial inducement for them to invest in serving the needs of a school. The free webspace offered by many is a healthy attempt to build their attractiveness to other customers – and it is very useful for sharing and learning skills, so long as all on the Internet and not just their own customers, can get to it. The established sites have so much going for them today that waiting no longer makes sense. Governors are now being asked, in some detail, what their school is doing with the Internet. Pleasingly fewer advisors leading INSET can get away with specious comment about how the Internet will affect schools.

Going public across the school

Articles in school magazines, fliers produced by IT-using pupils, a school competition to list Internet uses – all are useful in spreading the word. A PTA project to set up and staff the Internet terminal (sensible at first to have knowledgeable adult supervision to prevent expensive or mindless uses, or embarrassing pauses) can easily be started by any teacher with time and access to a computer with a lockable phoneline.

Be wary of letting pupils dial up their bulletin boards from school. This is sometimes a very useful exercise in comparing the BBS and the Internet, but can be surprisingly expensive. Full supervision is essential.

Many system managers and the friends attracted by the computer room will make excellent journalists. A regular account of new and ongoing Internet activities rides well with many readers in the school magazine. A sample article appears at the end of this chapter.

Ideas for system technicians

A portable radio-modem is available, but it is expensive, slow, and risky. Once set up, it could in theory be used free by outsiders with the right equipment, just as pupils with remote control watches have been overriding teachers' commands to the classroom video recorder in lessons. Handheld computers with built-in mobile phone features can be expected in 1997. If affordable packages can be put together for schools, these could become invaluable.

A clearly visible, out of easy reach switch in the phone line is much better than repeated unplugging. If you are still having to move a jack, a cheap T-piece and a spare lead can reduce the risk of breakdown.

How to find a pupil manager

It is hard for a pupil to cope with pressure from friends, bribery and threats. Qualities needed include discretion, subtlety, persistence, toughness, gentleness and level headedness. Fortunately, such wisdom can be learned.

A part of the "Driving Test" might be to teach a teacher how to use and feel comfortable with the system; and then to produce an instruction sheet for general use by visitors. Testing this manual with the author present gives a very clear idea of how well you will work together.

For an apparently light-hearted test of ability, ask the candidate to make a simple list of rules, for display, from "Emily Postnews" in Appendix 3.

Check with candidates before calling parents to confirm that they think the pupil is ready for the burden, and to ensure that they will be supportive without applying unwelcome pressure. Include the home bulletin board operator: he or she is well-used to helping answer questions.

Inform the pastoral staff responsible for the pupil and tell the pupil's subject teachers. It may be that the pupil could do a spot of mini-research for them, in return for credit towards a day-trip to an educational computer show perhaps.

Some technical ideas for system managers

A pocket-size, fast modem is currently available for about £120. (The same model is sometimes bundled with a computer for £60). For security this will have to be chained on or screwed down or locked in with the phoneline. A security hawser with glue tabs costs about £25.

Many modems have a row of useful indicator lights, among them On line, Carrier detect, Off hook, Sending data, Receiving data. Off hook (OH) is the one that costs while its alight; RD and SD flash while data is moving in and out of the system.

Older modems have fewer LEDs, and, of course, run much more slowly – which may explain part of the awful phone bills of the early experimenters. It is hard to predict whether higher speeds are possible with current phone lines: BT were stating that today's speeds were "probably impossible" only three years ago, and downward movement in their price of the next technology suggests that a competitor is in sight. Watch for politically motivated price drops in normal and ISDN lines, and better still for fibre-optic cable in your area. Meanwhile lobby your MP for a fully free service to schools.

How to keep the phone costs down

- Keep time-consuming tasks for low-cost phone times.
- Make sure all Email is composed and read off-line.
- Ensure that the user is never interrupted or side-tracked.
- Adult supervision always. Ideally a knowledgeable, respected adult.
- All supervisors must know the "Disconnect" button or routine, and use it instantly.
- Download centrally onto disc, pass on for reading at other terminals.
- Ensure that any automatic dialup features on your software (particularly Email packages) are disabled, or the modem is turned off.

Seeking help with connecting

There is often good free technical help amongst friends and spouses of teachers. Make sure you stay in the driving seat though: outside influence can hinder progress.

Technical support helplines at information providers are there to be used. Many tech support people are students and keen to help. If you find a good one, get her or his name and ask if you can call back. They understand how hard first time set up is. Not all are just making sales.

Larger older providers do a regular free if (mainly advertorial) magazine. A couple of Internet magazines can be useful too, although some are over-priced and over-glossy, with little useful content. The exceptions make excellent train-journey reading.

Try also the county advisor, the Head's Union, the local schools' group, and bulletin boards. Some of the system operators have much experience to share. Ask pupils for the names of schools online already, and what they are doing. Don't just follow their advice, though: do what suits you. Consider the offers of "free" connection from large companies carefully – seek out the strings. Consider also the downsides of the "protected" services: the walls may just keep you in, and keep valuable contacts out. As we go to press, the best offer seems to be the three months no-strings trial at Internet For Learning, with its educational topic directory, free web space, and several hundred school web pages as samples for your pupils to analyse, emulate and improve upon.

Final musings for managers

Keep your head well down – they will throw everything at you. A school is the toughest testing environment in the known universe, and it all seems aimed at you.

That said, for the experience, the job is worth hanging onto. Much wisdom is needed, but most of it can be learnt. Discuss all mistakes with the teacher in charge: your respect rating will increase no end.

Try not to react when people get uppity: they need therapy, not a row, and a sympathetic poker face is your best defence. Do not laugh at demands to do the impossible. Answer requests from friends last – true friends will wait till you are free. Ignore or seek help about bribery, bullying or threats. You can be a powerful influence for good in the school if you work at it. Do not weep when an hour's downloading vanishes without trace. Just practise yoga or breathe steadily during tirades. If you are a pupil put in a position of Internet responsibility, do not smile when the team captain's Email disappears and do not spend extra time on the glamour girl's homework research. Your credibility depends on all of these.

Find a friend or three: the IT or computer teacher, the technician, the cleaner, the caretaker, the Head of Year, the Deputy or the Head herself. Show them what the Net can do for them when they visit – they'll enjoy that, as will you. Then you can share problems with them. You may get good answers, or at least know someone who sees it from where you are – don't be over evangelistic when headaches abound, though. Also, remember they have their own axes to grind. Your real job is to show them that an axe sharpened on a cyberstone cuts better and stays sharper longer. And keep your jolliest smile ready for when the machine crashes in the middle of the demonstration to the Head and her distinguished visitors. The smile will not be wasted. This is where your wisdom in keeping a pinboard to display the latest high quality printouts and photographs, the fruits of pupil-driven online research, comes into its own – and with any luck the Head can conduct her own tours from then on, comforted by knowing that paper will be around for at least as long as she is.

The second terminal and beyond

The following is the text of an article that appeared in Educational Computing and Technology in 1996.

In some schools, one computer had to be on the Head's desk before the rest became respectable. With Internet, many teachers see the potential but few of us can take the responsibility of standard bearing for an educational revolution without total support and insurance. The school team needs to advance together, so that the school's teaching community – which includes the parents, the governors, the computer-literate pupils, the secretaries and other ancillary staff, the advisors and the INSET leaders, the inspectorate, and the media – can all be in step. Who would want to co-ordinate this lot?

One method is the pincer movement of a terminal in the marking room or near pigeon holes with another in the library, so that teachers and pupils can experiment in small groups, building the skills of logging on and off, handling the daily Email, reading and contributing to newsgroups, and investigating and contributing to the wide-ranging web. One can emerge with a photocopiable sheet for class use, or a disc with, say, questions from an electronic exchange class, perhaps in a modern language, for pupils to answer or otherwise handle. The terminal must be accessible, so that replies can be pasted into the Email package as soon as possible, before the corresponding class moves on past the topic being shared.

The second terminal is far more important: in a welcoming and encouraging library, for example, so that pupils may be directed to it, with a cheerful, no-nonsense but not overly dominating auxiliary available. This would enable teachers with limited confidence in the system or the Internet to feel tempted to direct a trusted pupil to do the research in or out of class time and return with the good news on paper. Enhancement of pupil and teacher.

Pupils with solo research needs can also book into the system, and pass on to other learners the skills of both computer control, research, and interaction on the greater Internet. For schools with a busy Information Technology co-ordinator, this might solve several problems.

Don't go beyond these two terminals without much thought: advancing further than a Plain Old Telephone Service (POTS) line will give BT a large chunk of school money in the first year, before you buy the extra hardware, with no promise of future reductions. Other communications companies claim to be offering very much better arrangements soon, from American style free local calls, to fractional prices (25%) of current offerings. Perhaps BT will, after some further persuasion, offer some cheap or free connectivity to schools. Until then, it is cable, with its promise of "broadband" connectivity, which is catching the headlines.

Using a normal phoneline, it is possible to offer school-wide Internet access on the local network – to a point. A modem connected to your file-server, and some sensible software (like, for example, Acorn's Intertalk), will allow school-wide Email and Newsgroup distribution to any user groups or even individual pupils, but not, of course, multi-user access to the realtime and interactive services like the web. With such systems, Email is batched on your server until some specified time, when the server will dial up your Internet Service Provider and deal with batch sending and receiving automatically.

In order to achieve multiuser interactivity, the first option is ISDN. This service, although utilising the normal phonelines, is up to ten times as fast as a modem. Unfortunately, there are higher rental charges from BT as well, and the hardware required (a router) is still an expensive piece of kit. Unfortunately, a leased line, which will offer fast and non-metered access to the Internet, is prohibitively expensive, costing over £5000 a year at least to run and maintain. For those schools with ISDN already installed in an established computer room, and already running a fast network, all that is required is well tested software. The market leaders in this are the PC players – ICL, RM and the rest. A common question remains "is all this possible with Acorns"? The answer is yes. An Acorn employee set up a full network of Internet stations in under two hours at a BT conference. Apple's sales staff describe a similar system, running over their computer's new "Open Transport" system, which simplifies local and distance networking. In the PC world, in addition to RM, other supplies are worth a look. ICL have been deeply involved in several far-reaching Internet in-schools trials recently, and should be reporting soon on their experiences and future products.

What, though, for the teacher who wants to wait? At the moment, rumours abound but facts only tiptoe. BT's platform announcement at an in-house conference was "for schools, we can expect some sort of ISDN package". Only a brave man, or a showman, or a school with much money to spend and insider support, including perhaps a very able technical team or loan-staff from a company trialling its own technology, rushes into this minefield without solid research. There are places which would offer their community the adventure of doing this.

This advice may sound messy and specious, but an hour's research at an Internet terminal will produce accurate answers, by those concerned, to questions technical, educational, financial, or any other, including managerial. It will also produce comments on your plan of action. If it doesn't, Email us at **`koekie@koekie.org.uk`**. We'd like to help.

Although the way ahead is unclear, some patterns are emerging: TV set-tops are already here, at perhaps under £500 per terminal. These "Java boxes" have received much press attention, but it remains to be seen whether the idea of a "network computer" will be viable with a normal dialup phoneline as the only method of connecting with its programs and storage. Nevertheless, they attempt to blend with current classroom technology (sharing a large TV screen, say), giving an improvement on the microcomputer in ways, but lacking the latter's flexibility and minimising their interactive potential. Fully portable radio-linked colour terminals will take longer, and cost much more in the short term, but it is quite possible that the connected laptop-per-desk, so beloved of politicians left and right, might well be a practical possibility in five years time, perhaps sooner.

Today, the room of twenty Internet terminals is alluring, and is available now, at a price, and in good hands should be effective: again, the few reports or documented trials are encouraging. One real-world problem is keeping the good hands in the school. The ICL equipment in the science department at Brakenhale School in Berkshire (See their Web pages at **`http://www.Brakenhale.berks.sch.uk/`**) has splendid potential.

Other Schools Online Project test-beds on show are always at BETT and other education technology exhibitions.

To hold networks of computers and pupils together and in some semblance of order, schools are putting together home-written acceptable use policies. A good AUP gives access without undue restriction or the need for continual teacher supervision for older pupils, and encourages sensible use of a school cybercafé. It achieves this through a balance of powers and trust, rather than any overbearing regulation or threat, and early signs in the schools brave enough to trust their pupils to be responsible are promising.

Scenarios to avoid include allowing the small class set of Internetted terminals to be dominated by the driven computer scientist, the over-stretched IT co-ordinator, or the moralising puritan. Most computer room staff will recognise the feelings – been there, done that, got the computer-clan T-shirt. Some of us will even admit to it. A sensible way out is to involve the Head or Deputy in the setting up and training, so that all staff feel happy with the medium and able to gather experience with fewer stresses. Regrettably, pupils will not be slow to say "But Sir, Miss Smith lets us look at the Internet ..." At which point sir might consider sending the lippy one to the library to sharpen her or his research skills on the public network terminal, instructed to come back with a useful search result on hard-copy after the lesson.

Perhaps the hardest part of going beyond the first Internet terminal is the challenge of realising the interactive nature of the medium, what it offers and what to avoid. A sublime confidence in one's pupils is needed before letting them fly solo, and the stimulation of intellectual joy is vital in appreciating the profundity of the experience of cross-world interaction.

We find it very hard to condone the blocking, through financial or ideological constraints, of this form of education from those who would clearly profit. But what of the possible damage to the vulnerable many? The school community has, again, to find its own equilibrium and to make choices for itself. There is no safely walled-off adventure playground in life, and to believe such an idea is practical on the Internet is to ignore both the technical and social realities of the system, as well as to deny the serendipities only accessible beyond the playground's gates. So it behoves all in responsibility to seek and weigh the arguments. Complete delay is too easy a decision, although in some cases it is possibly the correct one. Lack of finance can be given as a reason, or facilities, or staffing; or morality, or insurance fears, or pioneerophobia. The scenario for accidents to pupils is serious – but letting them by default experiment alone and unsupervised at home or in a commercial cybercafé environment breeds other problems which might be averted by an early installation at school.

A mini case study

The Internet-active school could definitely use more than a POTS connection – seek out the Web pages from Hinchingbrooke School in Huntingdon, at which Duncan Grey is developing dozens of different types of projects, many of which require multi-terminal access for efficient application. The URL is **`http://www.worldserver.pipex.com/`**

We hear of one independent school with eight separate Internet accounts. A co-ordinating committee of Internet enthusiasts was formed, which was at first not able to drag in the IT co-ordinator. That luckless person had doubtless been so taunted by colleagues about the devil's new medium that he wanted to lurk behind a safety screen while others tested the water. Perhaps tomorrow would be more opportune to tackle management with another request to subvert the school's academic structure in the interests of popularly driven eclectic education?

A compromise: The happy persona in the library – perhaps a friendly volunteer parent looking after a few terminals – is perhaps the best halfway house for those schools unable to afford the fiendish set-up charges of both BT – for its ISDN line, and then the internal network costs.

Finally, if the Internet system you are planning has a three year lifetime and is affordable, do it now. Your teachers and pupils will still be thanking you well beyond their working lives. The investment in our good young people's future seems right. Our in-school planners need to practice the Email skills, to be comfortable in netiquette, to be able to work in virtual groups of all ages and persuasions, to be able to overcome the disorienting effects of real-time communication in Chatgroups, and to use Internet realtime-audio voice-overs as a normal part of teaching and learning. This is an area where the professional advisor is driven by so many conflicting forces that no blanket solution can be offered to a school. It is also an issue that cannot be deferred *sine die*, but one that demands a personal solution by all who would be involved in the educative process changes surrounding our schools today.

Acceptable Use Policy

The Internet is an online community, available for and interacting with all its users. Like all of society beyond school, it offers much and demands much, and has risks and penalties.

Most Acceptable Use Policies seek to protect the pupil and the school. Ours encourages pupils to experiment wisely, initially with guidance, until positive contributions via her or his Internet research show that the pupil perceives the values and has a deep sense of the etiquette of the medium, and of its pitfalls.

A simple but demanding driving test is required before going solo: fulsome printed evidence of on-going caring, intelligent contributions to academic or cultural newsgroups, an ability to reply to questions constructively in newsgroups like alt.homework, or other creative interaction with outsiders at a similar level.

Two senior pupils will always be on site: a "keyholder" and a "courier". The keyholder looks after the welcoming of visitors and casual users, and takes care of room security, logging usage and problems, key control, and so forth. The courier helps users to get the best from being online.

Unconstructive downloads, Email or postings are off-side: the goodwill of the school is crucial to this venture. Infringers and borderliners will need to seek arbitration.

Copies of this will be posted in the Net room area. Pupils and parents will be asked to accept it before using a school Internet system, and are warmly invited to suggest improvements.

Before settling on the Acceptable Use Policy in the box, we had several steps at producing a pupil-run AUP, but found that in early 1996 Internet experience was not wide enough for youngsters to make coherent suggestions. If we were starting from scratch today, we would issue the above and ask for improvements before implementing. And of course we would include in the licence test for keyholders and couriers an ability to use a search engine to find addresses for and details of other peoples' Acceptable Use Policies on both web pages and newsgroups.

Obstacles are sometimes not simple, and can easily get out of proportion: the legalistic problems that are faced by some school communities would be farcical were it not that we need to take them seriously. One has to hope that the following, published on a listserver, is a send-up:

```
K-12 Acceptable Use Policies
http://www.erehwon.com/k12aup
A new web site has been established addressing K-12 Acceptable Use
Policies. This site includes an extensive legal analysis of K-12
AUPs, including issues relating to due process, search and seizure,
liability, copyright, and First Amendment rights.
```

Choosing a Service Provider

The school will obviously choose a Service Provider on a cost effective basis: part of the effective side of the balance must be the quality of the material. We are not arguing for bland censorship, with everything so nailed down that one might be using a pre-digested CD-ROM, the so-called "walled garden" approach. There lies parochial insularity, and, worse, failure. A trapped community will either become narrow, or resistive. Pupils will not be able to explore the opportunities of independent education the Net offers. The cyber-police employed by some of the free Service Providers are not the encouraging influence one would wish for, either; a search on America Online revealed a raft of problems in policing the police. It may be that the UK version of America Online will solve this problem, but the jury is still out. It is hard to see through the hype, and the undeniable good work being done by the high quality British fans makes it an attractive offer. The other free services, with the Internet Service as a loss leader, are likely to have less educational input, and a thinner layer before the sales pitch. The acceptability of the service has a moral overtone: what is free at school may well be expensive when bought at home. It is likely, though, that the drives of advertisers to reach into homes with computers online will keep the charge well down.

Snippets

Some short tips as you leave the chapter.

Fund raising

A sympathetic bursar may let you slip it in with the general phonebill at first, but if only to help with budgeting for the type of access you will need, it is worth going official. Money-raising from pupils is ethically problematic, but like charging for the photocopier, or for components used in technology, it shows the community that the system is needed and appreciated. An insight into a society that charges children for seeking to grow up well.

Going public across a school

Is general pupil access educationally good? Many believe so, but the official jury is out. For a judicial analysis of many of the problems – and a crystal-clear exposition of what the Net is and offers, search for the 1996 ruling on the American Communications Decency Act by the Pennsylvania Circuit Court. The judges deemed the Act both unconstitutional and harmful.

Helping boost an A level grade

Use the various online homework services well before revision time. Seek revision suggestions for topics in which help is required – some will offer books, some expositions or just ways of looking at topics. But there is no royal road – hard work is still vital, examples must be practised, and mistakes learned from. Extra tuition by Email should be sought only if the tutor is qualified and known to other teachers. Before A levels, "approved" knowledge becomes uncomfortably necessary.

More ideas for keeping phone costs down

- ☎ Make sure the call to your ISP is local.
- ☎ Read all mail and type all replies off-line. Batch replies for sending.
- ☎ No aimless cyber-surfing.
- ☎ Set up a local network cache of frequently accessed sites. Some CD-ROMs do this for you.
- ☎ Discipline your users. Book online times to users, and impose call charges or use the detailed BT account. Charge an amount in advance to users, either lump sum or deposit against time of use.
- ☎ Keep an eye on new technologies, like radioing Email internally to a central point where it is batched for normal exchanging. Monitor price changes, like ISDN, leased line, and cable.
- ☎ Find a body that would sponsor part of your phone bill in exchange for a share in an educational venture like an in-school competition. Two computer companies and two supermarkets are doing very well out of their schools sponsorship projects.
- ☎ Tell your MP how many votes he will gain next election if his party persuades Oftel to allow BT to give all schools free calls. Perhaps also tell him also how much better educated the electorate will be thereafter. Unless he is afraid this will make him unelectable.

Organisation

So much depends on the trust between you, the school and the pupil community. There will always be mistakes, but they must not be terminal. The worst case is for trust to be reduced. Openness and enthusiastic, honest exploration is a great builder, committees breed boredom, secrecy builds suspicion. The School Internet Council, meeting weekly one lunchtime, to consider a posted agenda of questions, with rota of pupils, PTA, Governors and staff could be a very useful forum in ways unpredictable now, as long as the Council doesn't solidify.

Setting up an "Intranet"

Although the word Intranet can be a cloying piece of jargon, using Internet programs and interfaces to communicate over a local area network will prove attractive to many schools – integrating local web pages of school information and revision resources, for example, with internal links. No additional training in complex database packages is necessary – it's all there in the world wide web browser.

The good school website

A quality site gives the browser good experiences, mirroring the dynamism of the pupils and the school. It contains more than a prospectus or a photograph of a grimly visaged Head. It contains pupil work, images and sounds. You can examine the school's position in the league table, but you can also read the results of Year 3's collaborative poetry festival. Little guessing which will be more impressive in its inclusion.

Finally

As EM Forster might have had in his Email signature – only connect!

Magazine article

Our daily computer club meetings at the science laboratory Internet terminal give different ages and interest groups of pupils a focus for pursuing interests. They have, in the first four weeks of the year, all explored the browsers and search engines available on the Net, downloaded several programs – including a fully working and programmable model of the Psion 3 handheld computer – and had an Internet music player running within days of its appearance online. Snatches of CD quality music from all over the world have now become a part of the club's repertoire.

The teacher who runs these clubs finds that some pupils appear for their own interests only, while those who arrive several times each week make useful contributions across the board, as well as helping to get new members up to speed. There are days when the terminal is down, usually because of experiments with different Internet Providers – some of the 'free' ones have turned out to be quite expensive in this respect, as their software seems to take over the machine.

We keep a set of alternative exercises, like a pack of Internet training slides for the overhead projector, so that members can give talks on aspects of the Net such as Email or newsgroups. One afternoon club, with a pupil range from Sixth form to pre-GCSE, discussed a Science Across the World fax from a school in Malaysia: we completed their questionnaire on what the UK was doing about alternative energy sources, and worked on ways in which Internet could improve the project.

Left: An extract from an article appearing in a secondary school magazine.

'Learning the Internet' by Bruce Dickson and Nicholas Mailer is a pack containing OHP masters and a presenter's booklet of hints and tips, suitable for INSET, parents' evenings or secondary pupils. It is available from Questions Publishing, 27 Frederick Street, Birmingham, B1 3HH, price £14.95.

Starting Up

Some tips for getting a connection at school or at home, making sure it is secure and dealing with teething troubles.

Information about your computer system is included.

Chapter 10

The start-up path depends on your experience and your contacts. This chapter assumes neither.

Keep a list of your hardware, with technical details of the computer and modem for reference next to the telephone. Check little details like the shape and number of pins of the modem socket on the computer. For effective Internet use, a hard drive or local area network server is necessary.

Six steps to starting up

Who to contact first

Choose an Internet service provider (see Appendix 1). Word of mouth is useful in this context – ask connected friends what experiences they've had with their ISPs. You should bear the following points in mind:

- A flat-rate monthly or annual charge is a must, with no time or metered extra costs.

- They should have "sufficient bandwidth" – if their connection to the Internet is not quick, neither will yours be. Ask them to describe their connection to the States. Can you access the Library of Congress when America is awake, for instance? Ask if they have a "bandwidth guarantee": some ISPs will guarantee their system's possible capacity will never be saturated. A competent ISP should respond without confusing you or resorting to jargon.

- They should have a good "user to modem ratio". Too few modems at their end in proportion to the number of subscribers will lead to a frustrating number of engaged signals. Between twenty to thirty users to one modem is acceptable. Below that is excellent.

- Ensure the modems at their end will allow you to connect at least 28.8k. Some ISPs now allow 33.6k connection, if you have a 33.6k modem, with a few going even faster.

- They should have a local point of presence in your school's area: you don't want to dial up with national call charges. Many ISPs today offer local call access to 100% of the country.

- They should provide free technical support by phone and Email. Some ISPs offer weekend technical support.

- If you wish to put web pages up, ensure they offer at least two megabytes of web space free. Some ISPs offer more, with a few offering unlimited space free to non-commercial customers.

- They should provide software for your connection. This should include an Email package, Usenet reader and web browser. Ask if these are registered, full versions or shareware versions. Ask if they release the latest versions, or older software.

- Even if they do not "officially" support your computer, or a particular Internet program on it, make sure your ISP will be willing to help when things go wrong. Good support departments will not be officious about such things.

Whose phone numbers to collect

Make a note of contact names and numbers of your local user-group, your area advisor, bulletin board operator, pupils, suppliers and anyone else who will be able to help you in the first few weeks of your Internet connection. Ask around school and see who has connected privately. Collect their Email addresses, which will be valuable through the teething problems. Someone is bound to have gone through them before. The technical support help-line at your ISP should be by far the best source of advice.

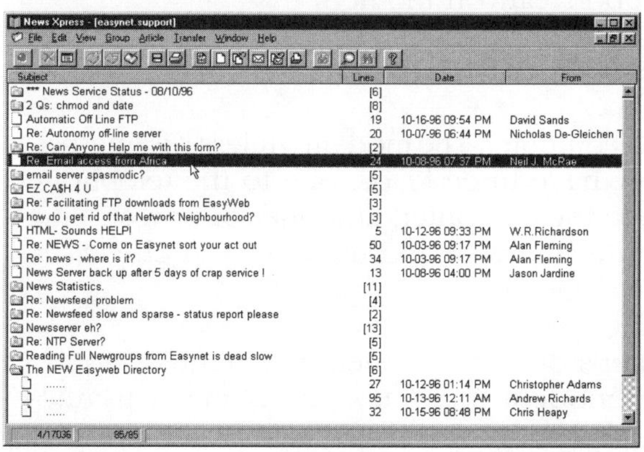

Left: Most ISPs now provide technical support through Usenet newsgroups where staff reply to messages and comments. These are run in conjunction with the phone service, so that those users who can get online, but want further support, can post a question in such a newsgroup and receive responses from employees and fellow subscribers.

Connection Routes

The most common way for an individual or school to connect to the Internet remains via a modem, over the telephone line. The disadvantages of this are a non-speedy connection and metered phone calls. Above this, ISPs also offer ISDN (using the same phone line, but sending the data at much higher speeds without a modem) or a dedicated leased line. The former is expensive. The latter is very expensive indeed. Cable TV companies are beginning to experiment with offering Internet connection over their services via "cable modems", which offer much higher speeds than conventional modems. It remains to be seen how successful these will be in real-world situations.

For more information on connection possibilities, see the ISP's Appendix 1.

What to buy

A year's subscription to the Internet will often cost less than when paying on a monthly basis. Nevertheless, if you are unhappy with your service, it is usually easier to pull out of the latter (although, of course, if there is a genuine case of "merchantable quality" or fraudulent claims, your statutory rights remain unaffected).

Purchase at least a 28.8 modem. If you can afford it, a new 33.4 modem might be able to squeeze that extra bit of speed out of the phone-line, but that small increase may not be worth the price difference. Make sure you have a lead that can connect your modem to your computer's serial port.

You might want to visit a cyber-café and get used to browsing the Internet before getting connected.

It may be worth while investing in an additional phone-line, dedicated to Internet use. Not only is this convenient, but it also makes it easy to budget for Internet phone-bills. Extension sockets may be placed in several classrooms, for easy access by your trolleyed Net terminal.

What to provide on site

Arrange a phone point (secured with a remote disconnect switch or key) and power points sufficient for computer, monitor, printer and modem. It is convenient to have a telephone handy to use during startup – preferably on a separate line, so you can dial up with your modem on one line while talking to your ISP's technical support team on another.

The physical connection

Switch off the computer. The modem (unless it is internal) will probably have three leads, one to the telephone socket, one to the computer, and one for power. Plug in, switch on at the wall and modem, and check the power lights come on.

You computer's operating system may require you to set up your modem in some way. Some will auto-detect your modem.

Setting up and testing

Connect in the manner suggested by your ISP – they should have sent you software, with easy-to-follow installation instructions. The modem should dial your ISP's number for you. You may have to log in manually by giving your username and password. If you are lucky, your service provider will have supplied you with instructions to automate the process.

Run an Email package, which should be supplied and set up as per your ISP's instructions. Try sending a test message to **`koekie@koekie.org.uk`**. We'll send you a friendly note back in response!

FTP is probably the next to test. Even in these days of the Java-enabled web, honing your FTP skills is useful, as you will be able to download new Internet software. For a first test, though, do something simple like downloading a small text file, rather than trying for a large program, which will take many minutes. Again, don't be afraid of phoning technical support if you stumble.

Afterwards, browsing the web should be an enjoyable, if baffling, experience. Try a few sites illustrated in this book, or simply follow some links from the page that opens when you load your browser.

Remember to close down the phone connection when you have finished, preferably using the software. If the computer appears to have hung, you may have to hang up by turning off your modem, or, if it is internal, by pulling the plug out of the phone-socket.

Make lists of the routines that work. These will become your school's instruction sheets, perhaps pinned up at the terminal for all users to follow. As well as specific sheets for specific applications, there should be a copy of your Acceptable Use Policy, and clear instructions concerning the following:

Logging on
Logging off
Saving and printing data from the Internet
Routine for closing down the terminal

Computer systems

Acorn

In their bid to survive in the cut throat competitive IT world, Acorn have adopted the divide and conquer tactic, except they have decided to divide themselves rather than their enemies. As such, the Acorn group now consists of several ever-changing entities, each of which deals with a different part of the market. Xemplar, its joint company with Apple, is the closest we have to old Acorn Computers. Along with their Online Media and Network Computer divisions, they aim to provide low-cost Internet options, already offering an Acorn network computer. Some question the power of this computer – certainly, the underlying StrongARM microprocessor is powerful, but it remains to be seen whether, even with Apple and Oracle (a company currently on a "Internetted network appliance v Microsoft" crusade), they will be able to achieve some large-scale market acceptance.

Nevertheless, in contrast with just two years ago, Acorn are now trying hard to integrate the Internet into their systems. They may well emerge at the forefront of educational developments, if they are able to achieve with their Online Media and Network Computer divisions a cost-effective and highly integrated solution which can be slotted into every British classroom – and perhaps beyond. With many schools wondering whether to jump to Macintosh or PC machines, Acorn know this is their last chance to carve a secure niche in the computing business. With their sister company's chips now looked at with interest by companies all over the world for "Internet appliances", the future should be at least interesting for this British-Italian company.

At the moment, Internet software is available through many British websites, and from several Acorn-specialising companies. In particular, Ant's Internet suite is becoming the de-facto standard for the RiscPC machines, and a version of the web browser is built into the new Acorn network computer. Although polished, the software does not have all the features of Netscape and Microsoft Internet Explorer, and it seems unrealistic to assume it will ever gain them, not least because the number of third party additions and plug-ins which will not be converted to the Acorn machines. Nevertheless, the Acorn public domain and shareware community is thriving, and there are several healthy depositories on the web of Acorn information and software.

http://www.acorn.co.uk/
Acorn Group's web site

http://www.ant.co.uk/
Homepage of the popular software suite

http://www.cs.vu.nl/~gerben/acorn/
A large number of links to Acorn sites

http://www.idg.co.uk/acornuser/
Acorn user magazine's site – online information, software and more

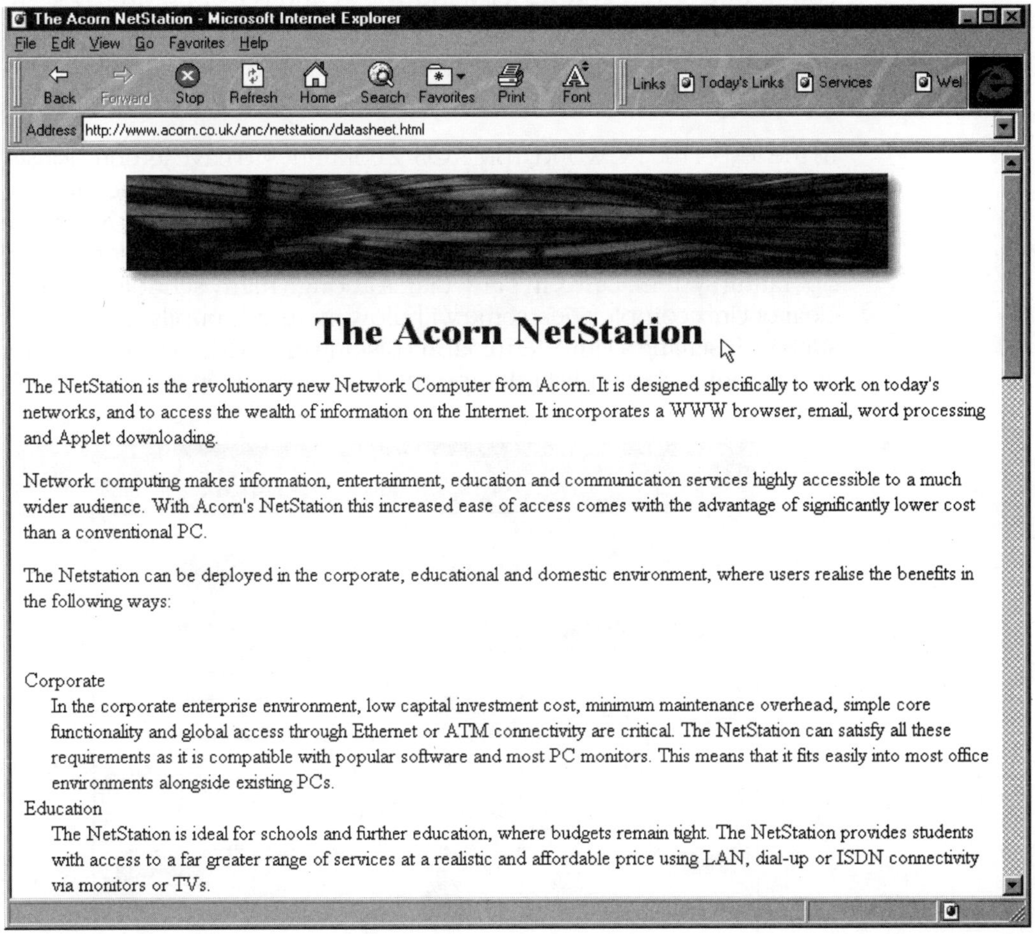

The PC

The PC world is dominated by Microsoft and its Windows operating system. Not long ago, it seemed Bill Gates was close to missing the boat by failing to recognise the Internet or its related developments, spending too much of his energy in promoting the proprietary Microsoft Network. But his company did an astounding about-turn, becoming a collection of born-again Internet zealots overnight: all Microsoft's programs are now constructed with the Internet in mind, and its quality Internet Explorer web-browsing software is being offered free in direct competition with Netscape's Navigator. The company claims to be committed to integrating its Windows95 and NT operating systems with Internet-based technology, such that you will eventually browse the web, your local network and your hard disc in the same environment almost seamlessly.

In the rest of the PC world, IBM's OS/2 continues to have its enthusiasts, and it remains quite capable of establishing a connection to the Internet, with Netscape continuing to develop a talking version of their Navigator software for it. Finally, there are the variants of the high-powered Unix operating system, Linux in particular. Although many schools will steer clear of Unix complexities, some will allow more able pupils to hone their skills by installing a Linux terminal and asking them to get on with it. After all, this highly accomplished, supported and popular operating system is completely free!

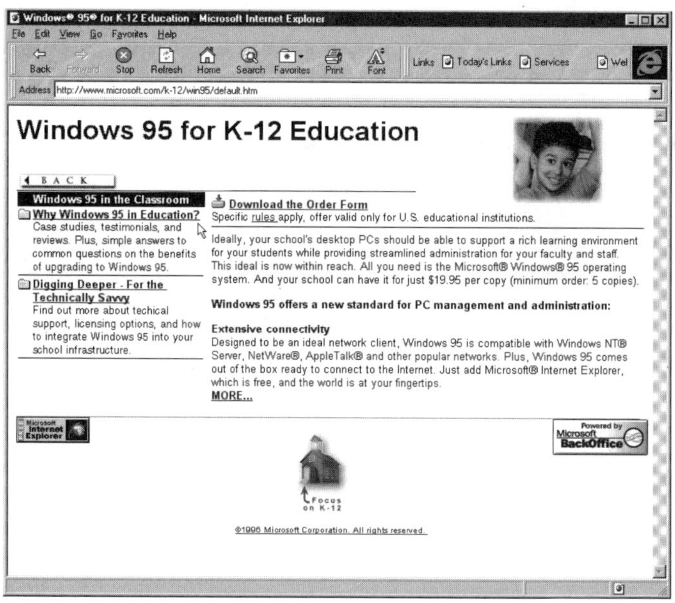

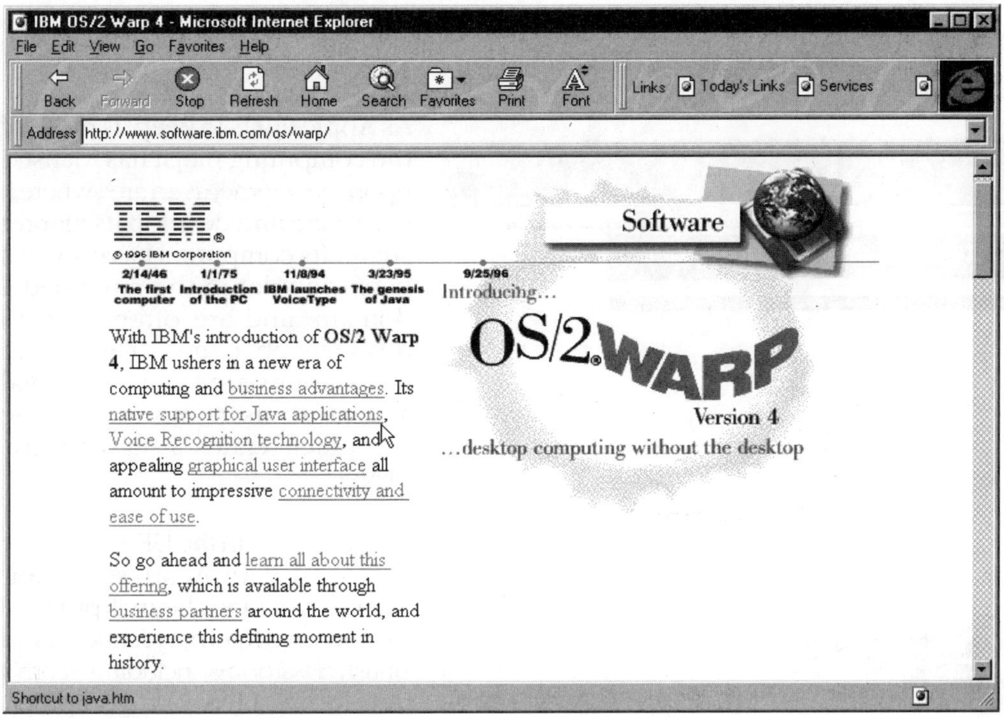

Above: IBM continues to develop its OS/2 Warp operating system, integrating it ever more closely to the Internet, in particular including Java as an integral part of its new release.

http://www.ibm.com/

http://www.microsoft.com/
Microsoft's web page has become extremely popular, offering files and information by the bucketfull.

http://www.tucows.com/
The best place to download any Internet software for Microsoft operating systems.

http://www.win95.com/
A huge resource for Windows95 users, with software, FAQs, magazines and links.

http://www.win95mag.com/
For the latest quality news and reviews for Windows95, the online Windows95 magazine is a good place to go.

Apple Macintosh

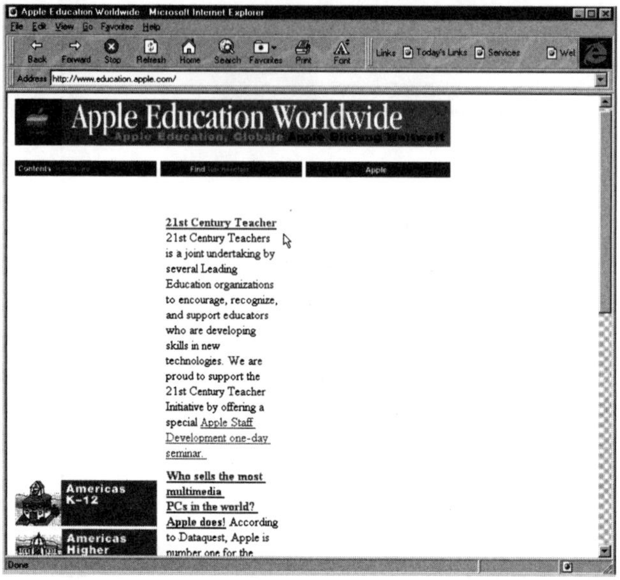

As Apple fights to keep its piece of the computing pie, it has focused upon the Internet as an area where it can retain and develop its market share. Its computers have always been popular in the multimedia domain, and are often used to design web pages. The Apple newsgroups are lively, and loyal Macintosh users ensure that the computer retains a high on line profile.

Apple's future in the UK is currently entwined with Acorn's, in their Xemplar venture. They will promote inexpensive Internet technology in British classrooms, including Acorn's developing Network Computer, which connects to a television screen and acts as a "network appliance".

`http://www.apple.com/`
Apple's homepage contains a wealth of information, including operating system components and Internet software available for downloading.

`http://aristotle2.isu.edu/MacResources.html`
Apple Macintosh resources. A link to programs, manuals and files galore.

`http://www.tidbits.com/`
A high quality online magazine with the latest information about the Mac and its development.

`http://www.elnet.com/~hanlon/mac/macresources.html`
Contains a good collection of Macintosh Internet software and utilities for download.

`http://hyperarchive.lcs.mit.edu/HyperArchive.html`
For even more software, the InfoMac archive represents a cornucopia. This site has a built in search engine to find the package you want.

Amiga

After the demise of Commodore, the Amiga is enjoying a vibrant after-life on the Internet – with software, support and news readily available. The Amiga newsgroups are always buzzing, and small companies and enthusiasts are creating quite respectable Internet connectivity software. This is important, because many pupils will own these machines and still use them, even today. The Amiga may even appear, as in a Trojan horse, in the set-top boxes and network computers currently being developed – its cheap and efficient graphical subsystem making it useful for these sort of applications.

`http://ftp.wustl.edu/~aminet/`
The Aminet software archive has been going for some time, and includes a huge bank of freely downloadable resources. There are mirrors of this site all over the world, with every category of Amiga software available.

`http://www.cucug.org/amiga.html`
A collection of hundreds of links to Amiga news items, reviews and web pages and other Internet resources all over the world.

`http://www.vistv.com/`
The homepage of Viscorp, the current owners of Amiga technology. They are developing the computer's chip-set into a set-top "information" box.

`http://www.qni.com/~dwaldr1/`
The Amiga Appreciation Page. Includes the "Amiga Image of the Week".

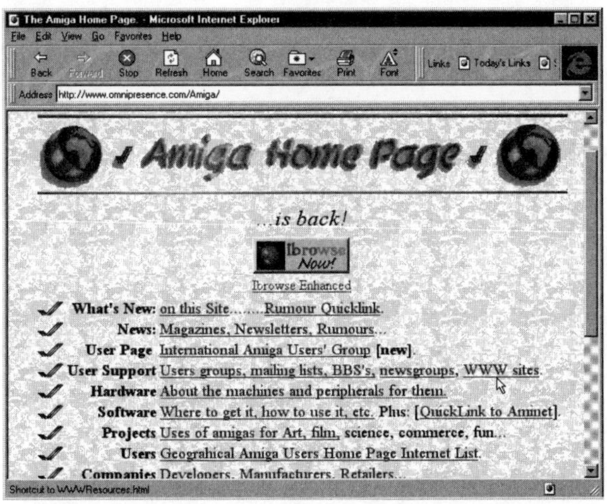

Left: The so-called "Amiga Homepage" contains links to those companies still developing software for the Amiga, as well as the latest rumours concerning the computer's fate.

http://www.omnipresence.com/

The Internet Future

Chapter 11

In the first edition of this book, we ended with a few homilies - some predictions for the distant future. We are happy and surprised to note that some of those predictions have already come to pass much more quickly than we predicted. Nevertheless, soothsaying is a difficult task, with every online Merlin having his or her own ideas about where the technology is leading us.

Simply put, we can now all agree that the Internet is more than a "blip". It is now not just possible, but likely that its continuing development will have profound effects on education and general culture. Rather than direct fortune-telling, though, we provide for your reading pleasure two stories of a pupil going to school in, say, the year 2010. The first story is generally optimistic. The second is not. We invite you to construct your own scenarios, which will probably lie somewhere in-between the two. Both have the characteristic of science fiction pieces in being caricatures of a milieu of possible worlds – basically narrating a *reductio ad absurdem.* Even so, some of the technical ideas within will probably be realised long before 2010. The social developments are more questionable.

Story one

Emma stepped off the coach as it slowed down at her school. A wisp of pure steam from the exhaust preceded her towards the gate. She was looking forward to finishing her music project that day – the improvisations on her simple theme should be arriving any moment from her Venezuelan friends. She hoped that the joint-markers (she wasn't sure yet whether they'd be fellow pupils or teachers) from both schools wouldn't mind her using those unconventional time-signatures! After submitting the MIDI file, she'd have the time to begin the research for her history assignment on the development of shared electronic learning from the last quarter of the 20th century onwards. One of her info guides would help in finding sites to obtain useful information, but she knew that the point of this project was selecting for herself the pivotal developments since those heady days at the end of the last century.

Emma didn't usually enjoy the formality of registration class – she couldn't fathom why it was necessary – after all, she had swiped her card through the machines at the school entrance and the classroom door, which she thought should have proved registration enough. With today's session, however, she began to realise the point – it was more than just being counted, but a time for the live guides to have a rare face-to-face meeting with their charges, which was an aspect of the day most learners cherished, even if only deep down. Today's registration meeting was shared with some kids in Goa, who, as usual, were showing off their advanced Netlang programming skills. Unlike most kids in the UK, they still seemed particularly interested in what happened under the bonnet.

Emma decided that she would give the Goan project now being discussed a miss. They wanted to build an info guide that could appreciate and understand both Western and Indian theatrical conventions – at the moment, the guides seemed slanted more towards Broadway than Belgaum. Although she quite enjoyed seeing all the advanced Net tricks the Goans played, she wanted to put more time into her history project – she decided it would be her major contribution to the knowledge pool for the year, and wanted it to be something special.

The Goans waved their goodbyes from the wall and the live guide, Jenny MacPherson, invited anyone needing further face-to-face contact time to return at 11am after the two hour free-research session. Emma didn't particularly worry about this – she could always contact a live or info guide on her slate while she was researching if she wanted – the live guides walked around the campus, keeping track, keeping an eye on learners as they researched, answering slate questions and occasionally chatting to children in other schools. Not to mention carrying on with *their*research – after all, they were still studying too, as were most of their fellow citizens.

Emma took one of the bigger class-slates to her favourite plum tree in the school orchard, which had been planted in the school's old car-park. She gave her main search agent the delimeters of her history project and told it to begin constructing a research plan. While it was busy, she had a chat with Cheaneta, a learner at the El Tigre Middle School in Venezuela. She enjoyed the improvisations which warbled out of the slate's speaker, particularly the Latin American rhythms, which rather masked her odd time signature and made it sound quite normal! She was glad that people around the world had fought hard to put music on the International Core Curriculum. After the adios, the search agent reported back the standard timeline highlights:

- The development of the then world wide web at CERN.
- The browser and bandwidth battles.
- The overbearing control legislation which toppled under its own inconsistencies.

- The final realisation (after the '99 depression) that a globally educated population was the only valid counter to the bust-and-boom cycle.
- The establishment of the Interactive Peripatetic Parliament as Britain's third chamber within the European Federation (Emma had already participated as a consultant for one of its Green Papers).
- The so-called Rockerfellering of Gates: Microsoft's historic policy to select as its primary motivation to act as a catalyst for free and universal educational access to any electronic resource (now enshrined in the UNICEF charter). Cynics were confounded as Gates mellowed. He even apologised for MS-DOS.
- The Net controllable labs on the moon and Mars (although no human had made it to the red planet yet – far too expensive). Emma was scheduled to help conduct some lunar experiments in two months time.

As a plum dropped past her, improvising a puddle of damson jam, an info guide popped up on the slate, to remind her of her project's remit – to discuss whether the development of GIVE (Global Interactive and Versatile Education) and the Internet which underlay it was purely serendipitous or a part of an inevitable cultural evolution. A few months earlier, she had completed a biology project with the Darwin Institute (she had just received the Merit Certificate, which she printed out for her proud grandmother, who was running out of wall-space. The old lady's immediate comment was that in her day of the rigorous "pre-nonsense" O level system, the certificates were properly printed on quality bond paper).

To earn that certificate, Emma had to learn quite a bit about natural evolution, and she had noted that many evolutionary chains began as a kind of opportunist response to a cataclysm. Perhaps the chain of cultural evolution which lead to GIVE and the Internet which underlay it had its roots in the Cuban Missile crisis. After all, everyone knew the Internet had been a product of the Cold War. Perhaps it wasn't just the two leaders who needed to learn how to communicate more efficiently, but their communities as well. Yes, the official line was that the Internet had developed as a nuclear-proof network, but she wondered whether, in the subconscious realms of the founding computer scientists' minds, there was not the strong thread of something greater, more inclusive and social – much more profound than a research or military tool right from the beginning.

She dictated her thoughts to her slate and picked a greengage from a neighbouring branch. Her slate started bleeping out a commercial for the latest slimming fad – it had burrowed its way through the school's ad-filter disguised as a health program. She told her slate calmly to send the ad back to its owner, (several balance-agents had already popped up offering various sites dealing with anorexia, diet deficiencies and so forth). She bit into the greengage and noticed a worm had been there before her. The school's decision not to use pesticides had lead to a balance of life in its orchard.

As she was about to rise from her arcadian bliss, an independent netwide music-analyst agent popped up on her slate and informed her that her composition, which it had been considering after picking it up at one of Cheaneta's show-and-tell sites, had much in common with certain African dances. It played her an extract from a Liberian ceremony. The tonal system was different, of course, but the rhythms were very much the same. She stored the music on the school's main server, intending to play it to friends before orchestra practice the next day – perhaps they could perform it live; she told the scoring agent to produce some networked sheet-music out of it. She felt a tap on her shoulder. It was her best friend Sam.

"Come on, you'll miss tea. We've got those South African doughnut things today. Those ones soaked in the cinnamon syrup. You don't want to miss them".

Their slates chirped in unison that break was starting, and snippets from the top-ten singles of that week emanated from the tiny speakers. Sam particularly liked the slushy ballad about someone trapped in a series of virtual Net meetings, all with no logout. Emma paid for the download from her pocket E-Account, which had just been supplemented by payment for some gardening work she'd done.

During break, she remembered to mail the elderly gentleman who lived alone a few blocks from the school. According to the community service roster on the school canteen's wall-screen, it was her day to do his shopping. He replied almost immediately, claiming he was too busy to worry about such things at the moment, as he was busy "web surfing". The friends giggled at this quaint old expression from a previous millennium and Emma resolved to tackle him again before she left school.

Story Two

Emma dragged herself up the steps into the crumbling concrete monolyth through a cloud of diesel soot. She swiped her card through the machine at the door, which beeped at her alarmingly. Her slate beeped too, as though the devices were having some infernal conversation, which, in a sense, they were:

"2.38 minutes late. Reported to CentroNet. Penalty deduction. Please have a nice day and try harder" flashed yellow on the slate's little grey screen. She knew that if she had any further penalty deductions, she'd lose all research rights, and perhaps even her slate, being forced to use one of the under-powered public network terminals in the upstairs corridor.

She ran to the classroom and slid her card again. Same beep. Same message. The teacher glowered at her, and she sat down at a rickety desk in the front. It still had an inkwell. She decided not to use any E-vouchers for the first lesson (she'd spent too many on the maths sessions last term). Today she'd have to do without the fancy online holographic demonstrations and Edu+ international experts, but make do with the video-disked low-bandwidth version provided by the National Education Service for all those not able to afford these little extras. The teacher turned on a netscreen in the corner of the room, but no more than a familiar pre-recorded and rather morose face appeared on it:

"Sorry, no available Netchannel. Please try again later".

So much for the planned Netmeet with some students in Arizona – since the NES's tender for extra bandwidth allocation had failed, they had to share their sponsored link with Shopnet, Sportsco and GrendelNet – who took priority during business hours, when they sapped the link with extremely complex interactive 3D imaging and the high-density data-streams for the new networked "body-sense" suits, with which even the latest fibre-optic lines could not adequately cope. Inconveniently, school hours were business hours. This was also the sales season, so the line was pretty much saturated as it was with normal high-band commercial traffic. The teacher sighed and touched a "Disconnect" icon on the screen. The speaker retorted jollily, "thank you for using the Sportsco Network – quality sports information at a price you can afford! Please come again soon" and flickered into a replay of last Tuesday's maths lesson, enlivened with product endorsements scrolling across the screen's bottom.

The bell tolled and those children who, along with Emma, didn't have the current purchasing power to afford the Edu+ experience filed into a little prefab alongside the car-park. Some claimed that the History Department was riddled with asbestos. There had been some scurrilous rumours circulating across the Net, but an MS Contentment-Agent had removed them "before they could do damage to minor's sense of well-being" (or so went the well-trodden phrase appearing on so many expunged sites). The pupils sat down and waited for a teacher, but none entered – apparently he was busy at a Schools' CRAMP (Curriculum for Remote Advertising, Marketing and Publicity) conference in Leicester.

A secretary arrived with a video-disk labelled "NES World War II" and slid it into the wall player. Another of those messages flashed across the screen:

"Curriculum Material Expired.
Please download updates after credit approval"

She ejected the disc from the slot and slid in another.

"NES Netlink Topic 4.23: Pending approval by curriculum board. Please purchase appropriate alternative Edu+ online materials for Licenced pupils. Alternatively, seek software on hard-media or approved non-interactive resource materials: videodisk, textbooks etc".

Some in the class began giggling. The school's remaining books were in three locked glass cases on the third floor.

The secretary banged an icon, and the screen flickered, but not much else happened. She slid in another disc. Third time lucky.
"NES Interactive History: Please select
1) The theme of your investigation
2) The period of your investigation"

"Dinosaurs!" shouted one of the pupils. "Doing Net Approval-Lookup" flashed the screen. A minute or two later, a slow recorded voice emerged from the speaker:

"Dinosaurs are now removed from the current Approved National Curriculum at this level. Please try again."

After much trial and error, with similar messages repeated, it became clear that all that was on offer was the industrial revolution, post cold-war communication studies and the history of modern Norwegian manufacturing industry.

The secretary chose the second option and walked out of the prefab – the Netcams would watch out for miscreants. The latest image-recognition algorithms were capable of identifying the guilty party and making penalty deductions from his or her account immediately – the Netcams had their own dedicated line apart from the Sportsco route. Unfortunately, the system was not quite capable of discovering the subtler forms of bullying which sometimes prevailed.

The NES tutorial continued, outlining:

- The development of the then world wide web in CERN.
- The browser and bandwidth battles.
- The stringent Netcontrol legislation becoming a part of most countries' constitutions.
- The commercial buyout of 86% of the Internet's backbones by one large corporation.
- The successful amalgamation of 93% of the world's service providers into two trans-nationals.
- The failure of a world bank project to get high-performance connections to developing nations.

An elderly man with a well trimmed moustache and a carnation in his lapel appeared on the screen: "They'd only have stolen the terminals. And they're all fighting with each other. Anyway, they don't even have chalk, so what do they want with the Internet?".

The timeline continued into the realisation that tendering corporations could provide electronically the sort of Western education popular with tabloid journalism more cost-effectively than schools could provide teachers. And the further realisation that metered online education was a more generous model than top-sliced funding. It would teach the pupils to be careful with their research time – knowledge was money.

The pre-recorded interactivity was suddenly interrupted – apparently there was a bit of extra bandwidth allocated on Sportsco's Net, and the screen flickered through the usual pre-connection advertisement. The commercial concluded, and it became clear that the children in Arizona had made contact! They waved. The American teacher was busy fixing a printer connected to an old Windows2000 terminal with only 256meg of RAM.

The children began talking, aware that the Netcams were monitoring their speech and actions and that each minute, even after sponsorship, was metered. The strong morning Arizona sunshine added freshness to the Amercian opinions and a grey British afternoon. They talked happily for the few (literally) precious moments, sharing opinions about the freedom they now enjoyed. When a class maverick in England quoted extracts from the year-2001 change to the United State Constitution's 1st Amendment, where freedom of speech was defined and delimited very clearly indeed, his slate informed him that because of his actions, the school was now being charged double-time for a non-relevant political discussion. This irresponsible side-track would, of course, be reported to Centronet.

To compound this, an automatic cyberagent popped onto the wallscreen, and smilingly suggested that this would be an opportune moment to discuss Bill Gates' altruistic 1996 assistance in helping to connect US public libraries to the Internet. The same class maverick reminded the assembled group that the libraries in both the US and the remaining few in Britain had been sold off little more than two years later to the largest information supplier in the world, which had turned them into "information clubs" where, for a nominal fee, you could find all manner of facts. Once they had been squeezed of all the positive press publicity they could muster, info clubs in the more deprived areas of New York had little financial incentive to remain open.

Before further discussions could be had, each pupil's slate reminded them of the metered cost of the discussion to their school. "Time is money. Discussion is Dollars. Parlance is Pound". A little cockney mascot popped into view with grating amiability: "It's good to talk!". The screen faded into the terminating advert and a mini-documentary by BBC plc about otters.

Internet Service Providers

An explanation of the sorts of Internet connections generally available today, with a fairly comprehensive list of UK Internet Service Providers.

Appendix 1

Internet service providers are beginning to pop up all over the UK.They offer different levels of service to different markets. These are the different kinds of Internet access routes you will encounter.

Free bulletin board

Yes, it is possible to gain a modicum of Internet access absolutely free. Electronic bulletin boards, which you dial up with your modem, have been around for quite a time. Many of them are now getting some kind of Internet connection. In effect, this means that, once you have registered with your local bulletin board, you will be allowed to receive Internet Email through its interface, as well as browse a selection of newsgroups and so forth. Of course, you won't be able to browse the web in any particularly useful fashion, because bulletin boards usually only allow for simple text and, at the most, very simple graphics. Nevertheless, if you have a good quality local enthusiasts' BBS service, it can be a useful way of obtaining a free Email address for making your first Internet contacts.

Information provider

Before the Internet became popular outside the military and for high-end research, computer telecommunications was divided between the free hobbyist bulletin board services and commercial information providers, to whom you dialled up and obtained share quotes, the latest news and so forth. The charges were high and metered. CompuServe is one of the veterans.

Of course, such service could not remain competitive in the world of the Internet. To keep their market shares, the information providers have provided connection through their service to the Internet, with America Online now available in the United Kingdom, with augmented European content. Nevertheless, these services can be pricey, slow to connect with the Internet, and overly paternalistic in their policing regimes. Nevertheless, some are working hard to integrate their content with the web, in many cases aiming to remove the propriatorial software interface to the service all together. Even so, with the quality unmetered access that dedicated Internet Service Providers now offer, the pay-per-hour information providers are going to have to go much further in adapting or dying.

Shell account

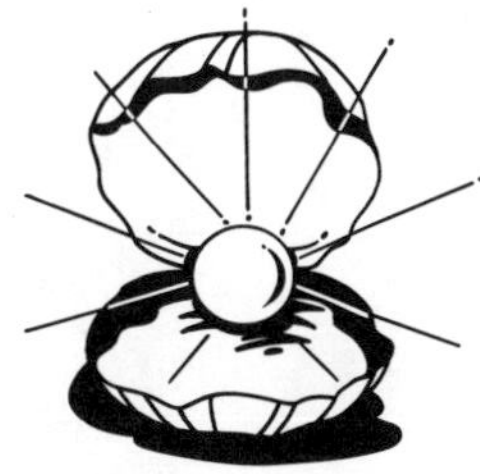

Sometimes, you might access the Internet by dialling up to a server machine and connecting as a user to its operating system - usually Unix. You type commands at the command-line "shell", as it is called. You issue these commands one at a time, running text-line based Internet mail packages and the like. Not the friendliest way of accessing the Internet, but beloved of university computer science departments and users of very old text-terminals with no hope of accessing anything much more sophisticated. The FTP command line (illustrated in the FTP chapter) is an example of something you might do with a shell account. Some commercial ISPs will provide shell accounts for specific tasks.

Dialup account

The most popular and cost-effective way to access the Internet is through a modem connected to an Internet Service Provider. Your computer, when online, will be assigned an Internet address, and will actually become a part of the "Greater Internet", and have full access to all Internet services, including the web.

To connect, your computer needs to have a *TCP/IP stack* installed. That is, it must have the software installed to allow your computer to "speak" the language of the Internet. Programs then communicate with the Internet through the TCP/IP stack. If you're connecting to the Internet over a modem, you have a few more acronyms to worry about - *PPP* or *SLIP*. PPP stands for point-to-point protocol. SLIP stands for Serial Line Input Protocol. Both are very similar (PPP is better in several ways, and has now supplanted SLIP with most ISPs). Simply, it is PPP (or SLIP) which packages up your data and makes sure it goes through your modem down the telephone line properly. That is why the dialup account is often called a PPP account. There are free TCP/IP stacks and PPP diallers available for most systems. They are built into Windows95, WindowsNT and the Macintosh as standard.

ISDN

Faster than a modem, and very quick to establish a connection to your ISP, ISDN (Integrated Services Digital Network) is a way of connecting to the Internet which quite a few schools are now looking into. The telephone copper-cables have mostly been updated in the past decade, and most exchanges are now computerised. ISDN is a technology which allows digital (computer) information to be sent down the telephone line, but without first needing to convert it into sound via a modem. The advantages of this are, of course, speed. Since the data is digital, it's almost as though you're plugged into the back of your ISP's server with a very long piece of cable (which happens to be the phone-line). Speeds are only four to eight times the speed of modems, though, because ISDN traffic has to share the cable with normal analogue phone-calls. ISDN comes in "channels", each of which allows 64,000 bits per second. A common combination is connecting with two channels at once, which allows 128,000 bits per second. The fastest modems currently connect at 33,600 bits per second.

You connect to an ISDN line with either a terminal adapter or a router. The terminal adapter is a small box or board which regulates the flow of ISDN information into your computer and establishes a connection. This is used if you want just one computer connected to an ISDN line at a time. A router is more expensive, but allows you to connect all the computers on your school's local network to the ISDN line at once. ISDN is speedy enough to cope with more than one Internet user accessing it at once, although, of course, too many users at once will cause the whole system to slow down.

Some ISPs allow ISDN dialback. This allows you to connect your own web servers and the like to the Internet - when someone on the Internet tries to access it, your ISP's server tells your router to dial up, and the ISP routes the request to your server, which deals with it appropriately. It then hangs up the line. Even at local call rates, a popular web server could produce high phone-bills!

The benefits of ISDN are obvious - a useful, quickish stopgap technology. Unfortunately, ISDN routers remain expensive (close to £1000) and the quarterly rental from the phone company is higher than for the normal phone line. Also, although call-charges remain the same as with normal local phone calls, the metered tariff still means unlimited web browsing is not a possibility for a cost conscious school.

Cable modem

Cable television companies around the world are beginning to realise that they can use their cables to connect people to the Internet. Although still very experimental, some cable companies are running tests in the UK with this technology, which, in theory, allows very quick Internet access - hundreds of times as fast as with modem or ISDN (although this is in the direction from the Internet Service Provider to the user - the return trip is much slower, as cable technology was only really envisaged for one-way broadcast traffic). It remains to be seen whether this theoretical speed can be maintained in a real-world environment, though. If they can, there will be few schools who do not access the Internet through a cable-modem by the turn of the century.

Leased line

Currently the pinnacle of Internet connection, the leased line is a direct, dedicated connection to the Internet. Few can afford one, but if the sky's the limit for money, so it is for speeds and capacities. Medium-speed leased lines can be obtained for several thousand pounds a year. High speed trunk lines (as used by popular Internet Service Providers themselves) can cost millions per year. If you have a leased line, you can put your own web and Email servers on the Internet, available for access throughout the world. Also, there are no call-charges (of course). Some people will only be satisfied when a free, almost unlimited capacity fibre-optic leased line is available from a plug-socket in every classroom. This science fiction proposal will, no doubt, turn into reality within a decade or two.

The ISP list

The following list of British Internet Service Providers is based on one available at http://www.limitless.co.uk/inetuk/ by Paola Kathuria, of ArcGlade Services Ltd (`paola@arcglade.co.uk`).

It has been edited for this book, and is relatively accurate for late 1996. Inevitably, though, the industry is changing very rapidly, and the list represents only some of the many companies coming into and going out of existence every month.

Explanation of a typical listing:

NetKonect Communcations Ltd ←	*Company name*
Tel 01420 542777 Fax 01420 542878 Email info@netkonect.net ←	*Contact details*
`http://www.netkonect.net/` ←	*Web site*
100% local ←	*Local-call access scope*
From £10 monthly ←	*Costs (excluding VAT)*
24 hour technical support ←	*Extra information*

AAP Internet
Tel 0181 427 1166 Fax 0181 427 1177
Email sales@aapi.co.uk
http://www.aapi.co.uk/
85% local
From £10 set-up, £8.51 monthly
Professional reputation.

Abbotsbury Software Ltd
Tel 01305 871543 Fax 01305 871688 Email sales@wdi.co.uk
http://www.wdi.co.uk/
Dorchester
From £12.50 monthly (paid annually)
On-site installation and support.

Abling.co.uk Ltd
Tel 01823 353771 Fax 01823 353772
Email info@abling.co.uk
http://www.abling.co.uk
Taunton only
£10 setup, £9.95 monthly.

ACE Ltd
Tel 01670 528204 Fax 01670 528211
Email info@ace.co.uk
http://www.ace.co.uk/
100% local
From £25 setup, £120 annual

Airtime Internet Services
Tel 01254 676921 Fax 01254 581574
Email sales@airtime.co.uk
http://www.airtime.co.uk/
Major cities
From £10 setup, £10 monthly

Aladdin
Tel 01489 782221 Fax 01489 782382
Email info@aladdin.co.uk
http://www.aladdin.co.uk/
50% local
From £20 setup, £10 monthly
Videotron Cable phone users in London get unmetered phone connection off peak.

Almac
Tel 01324 666336 Fax 01324 665155 Email info@almac.co.uk
`http://www.almac.co.uk/`
100% local
From £25 setup, £13.60 monthly
Combined BBS/Internet access.

Anglianet Ltd
Tel 01473 211922 Email tony@anglianet.co.uk
`http://www.anglianet.co.uk`
Ipswich
From £10 monthly
Local resource centre for advice. Shell accounts available too.

AOL
Tel 0800 279 1234 Email queryuk@aol.com
`http://www.aol.com/`
100% local
Metered charging, but some free offers for schools
Popular, but insidious, online service. Antithetical to the Internet?

Aspen Internet
Tel 01672 511388 Fax 01672 511290 Email admin@aspen-internet.net
`http://www.aspen-internet.net/`
Blackpool, Swansea, Swindon
Good modem/user ratio

Atlas Internet
Tel 0171 312 0400 Fax 0171 580 9510 Email mail@atlas.co.uk
`http://athena.atlas.co.uk/`
London
From £25 setup, £120 annually

Avel PiP
Tel 01872 262236 Fax 01872 262246 Email info@avel.net
`http://www.avel.com/`
Bidiford, Plymouth, St Austell, Truro
From £20 setup, £150 annually

Bournemouth Internet

Tel 01202 292900 Fax 01202 292700
Email sales@bournemouth-net.co.uk
http://www.bournemouth-net.co.uk/
Bournemouth
From £25 setup, £15 monthly

Brunel Internet

Tel 01922 59890 Fax 01922 51829 Email sales@brunel.co.uk
http://www.brunel.co.uk/
Aldridge
From £12.50 setup, £12.50 monthly

BT Internet

Tel 0800 800 001
http://www.bt.com/
100% local
From £17.03 setup, £12.77 monthly

Cable Internet

Tel 0500 336036 Email info@cablient.co.uk
http://www.cableinet.co.uk/
Most large cities
From £20.00 setup, £8.49 for TeleWest Cable customers, £10.99 for others
Fast CableModem access from late 1997.

CampusWorld

Tel 0345 626253 Email helpline.services@campus.bt.com
http://www.campus.bt.com/
100% local
From £15 monthly
Education "walled garden"

Cerbernet

Tel 0171 360 8010 Fax 0171 497 0679
Email sales@styx.cerbernet.co.uk
http://www.cerbernet.co.uk/
London
From £25 setup, £12 monthly

Cityscape
Tel 01223 566950 Fax 01223 566951 Email sales@cityscape.co.uk
http://www.cityscape.co.uk/
100% local
From £50 setup, £15 monthly

CIX
Tel 0181 296 9666 Fax 0181 296 9667 Email sales@compulink.co.uk
http://www.compulink.co.uk/
London
£25 registration then 4p/min off-peak, 6p/min peak
Very old text-based conference system, with new Internet capabilities.
Metered charging makes it a costly option.

Claranet Ltd
Tel 0181 962 1000 Email info@clara.net
http://www.clara.net/
Most large cities
From £9.99 per month - no setup fee.

CompuServe
Tel 0800 289378 Email 70006.101@compuserve.com
http://www.compuserve.com/
Major cities
$9.95 monthly for 5 hours and $2.95 per hour after that (international service, so calculated in dollars).
Old information provider tries to adapt to the Internet. Very slow and expensive. Not recommended.

Cygnet Internet Services Ltd
Tel 0181 880 4650 Fax 0181 880 4651
Email info@cygnet.co.uk
http://www.cygnet.co.uk/
London
From £15 setup, £10 monthly

Dean Software

Tel 01878 311044 Fax 01978 263014 Email info@deansoft.com
`http://www.deansoft.com/`
Chester, Corwen, Liverpool, Mold, Welshpool, Wrexham
From £25 setup, £10 monthly

Delphi Internet

Tel 0171 757 7080 Fax 0171 757 7160
Email ukservice@delphi.com
`http://www.delphi.co.uk/`
London. Outside more expensive.
From £10 monthly for 4 hours and £4 per hour after that.
Another outdated and expensive Murdoch-owned option.

Demon Internet

Tel 0181 371 1234 Fax 0181 371 1150 Email sales@demon.net
`http://www.demon.co.uk/`
100% local
From £12.50 setup, £10 monthly
Very big service provider. Can connect with ISDN for no extra cost.

Direct Connection

Tel 0181 297 2200 Fax 0181 297 0399
Email sales@dircon.co.uk
`http://www.dircon.co.uk/`
Most large cities
From £7.50 setup, £10 monthly
Shell accounts available. Free calls off-peak to Videotron Cable-Phone
subscribers in London.

Dungeon Network Systems

Tel 01638 711550 Fax 01638 718623 Email info@dungeon.com
`http://www.dungeon.com/`
Ipswich, Mildenhall
From £10 monthly - no setup fee

Easynet
Tel 0171 681 4321 Fax 0171 209 0891 Email admin@easynet.net
http://www.easynet.co.uk/
100% local
From £25 setup, £9.90 monthly
Unlimited amount of free webspace to each subscriber

Eclipse Networking
Tel 01392 424440 Fax 01392 491036
Email eclipse@eclipse.co.uk
http://www.eclipse.co.uk/
Exeter, Devon
From £15.00 setup, £8 monthly

EdNet
Tel 0131 466 7003 Fax 0131 466 7004 Email info@ednet.co.uk
http://www.ednet.co.uk/
Edinburgh
From £10 monthly - no setup fee

ElectricMail Ltd
Tel 01223 501333 Fax 01223 501444 Email info@elmail.co.uk
http://www.elmail.co.uk/
Major cities
From £95 quarterly
Specialises in professional network integration between your LAN and the Internet

Enterprise PLC
Tel 01624 677666 Fax 01624 613660 Email sales@enterprise.net
http://www.enterprise.net/
100% local
From £20 setup, £8 monthly

Epinet Data Networks
Tel 01242 821000 Fax 01242 821122 Email info@epinet.co.uk
http://www.epinet.co.uk/
Cheltenham
£99 per annum - no setup fee

EUNet GB

Tel 01227 266466 Fax 01227 266477 Email sales@Britain.EU.net
`http://www.britain.eu.net/`
Major cities
From £95 quarterly
Very expensive professional provider

ExNet

Tel 0181 244 0077 Fax 0181 244 0078 Email info@exnet.com
`http://www.exnet.com/`
London
From £10 monthly
Shell accounts and so forth, rather than full PPP

FastNet

Tel 01273 675314 Fax 01273 621631 Email sales@fastnet.co.uk
`http://www.fastnet.co.uk/`
Brighton
From £10 monthly

Foobar Internet

Tel 0116 2330033 Fax 0116 2330035
Email sales@foobar.co.uk
`http://www.foobar.co.uk/`
Leicester
From £12.50 setup, £10 monthly

Foremost Training

Tel 0141 248 6377
Email donald@scotnet.co.uk
Aberdeen, Glasgow
From £75 quarterly

Frontier Internet

Tel 0171 242 3383 Fax 0171 242 3384
Email info@ftech.co.uk
`http://www.ftech.net/`
95% local
From £25 setup, £10 monthly

Garden CityNet

Tel 01462 485624 Fax 01462 485224
Email colinb@gardencitynet.co.uk
http://www.gardencitynet.co.uk/
Hitchin, Letchworth, Luton, Royston, Stevenage,
Welwyn Garden City
From £35 setup, £15 monthly
Setup includes personal installation and tuition

Genesis Project Ltd

Tel 01232 560552 Fax 01232 560553
Email sales@gpl.com
http://www.gpl.net/
Belfast, Londonderry
From £12.50 setup, £10 monthly
Includes four POP3 mailboxes and options to restrict certain newsgroups

Gifford Internet Services

Tel 0117 939 7722 Email admin@gifford.co.uk
http://www.gifford.co.uk/
Bristol
From £8.50 monthly
Includes three POP3 mailboxes

Global Internet Ltd

Tel 0181 957 1005 Fax 0181 957 1100
Email info@globalnet.co.uk
http://www.globalnet.co.uk/
Most major cities
From £10 setup, £9.99

GMTnet Ltd

Tel 01509 269999 Fax 01509 218344 Email sales@gmtnet.co.uk
http://www.gmtnet.co.uk/
Derby, Leicester, London, Loughborough, Maidenhead,
Nottingham, Slough
From £25 setup, £30 quarterly

GreenNet

Tel 0171 713 1941 Fax 0171 833 1169 Email support@gn.apc.org
http://www.gn.apc.org/
London
From £15 setup, £20 monthly
Also has metered options. Part of an educational environmental organisation.

Griffin Internet

Tel 01332 60 61 60 Fax 01332 370 220 Email info@griffin.co.uk
http://www.griffin.co.uk/
Derby
From £17 setup, £12.50 monthly

Hiway

Tel 01635 550660 Fax 01635 521268
Email info@inform.hiway.co.uk
http://www.hiway.co.uk/
100% local
From £15 setup, £15 monthly

I-Way Limited

Tel 01734 580058 Fax 01734 512345 Email info@i-way.co.uk
http://www.i-way.co.uk/
Oxford, Reading
From £10 monthly

Internet Access Ltd

Tel 01536 414424 Fax 01536 411588 Email mailus@intac.co.uk
http://www.intac.co.uk/
Kettering
From £20 setup, £120 per annum

Internet Discovery

Tel 0181 694 2240 Fax 0181 694 8926 Email admin@idiscover.co.uk
http://www.idiscover.co.uk/
100% local
From £5 setup, £10 monthly (including VAT)

KENTnet Internet Services

Tel 01580 890089 Fax 01580 8935678 Email info@kentnet.co.uk
http://www.kentnet.co.uk/
Ashford, Hastings, Heathfield, Maidstone, Rye, Staplehurst, Tunbridge Wells
From £25 setup, £15 monthly (including VAT)

Manx Computer Bureau (MANNET)

Tel 01624 623841 Fax 01624 623004 Email postmaster@mcb.net
http://www.mcb.net/mannet/brochure.html
Douglas, Isle of Man
From £20 setup, £33 quarterly

MBC Internet Services Ltd

Tel 01902 651111 Fax 01902 651177 Email info@mbcis.co.uk
http://www.mbcis.co.uk/
Birmingham, Wolverhampton
From £12 monthly

MegaNet Internet Services Ltd

Tel 01483 31119 Fax 01483 31101 Email info@meganet.co.uk
http://www.meganet.co.uk/
Guildford
From £20 setup, £12.50 monthly

Mistral Internet

Email info@mistral.co.uk
http://www.mistral.co.uk/
Brighton, London
£9.90 monthly
Supports Amiga too

MKBBS

Tel 01908 604649 Email sysop@mkbbs.co.uk
Milton Keynes
£15 annually
BBS Internet access

NetDirect Internet
Tel 0171 732 3000 Fax 0171 732 2000
Email info@ndirect.co.uk
http://www.ndirect.co.uk/
London
From £9.99 setup, £9.99 monthly

Netforce Group plc
Tel 01245 257788 Fax 01245 257799
Email sales@netforce.net
http://www.netforce.net/
Most cities
From £150 annually

NetKonect Communications Ltd
Tel 01420 542777 Fax 01420 542878
Email info@netkonect.net
http://www.netkonect.net/
100% local
From £10 monthly
24 hour technical support

NewNet Ltd
Tel 01705 647400 Fax 01705 647111
Email sales@newnet.co.uk
http://www.newnet.co.uk/
98% local
From £12.50 monthly

Nildram On-Line
Tel 01442 891331 Fax 01442 890303 Email info@nildram.co.uk
http://www.nildram.co.uk/
Hemel Hempstead, London
From £30 quarterly

On-line
Tel 0181 558 6114 Fax 0181 558 3914
Email sysop@on-line.co.uk
http://www.on-line.co.uk/
London
From £9.99 monthly

Onyx Internet
Fax 01642 210 201 Email sales@onyxnet.co.uk
`http://www.onyxnet.co.uk/`
Barnard Castle, Belfast, Teesside, Tyneside
From £25 startup, £10 monthly

Paradise Internet Network Services
Tel 01256 414863 Fax 01256 462277 Email sales@pins.co.uk
`http://www.pins.co.uk/`
Basingstoke
From £15 setup, £8 monthly

Paston Chase
Tel 01603 502061 Fax 01603 502072 Email info@paston.co.uk
`http://www.paston.co.uk/`
Norwich
From £15 startup, £36 quarterly

PC User Group (CONNECT)
Tel 0181 863 1191 Fax 0181 863 6095
Email info@ibmpcug.co.uk
`http://www.ibmpcug.co.uk/`
London
From £7.50 monthly
BBS access

Pipex Dial
Tel 0500 474739 Fax 01223 250101 Email sales@pipex.net
`http://www.dial.pipex.com/`
100% local
From £19.99 setup, £15 monthly
Very large ISP

Poptel
Tel 0171 249 2948 Fax 0171 254 1102
Email info@geo2.poptel.org.uk
`http://www.poptel.org.uk/`
Dewsbury, London, Manchester
From £25 setup, £10 monthly

Reading Digital
Tel 01734 615379 Email sysop@Readdigit.win-uk.net
Reading
Free for Email account and facilities
BBS connection

RedNet
Tel 01494 513333,Fax 01494 443374 Email info@rednet.co.uk
`http://www.rednet.co.uk/`
Most cities
From £25 setup, £15 monthly

RM Internet for Learning
Tel 01235 826868 Fax 01235 826999 Email sales@rmplc.co.uk
`http://www.rmplc.co.uk/`
Most cities
From £25 startup, £150 annually
The first, and largest, educational Internet service

Sonnet Internet
Tel 0181 664 6000 Fax 0181 677 5757
Email enquire@sonnet.co.uk
`http://www.sonnet.co.uk/`
London
From £25 startup, £12.50 monthly

Spuddy's Xanadu
Email sweh@spuddy.mew.co.uk
Canvey Island
Completely Free
BBS-type enthusiasts' system offering 100% free and friendly Email, Usenet and more

Taynet
Tel 01382 561296 Fax 01382 561444 Email admin@taynet.co.uk
`http://www.taynet.co.uk/`
Dundee
From £20 setup, £12.75 monthly

Technocom plc
Tel 01753 730400 Fax 01753 730444
Email sales@technocom.co.uk
http://www.technocom.co.uk/
London, Maidenhead, Slough
From £5 monthly

Thames Global Internet Services
Tel 01344 641627 Fax 01344 412124 Email info@tgis.co.uk
http://www.tgis.co.uk/
Bracknell
From £8.50 monthly

The Internet in Nottingham
Tel 0115 956 2222 Fax 0115 956 1127 Email info@innotts.co.uk
http://www.innotts.co.uk/
Nottingham
From £15 setup, £12.50 monthly

Total Connectivity Providers
Tel 01703 393392 Fax 01703 366364 Email sales@tcp.co.uk
http://www.tcp.co.uk/
Most major cities
From £7 setup, £12 monthly

Tweednet
Email mike@scotborders.co.uk
http://calligrafix.co.uk/
Scottish borders
From £25 setup, £180 annually

U-NET Limited
Tel 01925 633144 Fax 01925 633847 Email hi@u-net.com
http://www.u-net.net/
100% local
From £12 setup, £12 monthly

UK Online Ltd
Tel 01749 333333 Fax 01749 333310 Email sales@ukonline.co.uk
http://www.ukonline.co.uk/
100% local
From £14.99 monthly (for unlimited hours and webspace)
Provides UK content

Voss Net plc
Tel 01753 737800 Fax 01753 737850 Email staff@vossnet.co.uk
http://www.vossnet.co.uk/
London, Slough
From £11.75 monthly

Wave Rider Internet
Tel 01564 795888 Fax 01564 795177 Email info@waverider.co.uk
http://www.waverider.co.uk/
From £18 startup, £10 monthly

WildNET Ltd
Tel 01604 36560 Fax 01604 36561 Email stuartj@wildnet.co.uk
http://www.wildnet.co.uk/
Bristol, Hereford, Milton Keynes, Northampton
£10 monthly

WinNET Communications Ltd
Tel 0181 863 1191 Fax 0181 863 6095 Email help@win-uk.net
http://www.ibmpcug.co.uk/
Most major cities
From £15 monthly
Special connect software

Wintermute Ltd
Tel 01224 595111 Fax 01224 595333 Email alex@wintermute.co.uk
http://www.wintermute.co.uk/
Aberdeen
£20 monthly

WiSS

Tel 01248 602405 Fax 01248 602405 Email enquiries@wiss.co.uk
`http://wiss.co.uk/`
Aberystwyth, Bangor, Chwilog, Dolgellau
From £20 setup, £11.75 monthly

ZetNet Services Ltd

Tel 01595 696667 Fax 01595 696548 Email info@zetnet.co.uk
`http://www.zetnet.co.uk/zetnet/`
100% local
From £25 setup, £6 monthly

Zynet

Tel 01392 209500 Fax 01392 421762 Email zynet@zynet.net
`http://www.zynet.co.uk/`
80% local
From £20 setup, £20 quarterly
Educational focus

Reviewed Web Sites

An eclectic selection of sites collected by Alan Wheatley of the University of Wales, Aberystwyth especially for this book.

Not exhaustive - no collection of web sites ever can be, but a stimulating and useful assemblage of starting points.

Appendix 2

Art and art history

ANU Art History Exhibit

An exhibit of art history materials collected and put online by Michael Greenhalgh of Australian National University. This site has thousands of images, with particular emphasis on the history of the print, and on the clasical architecture and sculpture of the eastern Mediterranean area

http://www.ncsa.uiuc.edu/SDG/Experimental/anu-art-history/home.html

Library of Congress Vatican Exhibit

An exhibit of materials from the Vatican Library. The scope includes Vatican history, the history of medicine, maths, humanities, etc

http://sunsite.unc.edu/expo/vatican.exhibit/Vatican.exhibit.html

The Getty Information Institute

Connections to the Institute's own resources and to databases for art and art history at other institutions. Gives access to images, information on artists, imaging techniques, bibliographies, provenance material, etc

http://www.gii.getty.edu/

Web Museum: Bienvenue!

Famous paintings, medieval art, Paris tour, about 130 artists' work, and biographies. Volunteers provide material for these non-official pages. Started by Nicilas Pioch to put more art on the web. Has lots of mirror sites for faster international response times

http://sunsite.doc.ic.ac.uk/wm/

World Wide Arts Resources

From the Metropolitan Museum of Art, a very comprehensive listing of arts information on the Internet; they say there are links to 100,000 pages here. Browse their headings or use the search engine

http://www.wwar.com/

Astronomy

Hubble Space Telescope Image Gallery

A collection of astonishing images from the Hubble orbiting telescope. Unlike many commercial sites, there are no fees for using this site. Whatever your interests, these images make it a "must see" site

http://quest.arc.nasa.gov/hst/photos-iii.html

Liftoff to Space Exploration

News of NASA's operations and plans, background, research announcements, lots of images, Kid's Space (quiz and pages for children's contributions), and virtual reality models

http://liftoff.msfc.nasa.gov/

The Nine Planets

A multimedia tour of the planets and moons of our Solar System, and comprehensive links to related sites. Very usefully, Nine Planets is also mirrored at several other sites for faster access; yes, it's good enough to warrant that

http://seds.lpl.arizona.edu/nineplanets/nineplanets/

The Planetary Society

Scientists Carl Sagan and Bruce Murray have founded a society to promote the exploration of the planets and the search for extraterrestrial life

http://www.transatlantech.com/tps/

Biology and botany

Biology Sites on the WWW

Pages and pages and pages of web and gopher sites for biology. Not all are US, and not all are schools level

http://www.usgs.gov/network/science/biology/index.html

Frog Dissection

An online dissection manual, with clear and progressive instructions, lots of high quality images of dissections to download. For the next dissection, log-on and save a frog. This site well deserves its excellent reputation and multiple awards for the quality of its content
http://curry.edschool.virginia.EDU/go/frog/home.html

Life Over Time

A museum's site for younger children to create dinosaur art and gain understanding through pleasure. Teachers notes are provided
http://rs6000.bvis.uic.edu:80/museum/exhibits/Exhibits.html

Victorian Dinosaurs on the Internet

These dinosaurs are from the Australian state of Victoria, not the Victorian era. The site is rich in dinosaur images and information from Victoria, and it has details of dinosaurs from elsewhere, but its failing is that it's not linked to other dinosaur sites
http://www.mov.vic.gov.au/dinoExhibit/intro.html

Visible Human

After execution, a Texas murderer, was cut into four-millimetre slices and scanned to generate 1,870 high resolution images (42Gb in total) that can be downloaded for the ultimate human anatomy study. Sample files for quick viewing give an idea of the images' potential. There are visible light images and also images produced by computer tomography and NMR scanning. A female body has been processed too. Agreement is required for downloading
http://www.nlm.nih.gov/research/visible/visible_human.html

Business studies

Business Cycle Indicators

Graphical presentations of data for 256 business cycle indicators, organised into 16 categories such as production, labour, prices, personal income, exports, imports, etc. The data cover the period 1948 to date
http://www.cris.com:80/~netlink/bci/bci.html

Business Pages

Concerned with many aspects of using the Web in a business context: covers example sites, business studies, statistics, analyses, etc

`http://www.owi.com/netvalue/`

Economics and Business Education

Interesting and useful economics and business education WWW sites for teachers and lecturers, and more

`http://savage.ecn.bris.ac.uk/ebea/`

Education Resources in Finance

Pages of links to courses, online texts, online calculators, clip art, videos, etc. [Note that the URL file extension is ".htm" not ".html"]

`http://www.cob.ohio-state.edu:80/dept/fin/educ.htm`

Financial Times

World and financial news, from a business perspective

`http://www.ft.com/`

UK Business Directory

Basic information about more than 26,000 UK and European organisations

`http://www.milfac.co.uk/milfac/`

Campaign groups

Amnesty International

Amnesty and its functions. Individual cases of human rights abuse are highlighted by Amnesty each month. Includes templates of letters in support of Amnesty's campaigns. Links from this main US Amnesty site reach to local Amnesty groups in countries around the world

`http://www.amnesty.org/`

Friends of the Earth

Has what is expected at FOE's site, including recent campaigns. There is a pollution map to be constructed for your area, if the data has been placed online. This is an award winning environmental site

`http://www.foe.co.uk/`

Greenpeace

Use this site to keep up to date with Greenpeace campaigns, and to see some of the information that underlies their views. More than just a rather nice campaign site, this one is conspicuously well organised in the Greenpeace manner, and it has won multiple awards

http://www.greenpeace.org/

Chemistry

ChemEd: Chemistry Education Resources

A sensible mix of safety, databases, software, history of chemistry, organisations, and chemical images

http://www-hpcc.astro.washington.edu/scied/chemistry.html

Chemistry Page

About 150 links to chemistry sites, organisations, publications, etc

http://www.chem.ucla.edu/chempointers.html

Internet Chemistry Resources List

Lists of fee and free information on teaching materials, catalogues, software, organisations, etc

http://www.rpi.edu:80/dept/chem/cheminfo/chemres.html

Web Elements

The periodic table online. Data is presented in categories such as physical, nuclear, electrical, biological, geological, crystallographic, etc

http://www2.shef.ac.uk:80/chemistry/web-elements/biol/periodic-table.html

Classics

Ancient City of Athens

Images and text for a virtual tour of the current remains of ancient Athens. An award winning site
http://www.indiana.edu:80/~kglowack/Athens/Athens.html

ROMARCH: Roman Art and Archaeology

Links to Internet resources indexed by province. Materials include information on excavations, bibliographies, images, news, etc
http://www-personal.umich.edu/~pfoss/ROMARC.html

The Internet Classics Archive

About 400 Greek and Roman texts and English translations, accessible by author, title, translator, and date
http://the-tech.mit.edu/Classics/index.html

Computing and electronics

Byte

Online access to the full text of one of the oldest magazines for "small" computers. Information is accessed by browsing categories or via a search engine. The text is published here about three months after the printed edition
http://www.byte.com/

E-Town: the Home Electronics Guide

Competent reviews of products, specifications, and locations for electronic stuff. Frequently updated. Good section with news of the DVD discs that will be replacing CD-ROMs in coming years
http://www.e-town.com/

RealAudio

Descriptions of the technology which delivers continuous sound of near-CD quality, from the company which invented it. There are also free files to download, and a list of sampler sites where RealAudio resources are offered
http://www.realaudio/com/

The Computer Museum

Historical exhibits, classes, careers, interactivities, and demonstrations of new technologies such as RealAudio and Virtual Reality modelling (these may require new software to be downloaded to your machine)
http://www.tcm.org/

Earth sciences

Earth Science Internet Sites

Sources of lesson plans, images, virtual museums, raw data, etc. etc.
http://www.ems.psu.edu/RelatedWebSites.html

Reducing Earthquake Hazards

A site from the US Geological Survey, with real depth of coverage. It has news of recent earthquakes, historical studies, ground movement maps, prediction data, details of current research projects, etc
http://quake.wr.usgs.gov/

US Geological Survey

Fact sheets, short reports, write-away-for-it addresses. Naturally there are maps, but landscape usage and environmental management materials expand the site's scope very usefully
http://info.er.usgs.gov/

VolcanoWorld

VolcanoWorld is funded by NASA and includes "Kid's Door," an 'Ask the Volcanologist' section, lesson plans, updates on current eruptions and more. An award winner
http://volcano.und.nodak.edu/

Environment

Environmental Education Network

Internet K-12 environmental education resources for teachers: birds, wolves, air quality, oceans, global warming, recycling, software, etc., and the Environmental Education Forum for exchanging views
http://envirolink.org/enviroed/envirok12.html

Environmental and Earth Science Resources

Multimedia resources that support instruction in Earth System Science; created and used for Pennsylvania State University's introductory earth science courses. Many of the items here, such as word processor files, are intended to be downloaded and are not suitable for immediate use
http://www.gis.psu.edu/Earth2/Earth2HTML/E2GenDescrip.html

Geography Resources

Images and maps are the strength of this site. Declassified intelligence images (satellite and air photos), also maps of world wide interest. Good remote sensing images and data, not just planet pretties
http://www.ems.psu.edu/geography.html

Sierra Club

One of the USA's oldest and most respected organisations concerned with conservation of natural areas. Environmental education, environmental politics, global warming, wetlands, wilderness, mountains, lots of images, resource lists, etc
http://www.sierraclub.org/

FTP sites

AskERIC (Educational Resources Info Center)

About 60 files and directories, making a large and varied collection of resources. Includes lesson plans, bibliographies, ERIC publications, etc. Most files are compressed
ftp://ericir.syr.edu/

CICA (Center for Innovative Computer Applications)

Three hundred megabytes of public domain and shareware utilities. Material here includes drivers, fonts, and applications for all versions of Windows 3, and also stuff for Word for Windows and Word Perfect. This is a very busy site, and access will be refused after the limit of fifty users are logged on
ftp://ftp.cica.indiana.edu/

Classroom Connect

About 50 directories and subdirectories of files. Material includes lesson plans, using the Internet, FAQ, stories, mailing lists, etc
ftp://ftp.wentworth.com/wentworth/Classroom-Connect/

EdRes (New Brunswick, Canada)

This URL gives access to the top directories of EdRes, and also to a range of materials concentrating on arts and educational resources, and some surprising further stuff on swimming and tourism. The EdRes database has reviews and resources catalogued under school subjects. Files can be FTPed, or the database can be searched by Email (archived documents desribe this)
ftp://jupiter.sun.csd.unb.ca/pub/faculty.ed/

Free University of Berlin

A vast collection of resources, carefully organised into directories and sub-directories and accessible through the medium of English. Material on physics, maths, German, games, maps, etc.
ftp://ftp.fu-berlin.de/

Geography

CIA World Information: World Factbook

Access to a vast amount of data about every place on earth (countries, oceans, regions, even the world itself). The information is organised by country

http://hoshi.cic.sfu.ca/cia/

The London Guide

General information about London: eating, drinking, travelling, listening, places, maps, images, etc

http://www.cs.ucl.ac.uk/misc/uk/london.html

The Virtual Tourist II

Clickable world, regional, and national maps which reveal tourist guides, pictures, write ups, etc. about each region and its countries. Material is contributed by volunteers, whose help is still needed

http://www.vtourist.com/vt/

Visit Egypt: Unofficial Egyptian Homepage

This site allows the viewer to take a tour of the different parts of Egypt

http://auc-amer.eun.eg/egypt.html

Gopher sites

CICNet (Committe on Institutional Co-operation)

Access to library catalogues, computer help files, a reference shelf, guides to Gopher and FTP resources, FAQs, telephone directories of US universities, etc

gopher://gopher.cic.net/

Disaster Information

A site maintained by "Volunteers in Technical Assistance," and offering information on emergencies of all kinds in all parts of the world. There are situation reports, appeals, information for volunteers, support services, etc

gopher://vita.org:70/

English Server

Amazingly wide ranging collection of materials on music, feminism, software, poetry, recipes, etc

gopher://english-server.hss.cmu.edu/

Internet Wiretap

An eclectic gopper site. There are e-journals, lists of organisations, newsgroup archive, US and foreign government documents, classic texts from Aesop, through the Bible and Quran, to Dickens and Sherlock Holmes, and an even more varied online library

gopher://wiretap.spies.com/

Marvel

This is the Library of Congress gopher, offering access to the library's catalogue and a seemingly bottomless pool of information resources. There are lists of Internet resources, Congressional information, bibliographies, a global electronic library, etc. and a tool for searching the titles of Marvel's documents

gopher://marvel.loc.gov/

History

American Memory

Historical documents, interpretations, and thousands of images from Library of Congress' collections of American history materials

http://lcweb2.loc.gov/

EuroDocs: Western

European Primary Historical Documents

Texts, images and translations of important documents from European history. Both geographical and chronological access is provided
http://library.byu.edu/~rdh/eurodocs/

Regia Anglorum

About 150 articles on Anglo-Saxon, Celtic, Viking, and Norman events, and life in early mediaeval Britain and northern Europe. The principal focus is on Anglo-Saxon Britain
http://www.ftech.net/~regia/

The History Net

An oddly balanced collection of materials with a very attractive approach. Presents articles on world history, history of some countries, personal accounts, letters, great events, travel, technology, etc. Visit this site for yourself, to see what is missing from the weaker approaches adopted by so many other sites
http://www.TheHistoryNet.com/

The World of the Vikings

Top scoring site, with information on runes, ships, museums, sagas, and it also has school and academic materials
http://www.demon.co.uk/past/vikings/

Internet and Web information

Internet Society

The frontage for a number of groups shaping the Internet. There is a wealth of information about the Internet here: history and technical documents, maps, statistics, etc
http://www.isoc.org/

InterNIC InfoGuide

A Web server run by the InterNIC (Internet Network Information Ceter), it's a good place to find general Internet information, lists of servers, directories, archives, etc

http://internic.net/

Virtual Tourist

Clickable world, regional, and national maps which reveal WWW and Internet information. Material is contributed by volunteers, whose help is still needed

http://www.vtourist.com/

Languages

CTI Centre for Modern Languages

The Computers in Teaching Initiative Centre for Modern Languages (CTICML). Links for languages, linguistics, newspapers, dictionaries, fonts for languages with special requirements, and world regions, etc

http://www.hull.ac.uk/cti/

French Pages (in French)

French language resources on the Web: the Virtual Baguette, software, the arts, etc,

http://web.cnam.fr/fr/Welcome.html

German Studies Trails on the Internet

A trail compiled by Andreas Lixl-Purcell (look closely at the URL). The trail leads to teaching tools, materials, and literature. It looks at many areas for the topics which act as vehicles for its studies, e.g. arts, science, business

http://www.uncg.edu/~lixlpurc/german.html

KidsCom

In English, Spanish, French, or German: an opportunities and information site for children of 4-15 years. Make electronic grafitti and pen pals, try some quizzes, etc.

http://www.kidscom.com/

Paris Pages

In French and English. Provides material and links to 7,000 pages and messages about Paris to add reality to learning French
`http://www.paris.org/`

Romance Languages Resource Page

Indexed in French, Italian, Portugese, Spanish, and English, this page provides links for all these languages, and for some less common ones too
`http://humanities.uchicago.edu/romance/`

Si, Spain

Resources for Spanish affairs, society, people, places, things, etc. to support the teaching of Spanish
`http://www.DocuWeb.ca/SiSpain/`

Tecla: Service of Spanish Language Texts

Texts in English and Spanish for teachers and learners of Spanish
`http://www.bbk.ac.uk/Departments/Spanish/TeclaHome.html`

Tennessee Bob's Famous French Links!

A no-nonsense site, without graphics or fancy presentation tricks. Instead you get about 200 links to sites concerned with France and the French language
`http://www.utm.edu/departments/french/french.html`

The Human Languages Page

A site to connect you to information about human languages including Spanish, Italian, French, Japanese, Estonian, Maori, Urdu, Tagalog, Croatian, Greek, Thai, Swedish, Hebrew, and Serbian. It continues to grow bigger and better, and now has over 1,000 resources
`http://www.willamette.edu/~tjones/Language-Page.html`

Lifestyles

duPont Registry

Heart aching cars, and most of them are big, bad, and expensive. Perhaps this is a sample of the commercial Internet sites to come

http://www.dupontregistry.com/

FiX

A London based fashion and lifestyle web magazine, covering clothes, hair, café culture, pollution, etc

http://www.widemedia.com/fix/

Madonna Pages

Guess who might be getting some more publicity out of this posting? This is a fan-produced, fanzine, not the oily politician-speak of so many official commercial sites

http://www.mit.edu:8001/people/jwb/Madonna.html

N-touch

A magazine produced by students of the London College of Fashion. This is fashion with attitude and London style

http://www.dircon.co.uk/lcf/ntouch.html

Postmodern Culture

Postmodern Culture is an edited journal distributed over the Internet

http://jefferson.village.virginia.edu/pmc/

Streetstyle

A photographic fashion magazine. Text is not important here, much of the content is readers' photos of their own fashion worlds

http://www.best.com/~street/

Vegies Unite

Covers food, environment, ethics, recipes, book reviews, and links to related sites

http://www.vegweb.com/

Literature

British Poetry, 1780-1910

A modest but well prepared electronic text collection of mainstream poems, from Virginia University
http://etext.lib.virginia.edu/britpo.html

Children's Literature Web Guide

David Brown's superior and multiple prize winning site for children's literature, includes links for publishers, story tellers, parents, reviews, best sellers, research, book award lists, the classics, etc., etc. Visit here soon, visit here often
http://www.ucalgary.ca/~dkbrown/

CMU English Server (WWW)

From the staff and students of Carnegie Mellon University. Multiple topics are covered here, but the material is probably of greatest value in the context of literature
http://english-server.hss.cmu.edu/

Electronic Poetry Center

Authors, sound files, the small press, poetics discussion, and poems from about 120 poets
http://wings.buffalo.edu/epc/

Oxford Text Archive

Wide range of electronic texts, mostly originating from academic projects and needs. Hundreds of authors, thousands of titles, and about fifteen languages
http://ota.ox.ac.uk/ota/

Project Gutenberg Index

An index of the 2,000 documents in the Project Guttenberg archive of machine readable texts. They include work by Aristole, Bunyan, Edgar Rice Burroughs, etc. (it's a very "etc" list of out-of-copyright materials contributed by volunteers who keyboard or scan materials for the archive)
http://www.w3.org/pub/DataSources/bySubject/Literature/Gutenberg/Overview.html

The Internet Poetry Archive

Online access to poetry texts (just three modern poets at the moment), with some images and sound
`http://sunsite.unc.edu/ipa/index.html`

Mass media

America's Public Broadcasting Service

Educational materials and projects, including some very imaginative and interactive ways of using the Internet's capabilities. The USA viewpoint is instructive
`http://www.pbs.org/`

Critical analysis of communications media

Good reading list for critical analysis of communications media and their impact on changing the way we think and live. Read and digest
`http://www.seas.upenn.edu/~mengwong/netsurf/`

Electronic Telegraph

The Daily Telegraph on the Web. Barely recognisable as a child of its staider paper parent. Very complete electronic edition, with most of the paper version's text
`http://www.telegraph.co.uk/`

Jr. Seahawk News: Student Newspaper

Student newspaper from Arbor Heights School, Washington state, U.S.A
`http://www.halcyon.com/arborhts/arborhts.html`

News: Daily European and International

A daily news page for Europe and International countries. Quick links page for online newspapers in Europe, Africa, Asia, Oceania, and north and south America
`http://www.cs.vu.nl/~gerben/news.html`

North Wales Newspapers

English and Welsh language material. News, sport, horoscopes, etc. in English from this north Wales and Chester publishing group, and "Y Cymro" in Welsh
`http://www.nwn.co.uk/`

Sony Movies

Sony controls a lot of Hollywood, and this is their site on the web. Movie news and previews, music, TV, consumer goodies, and games
http://www.sony.com/

Steve Opfer's Home Page

A rich set of links to news related sites. Links are helpfully organised into subject categories, such as "hot topics" for current headline matters and categories such as "sports" for continuing topics. The emphasis of the links is on American news resources. [Note the "htm" not "html" file extension in the URL.]
http://www.infi.net/~opfer/daily.htm

The Daily Record and Sunday Mail

Probably the best of the Scottish newspaper sites
http://www.record-mail.co.uk/rm/drsm/front1.html

The Guardian

Main news stories, excellent special analyses for some of the major news stories, and also includes *The Guardian Weekly* and each week's *Guardian Online* supplement
http://www.guardian.co.uk/

The Hindu

Daily edition of *The Hindu*, and archives of the discontinued (electronic) weekly edition. Sections for the front page, sports, stock exchange, etc. A prize winning site
http://www.webpage.com/hindu/

The Internet Movies Database

Information on films from all ages: FAQ, reviews, casting, Oscars, quotations, and a search engine to help you find all these things
http://uk.imdb.com/

The Times and Sunday Times

The Times newspapers, redesigned for the Web. Contains most of the information in the printed editions (gulp), and it has a search engine too
http://www.the-times.co.uk/

The Vocal Point: Boulder's First Electronic Student Newspaper

One of the first on-line newspapers produced entirely by K-12 students. Generally one topic per issue, and six issues per year. Granted an award by the children and teenagers "Thumbs up" scheme
http://bvsd.k12.co.us/cent/Newspaper/Newspaper.html

Universal Studios

Web site for MCA/Universal, the Hollywood movie giant. Has an online music magazine (beware of lengthy download times), previews of new movie releases (these can be well in advance of UK release dates) with video clips (again, be wary of lengthy downloads), gifts, Kid's Club, and shops. A very graphic site, it can be slow to load
http://www.mca.com/

Maths

MacTutor History of Mathematics Archive

Biographies, histories of mathematical problems, anniversaries, birthplace map, and links to other maths sites. This site has won several awards
http://www-groups.dcs.st-and.ac.uk:80/~history/

MegaMath Project

An excellent source for some challenging problems
http://www.c3.lanl.gov/mega-math/welcome.html

The Math Forum

A site funded by the National Science Foundation and dedicated to geometry and math education. Resources for students, teachers, and parents. Includes "Mathmagic" offering the K-12 problem solving project
http://www.forum.swarthmore.edu/

Multi-topic sites

AskERIC Virtual Library (US Educational Resources Information Center)

Amazing collection of lesson plans, information, virtual library, search service, frequently asked questions, gopher and web links to the world, discussion groups, full text of recent articles on educational topics, a reference collection. There is also the ERIC database of educational articles, reports, etc. (850,000 citations, 1982-1996 only at this stage), complete with a search engine
`http://ericir.syr.edu/`

BBC Education

A developing site for a wide audience, with material for pre-school, school, and adult education. Has a useful directory of Internet resources for children. A sister site is the BBC's "Learning Zone" located at
`http://www.bbc.co.uk/education/lzone/`
`http://www.bbc.co.uk/education/`

Education Virtual Library

Lists hundreds of sites with educational materials on many topics. Can be searched or browsed by educational level, country, etc
`http://www.csu.edu.au/education/library.html`

Guide to NASA Online Resources

The Guide lists scientific, educational, and government resources, stressing scientific matters but including other things too. There are specific entries for K-12 items
`http://naic.nasa.gov/naic/guide/`

Internet Public Library

Not specifically a childrens or educational resource, but there are areas for youth and children which are relevant to the school context
`http://ipl.sils.umich.edu/`

List of UseNet FAQs

From "Abdominal training" to "Zoroastrianism," the 500 or so FAQs listed here are a reference resource of ordinary and wonderful information. Search or browse them all quickly at this site
http://www.cis.ohio-state.edu/hypertext/faq/usenet/FAQ-List.html

NCSA Home Page

The home page for the National Center for Supercomputing Applications at the University of Illinois at Urbana-Champaign. There are numerous links from here to other WWW sites and resources. The front page has an area for education
http://www.ncsa.uiuc.edu/General/NCSAHome.html

Portico

From the British Library. Of course there is lots of formal information here, but the images of manuscripts and treasures such as Beowolf and Magna Carta are also pure visual pleasure. A rich and growing resource
http://portico.bl.uk/

RM Internet for Learning

Operated by Research Machines, the Oxford-based hardware company building its own PCs for the schools market. This is an Internet access service offering normal Internet services. Its provides access software which incorporates some "censorship" of news groups with schools needs in mind, and the access time can be pre-limited to control costs. More information on the home page noted below.
http://www.rmplc.co.uk/

Rob's Neat Links Page

Rob Muir's personal list of links to good things on the net, many of them valuable for the educational world. There are many more such lists, but this is a particularly good one, and its "large print" display makes every point seem so obvious
http://chs.cusd.claremont.edu/www/people/rmuir/WWW_goodies.html

The Ultimate Children's Internet Sites
A list of lists: pre-school and younger, 4-9 year olds, middle school, teenage, etc
http://www.vividus.com/ucis.html

Music

IUMA — Internet Underground Music Archive
Downloadable files of current music, particularly world music, much from new and unpublished people. Also has lots of related information: bands, labels, sound files, and Real Audio. Be warned, the graphics are truly heavy duty, the site is very popular, and can demand lots of loading time. There is a fast version for slower modems
http://www.iuma.com/

Jazz
Read about Jazz musicians, the nightclub scene and the West Coast Jazz movement in the 1950s
http://www.book.uci.edu/Jazz/JPRA2.html

MTV
The content is just as you might expect from MTV
http://www.mtv.com/

Music Virtual Library
Has a search engine for this database of music related materials. Search by instrument, performer, composer, label, etc. Covers all types of music, but it's largely popular
http://syy.oulu.fi/music.html

RISM: US Office of the Repertoire International des Sources Musicales
Access to various of RISM's databases and information files on music resources from the earliest times to about 1825
http://www.rism.harvard.edu/RISM/

The Ultimate Band List

Music information on the net: artists, charts, stores, magazines, discographies. You would have to be catatonic or very esoteric to fail to find fascination here

http://ubl.com/ubl.html

Physics

CERN Home Page

CERN (European Nuclear Research Centre, Switzerland) is where the Web was developed. These pages are a good starting point for information about particle physics and related stuff

http://www.cern.ch/

MicroWorlds: Exploring the Structure of Materials

An attractively presented and sensibly selective view of materials science, well illustrated, and with an interactive approach and exercises to explore

http://www.lbl.gov/MicroWorlds/

Physics Around the World

A searchable major listing of physics resources. Journals, textbooks, companies, physical constants, societies, biographies, newsgroups, etc. make this a very wide ranging collection of links

http://www.physics.mcgill.ca:8081/physics-services/

Physics Ed: Physics Education Resources

Courses, software, textbooks, FAQ, bibliographies, and a handy reference shelf

http://www-hpcc.astro.washington.edu/scied/physics.html

Politics and government

All Politics (USA)

An object lesson in presenting a vast topic in a thorough and entertaining manner. This is the kind of presentation that only the Web can do: there are links to an eclectic selection of worthwhile information resources at other sites. Especially useful for UK users is the "Issues" page where during the Presidential election, the themes of the election were explained and related to each other. CNN and Time are the powers behind this site, and their experience is very evident
http://www.allpolitics.com/

Conservative Party

Constituencies, MPs, organisations, press releases, etc
http://www.conservative-party.org.uk/

Houses of Parliament

An excellent site, if you know what you are looking for, and if it's likely to be of national or local government origin. This is the obvious place to look if you are asking questions like "does English Heritage or Manchester have a Web page?" The site is not so suitable for simply browsing the long alphabetised lists
http://www.open.gov.uk/

Labour Party

Road to the Manifesto, MPs, women, policies, local government, etc
http://www.poptel.org.uk/labour-party/

Liberal Democrat Party

Links for policy, people, MPs, local councillors, etc
http://www.libdems.org.uk/

Plaid Cymru

Pages in English or Welsh, history, people, MPs, policies, news, etc
http://www.plaid-cymru.wales.com/

Scottish National Party

People, MPs, election, news, policies, and an online library of the party's publications, etc. SNP seems to be the only political party whose site bears a trace of humour

http://www.snp.org.uk/

United Nations

This is the best starting point for discovering how to penetrate the labyrinth of about 70 UN organisations (about 40 of them have Web pages). All the organisations are indexed alphabetically and by category, and there is also an FAQ

http://www.unsystem.org/

Religions and ethics

All Religions

The "Society and Culture — Religion" section of Yahoo's subject tree. A balanced and high quality set of sites

http://www.yahoo.com/Society_and_culture/Religion/

Boys Brigade

Well focused modest size lists of Christian and Christian oriented youth sites

http://www.gold.net/users/dm59/bb.html

Christian Internet Directory

A subject tree for Christian matters and theology, with its own search engine

http://www.bakerbooks.com/ccc/appcmain.html

Christian Resources on the Internet

Resource listings, grouped by organisation, international, etc. The site has its own search engine

http://www.iugm.org/iugm/christian-links.html

GOSHEN Christian Resource Directory

Large lists of resources, and a necessary search engine. Possibly the most comprehensive starting point for Christian studies on the Net
`http://www.goshen.net/`

IslamNet

Developed by The World Assembly of Muslim Youth, this site offers databases of the Quran, Hadith, and Fiqeh, and also people, events, magazines, organisations, etc
`http://www.cais.com/islamic/`

Maven

A well orgainised guide to innumerable Judaic and Israeli links
`http://www.maven.co.il/`

Qibla and Prayer Times

A thoroughly practical page with a clear purpose: it supplies local Qibla and prayer times, and the direction of Mecca, for anywhere in the world. Just specify the location and the site's software does the rest
`http://www.arabia.com/prayer.html`

Resources for the Study of Buddhism, Confucianism, and Taoism

You will probably need special software to display the non-latin character sets required to fully explore the resources listed here. There are discussions, classic texts, English translations, history, philosophy, etc
`http://www2.gol.com/users/acmuller/`

Skeptics Society Web

Explores our beliefs about faith, science, philosophy, psychology, religion and the paranormal. Its speciality is doubts about recieved wisdom
`http://www.skeptic.com/`

The Secular Web

Public domain e-texts on the common theme of free thought, and other resources such as debates, pointers, FAQ, historical documents, and newsgroups
http://freethought.tamu.edu/

Science

Explorer Home Page

Pointers for software, laboratory activities, multimedia resources, and special provision for curriculum browsing in the areas of science and mathematics. Some resources are in Adobe Acrobat format (you may need to download this software before viewing them), and others are restricted to users at the site's home locality
http://unite.ukans.edu/

NASA Kennedy Space Center

Largely an historical archive of technical and scientific materials. Includes the Space Shuttle Reference Manual, a FAQ, and information on planned and recent NASA missions
http://www.ksc.nasa.gov/

NASA Spacelink

Offers a wide range of materials related to the space program, including documents on science, maths, engineering, and technology. The principle focus is on the Space Shuttle and related matters rather than astronomy
http://spacelink.msfc.nasa.gov/

New Scientist: Planet Science

New Scientist magazine's WWW site. Still the only publication to responsibly blend political and science reporting. Has items from the magazine, jobs, background, etc. Fee and free services from a colourful and worthwhile site
http://www.newscientist.com/

New South Polar Times

Serious science here. Information on meteorology and ozone measurement coexists with glimpses of daily life in a dome, and a glossary of South Pole lingo. Includes specific materials and ideas for teaching. [Note the UR's "htm" file extentsion, not "html"]
`http://205.174.118.254/nspt/home.htm`

Science Museum

This is the South Kensington science museum's presence on the web. A new site under constant development as a remote arm of the museum. News of the museum and exhibitions, electronic exhibitions, services, and a programme of sponsored exhibitions
`http://www.nmsi.ac.uk/`

Search engines

Alta Vista

Perhaps this is the biggest search engine on the net, there are certainly many millions of documents represented. Use the default "Simple Search" interface by just typing words into the search box; the "Advanced Search" interface is more controllable – provided you have read and remembered the instructions on the Help pages
`http://www.altavista.digital.com/`

Excite

This site is unique in offering what it calls "concept based" searching as well as standard keyword searches. In concept searches its software tries to get behind the search words to their real meaning. Judge for yourself whether this works. Excite is a big search engine, covering more than 50,000,000 Web pages
`http://www.excite.com/`

Infoseek

Infoseek preserves original capital letters in its indexing, so searches for "John Major" won't result in lots of documents about the army rank
`http://www.infoseek.com/`

Lycos

The main rival to Alta Vista for the Net's champion heavyweight search engine. Very simple to use, but your success can be improved if you understand the search tips offered by the operators
http://www.lycos.com/

Society

Homelessness in the UK

Information and Web links for this problem: finding somewhere to live, organisations, the law, organisations that can help, advice
http://www.ris.org.uk/

HungerWeb

Information on the nature, distribution, causes and cures of hunger in the world. A section is aimed at the education world
http://www.brown.edu/Departments/World_Hunger_Program/

Kidlink

Home of a "grassroots project aimed at getting as many children in the age group 10-15 as possible in a global dialog." Numerous forums for individual and classroom dialogues in many languages
http://www.kidlink.org/

National Parent Information Network (NPIN)

Discusses issues related to parenting and child development
http://ericps.ed.uiuc.edu/npin/npinhome.html

The Electronic Frontier Foundation

One of the ten most-linked-to sites on the net. The premier source for information on censorship, liberties, privacy, security, the philosophies and responsibilities of freedom, and simplistic Big Brother fundamentalism
http://www.eff.org/

Urban Education Web

Deals with the problems and pressures of urban schooling and living: race, gender, culture, parents, families, etc. This site is American but the problems are universal
http://eric-web.tc.columbia.edu/

Youth Programs Division (British Columbia)

The Youth Programs Division works with youth to prevent youth crime and crimes on youth. It's particularly concerned with bullying, violence, gangs, drugs, school violence
http://www.harbour.com/crimprev/

Sports

Aquatica Index

Swimming, diving, rowing, windsurfing, canoeing, kayaking, life saving: Aquatica Index has links for just about everything that you can legally do on or in water. [Note the fourth "w" in this site's URL.]
http://wwww.aquatica.com/Aquatica/

Cricket World Monthly

National and international cricket: games, personalities, fantasy cricket, etc
http://www.cricketworld.com/

FIFA Online

World Cup, handbook, facts, competitions, results, etc
http://www.fifa.com/index.html

International Museum of the Horse

Exhibits and an exceptionally strong list of links to other Internet equestrian sites from this museum at Lexington, Kentucky
http://www.horseworld.com/imhmain.html

Major (American) Football League

Players, clubs, history, score cards, video, and there are sections for children and fans too. There is real money behind this site, and it shows

`http://www.nfl.com/`

Major League Baseball

Players, clubs, history, score cards, video, Real Audio. There is real money behind this site, and it shows

`http://www.majorleaguebaseball.com/`

The Tennis Server

You'll forgive this site's punning name after loading links to Rules of Tennis, Code of Tennis, clubs, players, equipment, FAQ, etc

`http://www.tennisserver.com/`

WWW Soccer

The ultimate list of all soccer related Internet sites? Club sites, magazines, fans pages, etc

`http://caesar.atm.ch.cam.ac.uk/sports/webs.html`

Subject trees of selected Internet sites

Infoseek

Infoseek covers about 200,000 documents from the Web. The screen always displays a useful list of related headings as well as those being browsed

`http://www.infoseek.com/`

Lycos a2z

Exceptionallty wide coverage is the a2z strength, but this makes attention to detail difficult to impose. Use it when you have time to browse its considerable resources

`http://a2z.lycos.com/`

WebCrawler Select

WebCrawler's "Select" is a small but perfectly formed subject tree. Its 4,000 or so carefully selected documents are the elite from many thousands more examined. Use WebCrawler Select when you want a few very good documents
`http://webcrawler.com/select/`

WWW Virtual Library

This subject tree is co-operatively maintained by libraries and other organisations around the world. Browsing the main index of about 150 subject headings can take you to places and resources all around the world. The tone is professional, but different organisations often do things quite differently from their fellows
`http://www.w3.org/vl/`

Yahoo!

One of the oldest, largest, and best of the subject trees. It has about 150,000 items represented, and the quality of materials and their organisation is thorough and consistent
`http://www.yahoo.com/`

Teaching oriented lists and resources

Busy Teachers' Web Site

An organised and collaborative place, with short cuts, pointers, resources, and ideas. Hierarchically organised into broader divisions, such as Physics, Art, and History, and narrower sub-divisions, such as Structure of Atoms, Ansell Adams, and Society in 1492. Best of all, they will Email you about their updates
`http://www.ceismc.gatech.edu/BusyT/`

Cisco Educational Archive

Examples of how the Internet is used in schools today
`http://sunsite.unc.edu/cisco/edu-arch.html`

Classroom Connect

An international Web site list of more than a thousand schools, but not many from the UK: find individual schools with the fussy search engine. Some resources and tips for using the Net in the classroom

`http://www.classroom.net/classweb/default.html`

Computer as Learning Partner (CLP) project

Resources for science teachers and students, with a focus on the integration of science activities and the innovative use of computers

`http://www.clp.berkeley.edu/CLP.html`

EdWeb

A starting point for education and the Internet. Tutorials, discussions, guides to resources, a search engine, and both tested and experimental teaching materials. Well worth an early visit

`http://edweb.cnidr.org/`

FYI22: K12 Internet User Questions

FYI22 is a "For Your Information" document discussing how to use the Internet in schools, with practical details, and some useful sites noted

`http://chs.cusd.claremont.edu/www/people/rmuir/rfc1578.html`

Global Network Academy

Includes a searchable list of materials, topics, hundreds of distance learning programmes, thousands of courses (most of them from the USA), and a teachers lounge for discussions by Email. Take time to explore this large site and its links

`http://uu-gna.mit.edu:8001/uu-gna/`

Global SchoolNet Foundation

An information cornucopia about the Internet in schools: tutorials, events, projects, resources lists, prizes, schools, etc

`http://www.gsn.org/`

GRADES (Global Resources And Directory of Educational Sites)

A subject tree and search engine for more than 1,000 educationally valuable sites
http://www.classroom.net/cgi/rofm/eduFind.html

Kids Web

World Wide Web reference for resources developed and indexed by the K-12 group
http://www.npac.syr.edu/textbook/kidsweb/tindex.html

KidsWeb

World Wide Web reference for resources in the arts, sciences, and social sciences. The site was developed and indexed by the K-12 group
http://www.npac.syr.edu/textbook/kidsweb/index.html

Learning Resource Server

Resources to help learners explore the Internet's resources. There are sections for pre-college education, teacher education, and for other forms of higher education. Resources, courses, articles, etc., and links to teachers, students, and researchers projects
http://www.ed.uiuc.edu/

Lesson Plans: Washington State

Curricular and instructional services
http://www.ospi.wednet.edu/

Magpie

A database of Internet resources for schools, and more. Created at the Department of Computer Science, University of Wales, Aberystwyth, and now supported by Research Machines, it was the source of many records in this listing.
http://www.dcs.aber.ac.uk/~magwww/index_ht1.html

NCET

NCET's (National Council for Educational Technology) home page. Holds IT and Internet resources, CD-ROM reviews, report texts, ordering details. Not always direct curriculum stuff but very much in support of the curriculum
http://ncet.csv.warwick.ac.uk/

SchoolNet (UK)

Provides a focal point for UK schools activities on the Internet. Links to several UK sites and resources of schools interest. Lists of UK schools on the Internet, Email addresses of UK schools, etc. This SchoolNet is not related to the Canadian SchoolNet projects
http://schools.sys.uea.ac.uk/schoolnet/

The Education Web Server

A well organised site consisting largely of links to Net resources for a wide range of topics
http://prometheus.ed.csuohio.edu/

Weather

Weather Pages (USA)

Offshore data, models, cross sections, movies, and a place to enter your own weather observations. An award winning site
http://www.ems.psu.edu/wx/

Weather: UK Sources

Up to date and archived satellite images for visible light, radar and infrared, and also animations
http://www.atm.ch.cam.ac.uk/current_weather.html

World Weather

Download Virtual Reality replays of last week's global weather. You may first need to download the QuickTime software too (available via this site)
http://www.ems.psu.edu/VRStuff/QTVR.html

Writing

KidPub WWW Publishing

Publishes writing by children 6-13 years, and it does it for free. Pen pals too. A friendly and easy-to-use site, with several awards for excellence

`http://www.en-garde.com/kidpub/`

The Online Writery

A student-oriented site with an impressive collection of writing resources, some specifically for teachers

`http://www.missouri.edu/~wleric/writery.html`

The Quotations Page

Keyword searchable quotes, a quote of the day, humourous quotes, randomly generated quotes and other quotation information

`http://www.starlingtech.com/quotes/`

Just Ask Emily Postnews

The following is an exerpt from a humorous online article by Brad Templeton.

It features a fictitious "Miss Manners" dealing with problems of "Netiquette", particularly in the newsgroups.

Polemics never tasted so sweet

Appendix 3

Q: Dear Miss Postnews: How long should my signature be?
- verbose@noisy

A: Dear Verbose: Please try and make your signature as long as you can. It's much more important than your article, of course, so try to have more lines of signature than actual text.

Try to include a large graphic made of ASCII characters, plus lots of cute quotes and slogans. People will never tire of reading these pearls of wisdom again and again, and you will soon become personally associated with the joy each reader feels at seeing yet another delightful repeat of your signature.

Be sure as well to include a complete map of Usenet with each signature, to show how anybody can get mail to you from any site in the world. Be sure to include Internet gateways as well.

Aside from your reply address, include your full name, company and organisation. It's just common courtesy — after all, in some newsreaders people have to type an *entire* keystroke to go back to the top of your article to see this information in the header.

By all means include your phone number and street address in every single article. People are always responding to Usenet articles with phone calls and letters. It would be silly to go to the extra trouble of including this information only in articles that need a response by conventional channels!

Q: Dear Emily: Today I posted an article and forgot to include my signature. What should I do?
- forgetful@myvax

A: Dear Forgetful: Rush to your terminal right away and post an article that says, "Oops, I forgot to post my signature with that last article. Here it is."

Since most people will have forgotten your earlier article, (particularly since it dared to be so boring as to not have a nice, juicy signature) this will remind them of it. Besides, people care much more about the signature anyway. See the previous letter for more important details.

Also, be sure to include your signature TWICE in each article. That way you're sure people will read it.

Q: Dear Ms. Postnews: I couldn't get mail through to somebody on another site. What should I do?
– eager@beaver.dam

A: Dear Eager: No problem, just post your message to a group that a lot of people read. Say, "This is for John Smith. I couldn't get mail through so I'm posting it. All others please ignore."

This way tens of thousands of people will spend a few seconds scanning over and ignoring your article, using up over 16 man-hours their collective time, but you will be saved the terrible trouble of checking through Usenet maps or looking for alternate routes. Just think, if you couldn't distribute your message to 30,000 other computers, you might actually have to (gasp) call directory assistance for 50p and even phone the person.

Don't forget. The world will end if your message doesn't get through, so post it as many places as you can.

Q: What about a test message?

A: It is important, when testing, to test the entire net. Never test merely a local distribution when the whole Net can be done. Also put "please ignore" on your test messages, since we all know that everybody always skips a message with a line like that. Don't use a subject like "My sex is female but I demand to be addressed as male." because such articles are read in depth by all USEnauts.

Q: Somebody just posted that Roman Polanski directed Star Wars. What should I do?
– smartaleck@some.site

A: Post the correct answer at once! We can't have people go on believing that! Very good of you to spot this. You'll probably be the only one to make the correction, so post as soon as you can. No time to lose, so certainly don't wait a day, or check to see if somebody else has made the correction.

And it's not good enough to send the message by mail. Since you're the only one who really knows that it was Francis Coppola, you have to inform the whole net right away!

Using the most confrontational and impolite language you can, don't forget to point out the folly of the error made by the person.

Q: I read an article that said, "reply by mail, I'll summarise." What should I do?

A: Post your response to the whole Net. That request applies only to dumb people who don't have something interesting to say. Your postings are much more worthwhile than other people's, so it would be a waste to reply by mail.

Q: I collected replies to an article I wrote, and now it's time to summarise. What should I do?

A: Simply concatenate all the articles together into a big file and post that. On Usenet, this is known as a summary. It lets people read all the replies without annoying newsreaders getting in the way. Do the same when summarising a vote.

Q: I saw a long article that I wish to rebut carefully, what should I do?

A: Include the entire text with your article, particularly the signature, and include your comments closely packed between the lines. Be sure to post, and not mail, even though your article looks like a reply to the original. Everybody *loves* to read those long point-by-point debates, especially when they evolve into name-calling and lots of "Is too!" — "Is not!" — "Is too, twizot!" exchanges.

Be sure to follow-up everything, and never let another person get in the last word on a net debate. Why, if people let other people have the last word, then discussions would actually stop! Remember, other net readers aren't nearly as clever as you, and if somebody posts something wrong, the readers can't possibly realize that on their own without your elucidations. If somebody gets insulting in their net postings, the best response is to get right down to their level and fire a return salvo. When I read one net person make an insulting attack on another, I always immediately take it as gospel unless a rebuttal is posted. It never makes me think less of the insulter, so it's your duty to respond.

Q: How can I choose what groups to post in?

A: Pick as many as you can, so that you get the widest audience. After all, the net exists to give you an audience. Ignore those who suggest you should only use groups where you think the article is highly appropriate. Pick all groups where anybody might even be slightly interested.

Always make sure followups go to all the groups. In the rare event that you post a followup which contains something original, make sure you expand the list of groups. Never include a "Followup-to:" line in the header, since some people might miss part of the valuable discussion in the fringe groups.

Q: I cant spell worth a dam. I hope your going too tell me what to do?

A: Don't worry about how your articles look. Remember it's the message that counts, not the way it's presented. Ignore the fact that sloppy spelling in a purely written forum sends out the same silent messages that soiled clothing would when addressing an audience.

Q: How should I pick a subject for my articles?

A: Keep it short and meaningless. That way people will be forced to actually read your article to find out what's in it. This means a bigger audience for you, and we all know that's what the net is for. If you do a followup, be sure and keep the same subject, even if it's totally meaningless and not part of the same discussion. If you don't, you won't catch all the people who are looking for stuff on the original topic, and that means less audience for you.

Q: What sort of tone should I take in my article?

A: Be as outrageous as possible. If you don't say outlandish things, and fill your article with libellous insults of net people, you may not stick out enough in the flood of articles to get a response. The more insane your posting looks, the more likely it is that you'll get lots of followups. The net is here, after all, so that you can get lots of attention.

If your article is polite, reasoned and to the point, you may only get mailed replies. Yuck!

Q: The posting software suggested I had too long a signature and too many lines of included text in my article. What's the best course?

A: Such restrictions were put in the software for no reason at all, so don't even try to figure out why they might apply to your article.

Turns out most people search the net to find nice articles that consist of the complete text of an earlier article plus a few lines.

In order to help these people, fill your article with dummy original lines to get past the restrictions. Everybody will thank you for it.

For your signature, I know it's tough, but you will have to read it in with the editor. Do this twice to make sure it's firmly in there. By the way, to show your support for the free distribution of information, be sure to include a copyright message forbidding transmission of your article to sites whose Usenet politics you don't like.

Also, if you do have a lot of free time and want to trim down the text in your article, be sure to delete some of the attribution lines so that it looks like the original author of – say – a plea for world peace actually wrote the followup calling for the nuking of Bermuda.

Q: They just announced on the radio that the United States has invaded Iraq. Should I post?

A: Of course. The net can reach people in as few as 3 to 5 days. It's the perfect way to inform people about such news events long after the broadcast networks have covered them. As you are probably the only person to have heard the news on the radio, be sure to post as soon as you can.

Q: I have this great joke. You see, these three strings walk into a bar...

A: Oh dear. Don't spoil it for me. Submit it to rec.humor, and post it to the moderator of rec.humor.funny at the same time. I'm sure he's never seen that joke.

Q: What second-hand computer should I buy? An Atari ST or an Amiga?

A: Cross post that question to the Atari and Amiga groups. It's an interesting and novel question that I am sure they would love to investigate in those groups. In fact, post your question at once, to as many technical groups as you can think of, concluding your request with the line "Please reply by mail, as I do not follow this group." (No one will find such a statement impertinent; remember, the net is a resource to help you.)

There is no need to read the groups in advance or examine the "frequently asked question" lists to see if the topic has already been dealt with. Any such warnings are for people without your innate sense of netiquette, and whose uninspired questions are bound to be repetitive. Your question is sure to be unique; no point checking the list to see if the answer might be there already. How could it be, when you only just thought of the question?

Q: What about other important questions? How should I know when to post?

A: Always post them. It would be a big waste of your time to find a knowledgeable user in one of the groups and ask through private mail if the topic has already come up. Much easier to bother thousands of people with the same question.

Q: Somebody just posted a query to the Net, and I want to get the answer too. What should I do?

A: Immediately post a following, including the complete text of the query. At the bottom add, "Me too!" If somebody else has done this, follow up their article and add "Me three," or whatever number is appropriate. Don't forget your full signature. After all, if you just mail the original poster and ask for a copy of the answers, you will simply clutter the poster's mailbox, and save people who do answer the question the joyful duty of noting all the "me (n)s" and sending off all the multiple copies.

Q: What is the measure of a worthwhile group?

A: Why, it's Volume, Volume, Volume. Any group that has lots of noise in it must be good. Remember, the higher the volume of material in a group, the higher percentage of useful, factual and insightful articles you will find. In fact, if a group can't demonstrate a high enough volume, it should be deleted from the net.

Q: Emily, I'm having a serious disagreement with somebody on the Net. I tried complaints to his system administrator, organising mail campaigns, called for his removal from the Net and phoning his employer to get him fired. Everybody laughed at me. What can I do?

A: Go to the daily papers. Most modern reporters are top-notch computer experts who will understand the Net, and your problems, perfectly. They will print careful, reasoned stories without any errors at all, and surely represent the situation properly to the public. The public will also all act wisely, as they are also fully cognisant of the subtle nature of net society.

Papers never sensationalise or distort, so be sure to point out things like racism and sexism wherever they might exist. Be sure as well that they understand that all things on the net, particularly insults, are meant literally. If regular papers won't take the story, go to a tabloid paper – they are always interested in good stories.

By arranging all this free publicity for the Net, you'll become very well known. People on the Net will wait in eager anticipation for your every posting, and refer to you constantly. You'll get more mail than you ever dreamed possible – the ultimate in Net success.

Q:Emily, I'm a man. how should I treat the women who post to the Net?

A:As babes for the taking! Women post to the Net to advertise their sexual availability to you. If they deny it they're just playing hard to get. One way to make sure that more women participate in the network world is to send them sexual advances wherever you see them. Women just love it. And they're sure to want to go out with you. There's nothing a woman finds more seductive than a come-on from a total stranger who knows nothing more about her than that she's female and can type. It's so flattering; guys that discriminating turn us all on.

If a women is open about her sexuality on the net, that's a double invitation. Send her lewd, explicit Email. That's sure to encourage women to participate on the Net on an even basis with men.

And don't forget, women are dumber than men, and don't understand technology and computers. So be as patronising as possible, and don't use technical terms. Follow this advice and the strange fear women have of the net is sure to change.

Q:How can I use the Internet for bulk mail?

A: Isn't it great? On the Net, Email is included in the price of admission, and that means it's a fabulous deal for bulk mail. Forget the pesky post-office that asks that people sending lots of mail pay for the cost — now the cost can be borne by everybody.

People don't get enough Email these days. Some people even go as much as 10 minutes without getting some Email. So they love it if you put them on new mailing lists without asking them. The more the better. Even better if they are mailing lists to promote commercial products, perhaps your products!

Imagine the joy when a mailbox normally full of boring personal and business correspondence contains a bright, perky ad from you. And not just you – there are millions of products out there that could benefit and with no cost in the way, soon nobody will go a minute without more Email. Joining this fray is sure to provide a positive image for your products and company.

Q: Emily, how can I put out my billboard on the information superhighway?

A: The best way to do it is to perform a spam. It's called that because everybody loves it as much as the customer in the Monty Python "Spam" sketch loves his spam.

The best way to do this is to find some naive programmer and ask it to write a script that posts your message to every newsgroup. You'll start by getting as big a list of newsgroups as you can find. The members of Usenet, hoping to see your ad, have prepared these lists just for you. It doesn't really matter what your product is. If people on the net might use it, they'll be happy to read about it in every group.

Now create a message promoting yourself. Be bold, be daring, and be sure to provide info on how to contact you in ways that people on the net can't shut off. (More on that later.)

Because the reaction is going to be so overwhelming, be sure to take the following steps:

a) Unlist your phone number. The networking public is going to want to contact you so much to talk about your product or service that they'll even try to call you at home. If they get your home phone or address, they'll be sure to share it with all the other people seeking to send you their admiration, and your fame may prove too much. You want business, of course, but do you want to take orders all night?

b) Get an account with some other Internet account providers. For reasons not quite certain, your provider probably has a clause in their contract with you saying not to do a spam. Even if they don't, they will probably delete your account a few hours after you announce your product, so be sure to get other accounts under assumed names so you can follow what's going on. This is the reason that expecting Email replies to your ad won't work.

c) Be sure you've lead a clean life. You and your product are going to become as famous as The Duchess of York and O.J. Simpson! But, as you know, such fame has its downsides, as your eager fans will research every tawdry episode from your past history. So be sure there are no skeletons in your closet. (Unless your product is skeletons!)

d) Load plenty of fax paper in your fax machine. Hire extra staff to load the rolls. There may be orders in all the faxes you will get.

e) Resign any memberships you may have in any professional associations you may have joined relating to your business that might have something as pesky as a code of ethics. Why put them through the trouble of handling all the calls from your adoring fans, looking for somebody to talk with about you?

Ok, now you're ready. Unleash the posting program. Have it send your message once to every group. There are thousands. Now picture in your mind the prospective customer. She starts her day, perhaps, reading a group about her hobby. And right there is your ad! The title is curious so she reads it. Your name is now inserted into her mind – you've got mindshare. It's true your product didn't have anything to do with her hobby, but the net is there to find customers for you, not for people to share their thoughts.

Then she goes to her next group, perhaps about her brand of computer. There's your ad again! You've sneaked into the great demographics of the high-tech world. As she goes on, she sees your ad again and again. Imagine her joy as she sees your now familiar headline everywhere she goes. "Wow, they must be really big and important," she'll think. "They're as famous as IBM." Soon that joy will be so much that she'll be ready to buy, buy, buy.

Now comes the bad news. Usenet is unreliable, and postings don't always work. So, for unknown reasons, a few hours after you make your postings they will all have disappeared. Normally you would just post them again, but by this time your internet mail access will have been deleted, as I said above, so you'll have to just sit back and bask in the adulation and orders. There is a theory that some people, who don't like your ad, will have a smarter program than your posting program root around the net and stamp it out,

but I hardly think it's likely anybody would do that.
There will be some people annoyed, it's true. But the Net has at least 10 million people on it, and you'll probably only *really* annoy perhaps 3 to 4 million of them – a minority!

Others who have tried this have reported not only that a mere minority show displeasure, but that vast numbers of people take the time to send back inquiries and orders just so you can have more to read. Unfortunately, they rarely actually pay. Some theorise that those in the vocal minority who don't like you are sending in pretend positive responses, to waste your time. Who would bother to do that? Perhaps just 1% out of the 3 to 4 million annoyed people, at most. That shouldn't bother you too much. A similar percentage may try to phone you, or fax you, or send bricks postage due, or subscribe you to magazines. Ignore them. They're just 40,000 or so of the lunatic fringe, communist element you find on the Net. They're just upset because you're making money and they're not. In fact, suckers that they are, they actually ended up paying to transmit your ad everywhere. Learn to ignore them. (That's not advice, it's just something you'll have to do.)

Now at this point you probably have to stop answering your phone, but keep those faxes coming in, and of course get ready for the mail. If you ever do get to see some of the Email you got sent – wow, what a flood!

When it settles a bit, threaten to sue anybody who didn't like you. That should put some fear of God into them. They should have known better than to build a system so open. Sure, they built the network as a co-operative effort, but if they didn't want your ads, why didn't they put in protections against them or enact laws to stop them? What you did was probably legal, so what's their complaint? They're like people who leave their keys in their cars and whine when they get stolen. Really, like they didn't deserve it. They just don't see the wonderful new purpose to which their network can be put, to help small, exciting firms like yours get famous. That's the American dream, after all, and you're living it, or will, when the time comes to come back out of your bunker and reconnect your phones.

Q: What does foobar stand for?

A: It stands for you, dear.

Glossary

A comprehensive explanation of the jargon that appears throughout the book

Appendix 4

A

Acceptable Use Policy (AUP)
This refers to policies that restrict the way in which a network may be used. Usually, a network administrator makes and enforces decisions dealing with acceptable use. Many schools have student-specific AUPs.

ActiveX
A method (developed by Microsoft) of downloading multimedia web plug-ins automatically.

Address
See either IP Address or Email Address.

Advanced Research Projects Agency Network (ARPANET)
A pioneering long-haul network funded by what's now-called DARPA. It was the foundation on which the Internet was built.

Agent
The part of a system that prepares information for use by a front-end program.

Alias
A type of nickname (usually short and easy to remember) that refers to a type of network resource. Aliases are used so you won't have to remember the long and difficult names typical of network resources.

Anonymous FTP
By using the word "anonymous" as your user ID and your Email address as the password when you log in to an FTP site, you can bypass local security checks and gain limited access to public files on the remote computer. This type of access is available on most FTP sites, but not all.

Application
Sometimes known as a client or an "app," it's a program that performs a specific function. FTP, EMail, Web, and Telnet clients are the common examples of Internet applications.

Archie
You'll usually hear this term referred to in the phrase "archie search." Archie is a way of automatically gathering, indexing and sometimes

even retrieving files on the Internet. Most good archie clients are able to FTP files once you've found the information you're looking for.

Archive
A collection of files stored on a machine. FTP sites are known as archives.

ARPANET
See Advanced Research Projects Agency Network.

ASCII
American Standard Code for Information Interchange. It refers to data containing only text: letters, numbers and punctuation.

Asynchronous Transfer Mode (ATM)
A method of transmitting data over a network. In certain circumstances, it can be particularly quick.

ATM
See Asynchronous Transfer Mode.

AUP
See Acceptable Use Policy.

Authentication
Any process that ensures that users are who they say they are. When you type your name and password, you are authenticated and allowed access.

Backbone
A high-speed connection within a network; it connects shorter, usually slower circuits.

Bandwidth
Technically, this refers to the difference (measured in Hz), between the highest and lowest frequencies of a transmission. Most people loosely refer to bandwidth as the amount of data that can be transferred over a network connection. The more bandwidth you have, therefore, the greater number of users will be able to get fast access to network resources simultaneously.

Baud rate
The speed at which a modem transmits data - the number of signals per second. It is not an exact measure of the number of bits of information per second, as there can be more than one bit per signal

(using different tones at a time), but in common use, it is often synonymous with "bits per second".

BBS
See Bulletin Board System.

Berkeley Internet Name Domain (BIND)
An early version of a DNS server developed by the University of California at Berkeley. Most Internet hosts run a version of BIND.

Binary
In the context of the Internet, binary data is that which can contain more than just textual information. Programs and other computer data are referred to as "binary information" on the Internet. In general terms, binary code is the basic system of 1s and 0s which the computer processes as information.

Bitnet
A large computer network devoted to academic use that provides Email and file transfer services. It has a connection to the Internet.

Bits per second (BPS)
The number of bits (on or off signals) transmitted over a line in one second. Modems commonly communicate from 300 bits per second to nearly 35 thousand BPS.

Bounce
If you send Email and it fails to arrive at its intended recipient for any reason (incorrect user name, network failure, etc.), the message "bounces" and returns to you. The subject line in a bounced message usually says something like: "Undeliverable Mail" or "Message Undeliverable."

BPS
See Bits per second

BTW
Acronym meaning "By The Way", one of the many used in Email messages, Usenet discussions and so forth.

Bulletin Board System (BBS)
A computer which typically provides Email services, file archives, and announcements of interest to the bulletin board system's operator (known as a sysop). BBSs started out as hobbies for computer enthusiasts, and were mostly only accessible directly by

modem. Recently, however, more and more BBSs are being connected to the Internet.

Cable modem
A special modem for sending and receiving data through cable providers (who usually provide television). They work at extremely high speeds, and some cable companies are thinking of providing Internet connections through their services.

Cache
Some web browsers (and servers) put aside some space on their hard disc to keep local copies of popular web pages - in particular, the graphics and so forth. That space is termed the "cache". When that page is next requested, the machine will first attempt to retrieve it from the cache, which is quicker than going across the world for it again.

CCIRN
See Coordinating Committee for Intercontinental Research Networks.

CCITR
See Comité Consultatif International de Télégraphique et Téléphonique.

CERT
See Computer Emergency Response Team.

Challenge-Handshake Authentication Protocol (CHAP)
An authentication method that can be used when connecting to an Internet Service Provider. CHAP allows you to log in to your provider automatically, without the need for inputting a password manually. It is more secure than the Password Authentication Protocol (another widely used authentication method) since it does not send passwords in normal text format.

CHAP
See Challenge-Handshake Authentication Protocol.

Chat
Another term for IRC. Also, an acronym meaning "Conversational Hypertext Access Technology."

CIX
An acronym meaning "Commercial Internet Exchange." A text-based service provider which predates most of the full Internet providers.

Client
In Internet terms, it's a program that performs a specific function, such as Telnet or FTP. It's the "front-end" to an Internet process. In more general terms, a client is computer system or process that requests a service of another computer system or process. The much talked about "client-server architecture" refers to a workstation requesting the contents of a file from a server.

Command line
A way of accessing a service where you type in commands, one at a time. This is the old fashioned way of using services (for example, through Telnet). If you have ever used MS-DOS, you have used a command line interface.

Comité Consultatif International de Télégraphique et Téléphonique (CCITT)
French for "International Telephone and Telegraph Advisory Council." It's an organization that plays a major role in the United National International Telecommunications Union (ITU). The CCITT is responsible for making technical recommendations about communications systems worldwide. Every four years, CCITT updates the standards, most recently in 1992.

Computer Emergency Response Team (CERT)
The CERT was formed by DARPA in November 1988 in response to a security incident. CERT exists to facilitate Internet-wide response to computer security events involving Internet hosts and to conduct research targeted at improving the security of existing systems. They maintain an archive of security-related issues on their FTP server at "cert.org." Their email address is "cert@cert.org".

Coordinating Committee for Intercontinental Research Networks (CCIRN)
A committee that provides a forum for North American and European network research organizations to co-operate and plan.

Corporation for Research and Educational Networking (CREN)
An organization formed in October 1989, when Bitnet and CSNET were combined. CSNET is no longer around, but CREN still operates Bitnet.

Cracker
Substantially different from "hackers," crackers are users who try to gain illegal access to computers. They are usually malicious in their intentions.

Cross posting
Articles posted to more than one Usenet Newsgroup at a time are said to be cross-posted.

Cyberspace
The "world of computers and the society that gathers around them," as referred to by William Gibson in his fantasy novel *Neuromancer*. It now loosely refers to the online world and even more loosely to the Internet.

Data Encryption Key (DEK)
Much like an actual key used for locking and re-opening doors, DEKs are used for the encryption and decoding of message text, sometimes in the form of a digital signature.

Data Encryption Standard (DES)
A standardized encryption method widely used on the Internet.

Datagram
A block of data that is "smart" enough (actually, which carries enough information) to travel from one Internet site to another without having to rely on earlier exchanges between the source and destination computers (not to be confused with a Candygram the 'syntactical sugar' that makes a programming language easy for humans to understand).

DDN
See Defense Data Network.

Dedicated Line
A communications line that is used solely for computer connections. If you buy an additional phone line for your modem, that's a dedicated line. There are other types of dedicated lines (such as T3s and T1s) that are used for larger network entities.

Defense Data Network (DDN)
A global communications network that serves the US Department of Defense. It is made up of a network called MILNET, other portions of the Internet, and classified networks which are not part of the Internet. The DDN is used to connect military installations and is managed by the Defense Information Systems Agency. It was originally developed by DARPA.

Dialup
A widely-used method of accessing the Internet. A dialup connection uses regular phone lines to connect one computer to another via modem.

DNS
See Domain Name System

Domain
A "logical" region of the Internet. People sometimes refer to them loosely as "sites." Generally, a domain corresponds to an IP address or an area on a host.

Domain Name System (DNS)
The DNS is a static, hierarchical name service used with TCP/IP hosts, and is housed on a number of servers on the Internet. Basically, it maintains a database for figuring out and finding (or resolving) host names and IP addresses on the Internet. This allows users to specify remote computers by host names rather than numerical IP addresses. The advantage of the DNS is that you don't have to remember numerical IP addresses for all the Internet sites you want to access.

Dot Address (*or* Dotted Decimal Notation *or* Dotted Quad)
The common notation for IP addresses of the form xxx.xxx.xxx.xxx; where each number represents one byte in the four-byte IP address. Eg: 194.72.6.51

Download
The transmission of a file from a remote computer to a local computer. You "download" software from the Internet, and install it on your computer, for example. A download (as a noun) is, literally, that which has been downloaded. For example, "today's downloads include a piece of maths software".

Electronic Frontier Foundation (EFF)
A foundation that addresses social and legal issues arising from the impact of computers on society.

Electronic Mail (Email)
A method by which computer users can exchange messages with each other over a network. Email is probably the most widely-used communications tool on the Internet. There are many quirky conventions to Email, but most entail a "To:", "From:", and "Subject:" line. One of Email's advantages is its ability to be forwarded and replied to easily.

Email
See Electronic Mail.

Email Address
Your Email address is made up of several parts. By convention, addresses use lowercase letters with no spaces. The first part of the address, the username, identifies a unique user on a server. The "@" (pronounced "at") separates the username from the host name. The host name uniquely identifies the server computer and is the last part of the Internet email address (for example, one of our Email addresses is nickm@koekie.org.uk). Large servers, such as those used at universities or large companies sometimes contain multiple parts, called subdomains. Subdomains and the host name are separated by a "." (pronounced "dot").

Encryption
The basis of network security. Encryption encodes network data as it is sent to prevent anyone except the intended recipient from accessing the data.

Ethernet
A standard and probably the most popular connection type for Local Area Networks (*LANs*). It was first developed by Xerox. Ethernet can transfer information at up to 10 Megabit-per-second (Mb/s).

FAQ
Acronym for "Frequently Asked Questions." FAQs are widely available on the Internet and usually take the form of large, instructional text files. They are written on a wide variety of topics, and are usually the most up-to-date source for specialised information.

File
A collection of computer data under one filename.

File Transfer Protocol (FTP)
The most widely-used way of downloading and uploading (getting and putting) files across an Internet connection. The File Transfer Protocol is a standardised way to connect computers so that files can be shared between them easily. There is a set of commands in FTP for making and changing directories, transferring, copying, moving, and deleting files. Formerly, all FTP connections were text based, but graphical applications are now available that make FTP commands as easy as dragging and dropping. Numerous FTP clients exist for a number of platforms.

Finger
A UNIX command that shows information about a user or group of users on the Internet. When executed, the Finger command

usually returns the user's real name, whether or not they have unread mail, and the time and date of their last login. Finger also displays two files (if they exist) located in the home directory of the user you fingered.

Firewall
Protective device and filtering program to prevent unwanted entry to a computer network.

Flame
A negative response to an Email message or newsgroup posting. If you post an article or send an Email message to an audience that deems your message inappropriate, expect to get "flamed." The most common recipients of flames are users who post commercial messages in public forums, those who post adult material in non-adult areas of the Internet, and users who post racial or gender-biased comments. The worst sort of flame is known as a "mail-bomb," which occurs when the user being flamed open his or her Email and receives a flood of letters with unusually long file attachments that make his or her computer "crash."

Follow-up
A reply to an Email or newsgroup posting that continues the conversation or idea, known as a *thread.*

Freenet
A network system made up of community-based bulletin board systems with Email, information services, interactive communications, and conferencing. They work to make computer networking services as freely available as public libraries - but in the days of fiscal miserliness, even that great Victorian ideal looks tragically threatened.

FTP
See File Transfer Protocol.

Gateway
A kind of "go-between" device or program that passes information between networks that normally couldn't communicate. What used to be called a gateway is now called a "router".

GIF
Graphics Interchange Format. A format often used on the Internet to distribute graphical files. It is also a standard graphics format of the world wide web.

Gopher
An information search and retrieval tool used for research. Gopher information is stored hierarchically on computers across the Internet. It uses a simple protocol that allows a client to access information from a multitude of numerous Gopher servers at one time, creating what's known as "gopher space." The most common search tools in gopher are Veronica and Jughead. Gopher clients exist for most platforms. This venerable attempt at placing a friendly and unified interface on the Internet has now been superseded by the world wide web.

Hacker
A computer user who works to understand the "ins and outs" of computers, networks, and the Internet in general. Hackers are generally benign, and are not to be confused with *crackers*.

Header
The top of an Email or Usenet message containing details about the sender, date, time, routing and other technical information. Much of the header is of limited interest to the average user, and is therefore sometimes filtered out by an Email or newsreader package.

Host
A computer that is attached to a network or the Internet. Hosts allow users on client machines to connect and share files or transfer information. Individual users communicate with hosts by using client application programs.

Host Address
The address of a host computer on the Internet.

Hostname
The name given a host computer connected to the Internet.

HTML
See HyperText Markup Language.

HTTP
See world wide web

Hypermedia
The combination of hypertext and multimedia in an online document.

Hypertext
A type of text that allows embedded "links" to other documents.

Clicking on or selecting a hypertext link displays another document or section of a document. Most world wide web documents contain hypertext.

Hypertext Markup Language (HTML)
The standard way to mark text documents for publishing on the world wide web. HTML is marked-up using "tags" surrounded by brackets.

Hypertext Transport Protocol (HTTP)
See world wide web

IMHO
Acronym for "In My Humble Opinion." Generally seen in IRC, Email, or Usenet postings.

Integrated Services Digital Network (ISDN)
A relatively new technology which combines voice and digital network services in a single medium. ISDN makes it possible for communications carriers to offer their customers digital data services as well as voice connections through a single line. You can connect to your ISP through ISDN between three to six times as fast as through a modem, but the subscription and phone line rental will cost more, as well as specialised equipment you'll need to make the connection.

International Organization for Standardization (ISO)
An organization of 89 member countries (founded in 1946) responsible for setting world standards in many electronics areas. Members of the ISO are the national standards organisations of the member countries.

Internet
It's not a corporation, organization, or entity in itself. When you connect to the Internet, you actually become part of it. Always capitalised, the word Internet can also be referred to colloquially as the "Net."

Internet Protocol (IP)
An industry standard protocol which is a part of the Internet's 'lingua franca'.

Internet Protocol Address (IP Address)
The 32-bit address defined by the Internet Protocol. Every resource on the Internet has a unique numerical IP address, represented in

dotted decimal notation. IP addresses are the closest thing the Internet has to phone numbers. When you "call" that number (using any number of connection methods such as FTP, HTTP, Gopher, etc.) you get connected to the computer that "owns" that IP address.

Internet Service Provider (ISP)
An ISP is a company that maintains a network that is linked to the Internet via a dedicated communication line, usually a high-speed link known as a T1. An ISP offers use of its dedicated communication lines to companies or individuals who can't afford thousands of pounds a month for a direct connection. Using a modem, you can dial up to a service provider whose computers will connect you to the Internet, typically for a monthly fee.

Internet Society (ISOC)
A non-profit, professional organisation that supports the technical evolution of the Internet and stimulates the interest of members of the scientific and academic communities, industry, and the public regarding technology and the applications of the Internet. The ISOC also promotes the development of new applications for the Internet by publishing a quarterly newsletter, the Internet Society News, and by holding an annual conference, called INET.

InterNIC
Meaning "Internet information Center," InterNIC is the combined name for the providers of registration, information, and database services to the Internet. InterNIC is who you contact if you want to register a domain name on the Internet.

IP
See Internet Protocol.

IP Address
See Internet Protocol Address.

IRC
IRC allows multiple users to converse in real time on different 'channels'. Channels (which have a "#" sign preceding their name) vary in traffic and content. Channel operators (or Ops) moderate the conversation, and have the ability to "kick" people from channels, or even ban them if their actions warrant it. IRC clients are available for nearly all platforms.

ISDN
See Integrated Services Digital Network.

ISO
See International Organization for Standardization.

ISOC
See Internet Society.

JANET
See Joint Academic Network

Java
A programming language (produced by Sun Microsystems) which is now proving popular as a language for making the world wide web more interactive. Java programs (called applets) download within the web-environment, and can run on a large number of machines.

Javascript
A simpler subset of Java (see above) which can be incorporated in the HTML code that makes up a web page.

Joint Academic Network (JANET)
Virtually all institutions of higher education in the United Kingdom are connected to JANET which is, in turn, connected to the Internet. The next generation upgrade to Janet is called SuperJanet, which produced much quicker connections between Janet sites, but the connection to the Internet can still be very slow.

JPEG
Standing for Joint Photographic Experts Group, this is a format of graphical file. Pictures in the JPEG format take up less memory than GIF pictures, but this compression is gained through a slight loss of clarity.

LAN
Acronym for Local Area Network. LANs are now commonplace in most businesses and many schools, allowing users to send Email and share resources such as files, printers, modems, etc. Currently, most larger companies are connecting their LANs to the Internet, allowing users to connect to resources within or outside the LAN.

Leased Line
A dedicated, full-time connection used to link a user or network to an Internet Service Provider or another network.

Listserv
An automated mailing list distribution system. Listservs exist for a

multitude of professional, educational, and special interest groups. Usually, you have to send an Email to a Listserver with the subject "SUBSCRIBE listname" or something to that effect. You are then "subscribed" to that "mailing list" and (depending on the service) will receive regular mail from a single source or from all members who send Email to the Listserver.

Log in
Logging in to a computer involves typing a username and password before access is given. To log in means to access a computer (usually over a network) and, as a noun, a login describes that state. For example, you could report that you achieved a successful login to an FTP site.

Lurking
Non-active participation on the part of a subscriber to a mailing list, a Usenet newsgroup, and IRC channel, or any other Internet communication device. If you're "lurking," you're generally just listening to the discussion. It's usually best to lurk if you're a beginner or if you are new to a communication group. This allows you to "get up to speed" on the history or acceptable behaviour of the group.

Mail Reflector
A program that distributes files or information in response to requests sent via Email. Many Listservs have mail reflectors. You can request documents of a reflector by sendinga message with the subject "SEND document name" or a similar command. Mail reflectors are also being used to provide FTP-like services for users with limited Internet access.

Mailing List
A list of Email addresses used to forward messages to groups of people. When you subscribe to a mailing list, you receive all mail sent to that list (*see also* Listserv).

MIME Encoding
See Multipurpose Internet Mail Extensions Encoding.

Mirror Site
Due to the popularity of some FTP and Web sites, mirror sites came into existence. They are areas on a computer that "mirror" or contain an exact replica of the directory structure of another computer. If you have trouble getting connected to an FTP site, for example, because of the traffic, you can usually connect to a mirror site that contains the same information on a different computer. Mirror sites are usually updated once a day.

Modem
Short for modulator/demodulator, a modem connects a computer to the phone system. It converts computer signals to audio pulses, which can be transmitted over the phone line.

Moderator
The person who manages moderated mailing lists, newsgroups, or online discussion forums for services such as AOL, CompuServe, or the Microsoft Network. They usually have some editorial control over that section of the service, which can lead them into contention at times.

Mosaic
A graphical browser for the world wide web that supports hypermedia. The NCSA (National SuperComputer Association) invented the Mosaic browser, which quickly became the industry standard. Now, however, its offshoot, Netscape has become much more popular, followed by Microsoft Internet Explorer.

MUD
Acronym for Multi-User Dungeon or Domain. MUDs are role-playing games and chat areas that take place on a computer. Users can Telnet to a MUD host, and create a character. MUDs can be action, adventure, or fantasy-based games, and allow you to save your character for future play. Some MUDs have thousands of registered characters, and most foster a community or culture of their own. These are highly-addictive areas of the Internet, and pupils might spend many hours enthralled in this type of activity.

Multipurpose Internet Mail Extensions Encoding (MIME Encoding)
When Internet (usually Email) software retrieves a file from a server, the server provides the MIME type of the file, and the file is decoded correctly when transferred to your machine.

Netiquette
The combination of the words "Net" and "etiquette," this refers to the proper behaviour on a network, and more generally the Internet. The key element in Netiquette is remembering that actual people are on the other end of a computer connection, and offensive comments or actions are just as offensive even if you can't see your recipient.

Netscape Navigator
Netscape Communications Corporation's popular web browser, Navigator, is currently the most popular in the world. *See also* Mosaic.

Network File System (NFS)
A protocol developed by Sun Microsystems. NFS allows a computer to access and use files over a network as if they were local. This protocol has been incorporated into the products of more two-hundred companies, and is now a *de facto* Internet standard.

Network News Transfer Protocol (NNTP)
An industry standard protocol for the distribution, inquiry, retrieval, and posting of Usenet news articles.

Newbie
A new user of the Internet or a particular Internet service is known as a newbie. This is not a derogatory term, unless the newbie is caught pretending he or she is not one.

Newsgroup
See Usenet.

Newsreader
A program which allows you access to the articles on a Usenet news server.

NFS
See Network File System.

NNTP
See Network News Transfer Protocol.

Node
A node is a computer or server attached to the network

Open Systems Interconnection (OSI)
A suite of protocols, designed by ISO committees to be the international standard computer network architecture.

OSI
See Open System Interconnection.

Packet
The common term for the standard unit of data sent across a network.

PAP
See Password Authentication Protocol.

Password Authentication Protocol (PAP)
One of the many authentication methods that can be used when connecting to an ISP. PAP allows you to log in automatically, without having to use a terminal window to type in your username and password. One warning about PAP: passwords are sent over the connection in text format, which means there is no protection if someone is "listening-in" ..

Ping
The simplest way to test or time the response of an Internet connection. PING sends a request to an Internet host and waits for a reply called a (you guessed it) PONG. When you PING an address, you get a response telling you the number of seconds it took to make the connection. PING clients exist for a number of platforms.

Plug-in (or plugin)
A small piece of software which augments another piece of software, adding additional features. Web browsers extend their multimedia (and other) capabilities through third-party plug-ins, which can be downloaded.

Point of Presence (PoP)
An installation of telecommunications equipment, usually digital leased lines and multi-protocol routers. You will dial up to your ISP's local PoP. Sometimes, these don't exist physically - the local number is routed to a central machine somewhere else in the country.

Point-to-Point Protocol (PPP)
PPP allows Internet data to be transmitted down the telephone line, and is one of the most popular methods for dialup connections to the Internet.

POP
See either Point Of Presence *or* Post Office Protocol.

Post Office Protocol (POP)
A protocol designed to allow single users to read mail from a server. The current version is POP3. When Email is sent to you, it is stored on the server until accessed by you. Once you are authenticated, the stored mail is transmitted from the server to your local client machine.

Posting
The sending of an article to a Usenet newsgroup or the placing of a message on a BBS.

Postmaster
The person who deals with Email and answers Email-related questions on an Internet site is named the postmaster. For example, sending mail to postmaster@aol.com will reach that provider's postmaster. Most organisations do the same.

PPP
See Point-to-Point Protocol.

Protocol
Simply, the "language" spoken between computers to help them exchange information. More technically, it's a formal description of message formats and the rules that two computers must follow to exchange those messages. Protocols can describe low-level details of machine-to-machine interfaces (like the order in which bits and bytes are sent across a wire) or high-level exchanges between allocation programs (the way in which two programs transfer a file across the Internet).

Proxy
Sometimes, instead of browsing the web directly, you may do it through a "proxy server", an intermediary machine. There are several reasons: for schools, it may be that the proxy server filters out inappropriate pages and so forth.

Request For Comments (RFC)
A document series, begun in 1969, which describes the Internet suite of protocols and related experiments. Not all (actually, very few) RFCs describe Internet standards, but all Internet standards are written up as RFCs.

RFC
See Request for Comments.

Route
The path (through routers and servers) through which mail or other information takes to get from source to destination.

Router
A device that forwards traffic between networks.

RTFM (Read the Flippin' Manual)
An acronym used to respond to a simple or common question.

Serial Line Internet Protocol (SLIP)
Similar to PPP, SLIP is the older standard protocol used to run TCP/IP

over telephone lines and so forth. Today, PPP is the protocol of choice.

Server
Simply, a computer that provides resources, such as files or other information. Common Internet servers include file servers and name servers running the Domain Name Service.

Service Provider
See Internet Service Provider.

SIG
Acronym for *Special Interest Group.* SIGs sponsor a variety of Listservs, IRC channels, and Internet sites.

Signature
An ASCII text file that can be automatically attached to the bottom of a piece of Email or newsgroup posting that identifies the sender. Many signatures (or “sigs”) use symbols and characters to create images or words to make the sig more interesting.

Simple Mail Transfer Protocol (SMTP)
A protocol used to transfer email. SMTP transfers mail from server to server, and the end user must use POP (*see also* Post Office Protocol) to transfer the messages to their machine.

SLIP
See Serial Line Internet Protocol.

Smiley
The use of punctuation marks and other symbols or characters to portray moods when typing, especially in Email messages and IRC. Here’s an example of a simple smiley:) . If you don’t see it, tilt your head to the left and look at it. The colon makes the eyes and the parenthesis makes the smiley mouth. The smile means happiness (like if someone says something funny) or it often denotes sarcasm. Other combinations of characters can express many other emotions. You may also hear them referred to as “emoticons”.

Snailmail
Internet term for post that requires the moistening of a postage stamp.

Streaming
When a system is capable of outputting data as it downloads, instead

of only once it has fully downloaded, the data is said to be streamed. For example, RealAudio allows you to listen to specially prepared and compressed audio files as they are downloaded via your modem, instead of waiting minutes (or hours) before the whole lot is placed on your hard disc.

Sysop (system operator)
The sysop is the person in charge of running and maintaining an electronic bulletin board service (BBS).

T1
A T1 denotes a leased line which allows 1.544 megabits per second to be transmitted over it.

T3
A T3 denotes a leased line which allows 44.746 megabits per second to be transmitted over it.

TCP/IP
See Transmission Control Protocol/Internet Protocol.

TCP/IP Stack
To properly use the TCP/IP protocol, PCs require a TCP/IP stack, which contains the whole protocol suite and other bits and pieces, through which Internet programs and dialup utilities can connect.

Telnet
The Internet standard protocol to connect to remote computer by typing commands. Telnet clients are available for most platforms. When you Telnet to a UNIX site, for example, you can issue commands at the prompt as if the machine were local.

Terminal emulator
A program which allows your computer to pretend it has the very primitive textual interface sometimes needed to connect to others. Telnet requires a terminal emulator.

Thread
A group of related Usenet articles or Email messages. Many threads tend to unravel.

Token Ring
A type of *LAN* in which networked computers are wired into a "ring." Each computer (or node) is in constant contact with the next computer in the ring. A control message, called a "token", is passed

from one computer to another, allowing the computer with the token to send a message out to the network. If the ring is "broken" by one computer losing contact, the network can no longer communicate. You can think of it as a kind of "pass the parcel" network.

Topology
The term is used to denote the "layout" of all the computers on a network and the links that join them.

Transmission Control Protocol/Internet Protocol (TCP/IP)
TCP/IP is the standard set of communications protocols required for computers to connect to the Internet. It is the Internet's 'lingua franca'.

UNIX
Popular academic computer operating system with many variants. Complicated but powerful, many of the Internet's server machines have this operating system running on them.

UNIX-to-UNIX Copy (UUCP)
Originally, UUCP was a program that allowed UNIX systems to transfer files over phone lines. Currently, the term is used to describe a protocol that is sometimes used to pass news and Email across the Internet.

Upload
The transmission of a file from one computer to another, usually remote, computer or server machine. An upload (as a noun) is, literally, that which has been uploaded. Eg, "today's uploads include a piece of maths software".

Usenet
Usenet groups are more commonly known as "newsgroups." There are thousands of groups hosted on hundreds of servers around the world, dealing with various topics. Newsreader software is required to properly download, view and post "articles" in the groups.

Utility
A small computer program which is of some utility to you or the machine is also termed a 'utility'. When a utility becomes an application is a semantic matter – a small text editor like 'Notepad' is usually termed a utility. A large wordprocessor like 'Microsoft Word' is usually termed an 'application'.

UUCP
See UNIX-to-UNIX Copy.

Uudecode
See Uuencode.

Uuencode
Uuencode is a common way of converting a binary file into one which can be transmitted via Email or Usenet as text. There are programs for most computers which can do this. When the data is converted back, it is uudecoded.

Veronica
A search engine (not unlike Archie) that is built into Gopher. It allows searches of all gopher sites for files, directories and other resources.

Virtual Reality Make-up Language (VRML)
VRML is a language for creating interactive 3D environments which can be manipulated over the Internet. Many web browsers now have VRML plug-ins, which allow you to view VRML worlds within the browser window.

VRML
See Virtual Reality Make-up Language

Universal Resource Locator (URL)
The URL, refers to the entire address that is recognized "universally" as the address for an Internet resource. Each resource on the Internet has a unique URL. URLs begin with letters that identify the resource type, such as http, ftp, gopher, etc. These types are followed by a colon and two slashes. Next, the computer's name is listed, followed by the directory and filename of the remote resource. For example, **http://www.koekie.org.uk/index.html**

W3
See world wide web.

WAIS
See Wide Area Information Service.

WAN (Wide Area Network)
As opposed to LAN. The Internet is the biggest WAN of them all.

White Pages
Databases containing Email addresses, telephone numbers, and postal

addresses of Internet users. You can search the Internet White Pages to find information about particular users.

WHOIS
An Internet program (related to Finger and the White Pages) that lets you enter an Internet entity (such as domains, networks, and hosts) and display information such as a person's company name, address, phone number and Email address - but only if they've set it up to do that!

Wide Area Information Service (WAIS)
A distributed information service and search engine that allows natural language input and searching. Many web search utilities use a WAIS engine.

Wide Area Network
See WAN.

Winsocks
Stands for "Windows Sockets." It is is a set of specifications or standards for programmers creating TCP/IP applications for use with Windows.

World wide web (WWW or W3)
The "Web" is a collection of online documents housed on Internet servers around the world. The concept of the web was created by researchers at CERN in Switzerland. Web documents are written or "coded" in HTML. To access these documents, you have to use a Web browser, such as Netscape. When these browsers access (or hit) a page, the server uses the HyperText Transfer Protocol (HTTP) to send the document to your computer.

Worm
A computer program that replicates itself and is self-propagating. While viruses are designed to cause problems on a local system, worms are designed to thrive in network environments. The most famous (or infamous) worm was the Internet Worm of November 1988.

WWW
See world wide web.

Glossary Invitation

If you find a piece of jargon not listed in this glossary, or not dealt with adequately, and if you wish to know its definition or simply want to let us know about it, the authors would be glad to hear from you. Simply send your questions or ponderings to:

koekie@koekie.org.uk

Index